iPad® For Seniors

10th Edition

by Dwight Spivey

A Wiley Brand

iPad® For Seniors For Dummies, 10th Edition

Published by: **John Wiley & Sons, Inc.,** 111 River Street, Hoboken, NJ 07030-5774, www.wiley.com

Copyright © 2018 by John Wiley & Sons, Inc., Hoboken, New Jersey

Published simultaneously in Canada

Table of Contents

Introduction

I f you bought this book (or are even thinking about buying it), you've probably already made the decision to buy an iPad. The iPad is designed to be easy to use, but you can still spend hours exploring the preinstalled apps, finding out how to change settings, and figuring out how to sync the device to your computer or through iCloud. I've invested those hours so that you don't have to — and I've added advice and tips for getting the most out of your iPad.

This book helps you get going with the iPad quickly and painlessly so that you can move directly to the fun part.

About This Book

This book is specifically written for mature people like you, folks who may be relatively new to using a tablet and want to discover the basics of buying an iPad, working with its preinstalled apps, getting on the Internet, and using social media. In writing this book, I've tried to consider the types of activities that might interest someone who is 50 years old or older and picking up an iPad for the first time.

Foolish Assumptions

This book is organized by sets of tasks. These tasks start from the beginning, assuming that you've never laid your hands on an iPad and guide you through basic steps using nontechnical language.

This book covers going online using either a Wi-Fi or 3G/4G connection, browsing the web (Chapter 9), and checking email (Chapter 10). I'm also assuming that you'll want to use the iBooks e-reader app, so I cover its features in Chapter 12. I also assume that you might be interested in getting to know Apple's personal assistant, Siri, so I give you an overview of it in Chapter 5. Not to mention covering other great things you can do with your iPad, such as taking and sharing your photos and videos (Chapters 14 and 15, respectively), getting the latest news (Chapter 19), and much more!

Icons Used in This Book

Icons are tiny pictures in the margin of pages that call your attention to special advice or information, such as

TIP

These brief pieces of advice help you to take a skill further or provide alternate ways of getting things done.

WARNING

Heads up! This may be difficult or expensive to undo.

REMEMBER

This is information that's so useful, it's worth keeping in your head, not just on your bookshelf.

TECHNICAL STUFF

Maybe this isn't essential information, but it's neat to know.

Beyond the Book

Like every *For Dummies* book, this one comes with free Cheat Sheets that bring together some of the most commonly needed information for people learning to use, in this case, the iPad. To get the Cheat Sheets, head for www.dummies.com and enter **iPad For Seniors For Dummies 10th Edition Cheat Sheets** in the Search box.

You'll also find two bonus chapters on the website.

Where to Go from Here

You can work through this book from beginning to end or simply open a chapter to solve a problem or acquire a specific new skill whenever you need it. The steps in every task quickly get you to where you want to go, without a lot of technical explanation.

At the time I wrote this book, all the information it contained was accurate for the 12.9-inch iPad Pro (1st and 2nd generations), 10.5-inch iPad Pro, 9.7-inch iPad Pro, iPad Air 2, iPad Air, iPad (5th generation, a.k.a. "iPad 2017"), iPad mini (models 2, 3, and 4), version 11 of iOS (the operating system used by the iPad), and version 12.5 of iTunes. Apple may introduce new iPad models and new versions of iOS and iTunes between book editions. If you've bought a new iPad and found that its hardware, user interface, or the version of iTunes on your computer looks a little different, be sure to check out what Apple has to say at www.apple.com/iPad. You'll no doubt find updates there on the company's latest releases.

1

Getting to Know Your iPad

iPads and iOS 11

» **Choosing the right iPad for you**

» **Understanding what you need to use your iPad**

» **Exploring what's in the box**

» **Taking a look at the gadget**

Chapter **1**

Buying Your iPad

You've read about it. You've seen on the news the lines at Apple Stores on the day a new version of the iPad is released. You're so intrigued that you've decided to get your own iPad, which offers lots of fun apps, such as games and exercise trackers; allows you to explore the online world; lets you read e-books, magazines, and other periodicals; allows you to take and organize photos and videos; plays music and movies, and a lot more.

Trust me: You've made a good decision, because the iPad redefines the mobile computing experience in an exciting way. It's also an absolutely perfect fit for many seniors.

In this chapter, you learn about the advantages of the iPad, as well as where to buy this little gem and associated data plans from providers for iPads that support cellular data. After you have one in your hands, I help you explore what's in the box and get an overview of the little buttons and slots you'll encounter — luckily, the iPad has very few of them.

Discover the Newest iPads and iOS 11

Apple's iPad gets its features from a combination of hardware and its software operating system (called *iOS*; the term is short for iPad operating system). The most current version of the operating system is iOS 11. It's helpful to understand which features the newest iPad models and iOS 11 bring to the table (all of which are covered in more detail in this book).

The iPad is currently available in various sizes, depending on the version of iPad. Here are the three basic sizes, by iPad type:

» **iPad:** The fifth-generation iPad features a touchscreen that measures 9.7 inches diagonally and sports a super-fast 64-bit desktop-class A9 processor.

» **iPad mini:** The iPad mini 4's screen measures 7.9 inches diagonally and uses a 64-bit A8 processor to do the behind-the-scenes work.

» **iPad Pro:** The two iPad Pro models are the fastest of the bunch. One measures 10.5 inches diagonally, and the other is 12.9 inches; they both come with blazing fast A10 processors.

TECHNICAL STUFF

Dimensions of devices are typically shown in the units of measurement commonly used in a region. This means, for example, that the basic iPad is shown on Apple's U.S. site as being 9.4 inches (240mm) high and 6.6 inches (169.5mm) wide. In metric-system countries, both dimensions are given, but the order is reversed. When it comes to screen sizes, however, the dimensions are given in inches.

In addition to the features of previous iPads, the latest iPad models offer

» **Screen resolution:** In addition to screen size, screen resolution has evolved so that Apple's *Retina display,* which supports very high-resolution graphics, now appears across the line. The name derives from the concept that individual pixels on the screen are so small that at normal viewing distance, they can't be distinguished.

» **Apple Pencil:** Designed exclusively for use with iPad Pro models, the Apple Pencil lets you draw and write on the screen with a familiar pencil-style tool rather than with your finger. The Apple Pencil contains a battery and sophisticated processing powers that make the experience of using it very much like (and sometimes better than) traditional pencils. Third-party pencils and drawing tools exist, but Apple's integration of Apple Pencil is remarkably smooth; the product has taken off quickly among graphic artists, illustrators, and designers. As other people have discovered its usability for marking up documents, it is becoming more and more common in business environments.

» **Faster motion coprocessor:** This coprocessor processes game features, such as the gyroscope and accelerometer. The iPad features the M9 coprocessor, the iPad mini 4 has an M8, and both iPad Pro models utilize a slightly faster M10 motion coprocessor.

» **Touch ID:** This security feature is included on all newer iPad models. Sensors in the Home button allow you to train the iPad to recognize your fingerprint and grant you access with a finger press. Touch ID also allows you to use the Apple Pay feature to buy items without having to enter your payment information every time.

» **Barometric sensor:** On all three iPad models, this sensor makes it possible for your iPad to sense air pressure around you. This feature is especially cool when you're hiking a mountain, where the weather may change as you climb. Perhaps more to the point, the changes in barometric pressure can be sensed on a smaller scale so that elevation can be sensed and measured as you move normally.

» **3D Touch:** This feature allows for three levels of pressure on the screen. Each level can be used for different input meanings. For example, the lightest tap on an object selects it; medium pressure displays a preview (called Peek by Apple); and the heaviest pressure opens the item (called Pop).

» **More keyboard options:** The iPad Pro has a full-size onscreen keyboard. Because the screen has more space, the top of the keyboard can contain extra commands for filling in passwords and using more advanced input techniques.

» **Smart Connector for Smart Keyboard:** Additionally, you can use a Smart Connector to hook up a Smart Keyboard, which makes getting complex work done much easier.

» **Live photos:** Using the 3D Touch feature, you can press a photo on the screen to make it play like a short video. The Camera app captures 1.5 seconds on either side of the moment when you capture the photo, so anything moving in the image you photographed, such as water flowing in a stream, seems to move when you press the still photo.

The iOS 11 update to the operating system adds many features, including

» **Much improved Control Center**: Control Center allows you to quickly access many of your iPad's features by simply swiping up on your screen. Control Center has been greatly streamlined, and the new interface is simpler to navigate. You can also customize Control Center to contain only the items that you use often.

» **Siri improvements**: Siri now sounds like a more natural voice and is able to translate into several languages.

» **Improvements to the Notes app**: With iOS 11, Notes takes another giant leap forward. New features allow you easy ways to add tables, handwriting is supported, and drag-and-drop is a great new tool. You can also use Notes to scan paper documents!

» **Files app**: Finally, Apple has delivered a great app called Files that allows you to browse the files stored on your iPad. You can also use it to browse and work with files you've stored on other cloud services, such as Google Drive, Dropbox, and others.

» **Improvements to Maps**: Maps has always been great for getting around on the road, but now it also shines when helping you navigate interiors. New maps are built-in, which help guide you in unfamiliar buildings, such as airports.

» **Store many more photos and videos than ever before:** iOS 11 is the first version of iOS that utilizes a new compression format for photos and videos. This format will allow you to take high-quality photos and videos, but they'll take up much less storage on your iPad.

TIP

Don't need or use all the built-in apps? If so, you can remove them from your Home screen. When you remove a built-in app from your Home screen, you aren't deleting it — you're hiding it. This is due to security reasons that are beyond the scope of this book. However, the built-in apps take up very little of your iPad's storage space, and you can easily add them back to your Home screen by searching for them in the App Store and tapping the Get button.

These are but a very few of the improvements made to the latest version of iOS. I suggest visiting www.apple.com/ios/ios-11 to find out more details.

Choose the Right iPad for You

The most obvious differences among iPad models are their thickness and weight, with the Pro being biggest, then iPad (see Figure 1-1), and finally the smallest, iPad mini 4. All three models come in space gray, silver, or gold, and the iPad Pro 10.5-inch offers a fourth option, rose gold.

All three models come in Wi-Fi only for accessing a Wi-Fi network for Internet access or Wi-Fi + Cellular for connecting to the Internet through Wi-Fi or a cellular network as your cellphone does. The iPad models also differ slightly in available memory and price based on that memory (prices are accurate as of this writing and are subject to change):

» **iPad Pro 10.5-inch:** Wi-Fi models come in 64GB for $649, 256GB for $749, and 512GB for $949; Wi-Fi + Cellular models come in 64GB for $779, 256GB for $879, and 512GB for $1,079.

Image courtesy of Apple, Inc.

FIGURE 1-1

» **iPad Pro 12.9-inch:** Wi-Fi models come in 64GB for $799, 256GB for $899, and 512GB for $1,099; Wi-Fi + Cellular models come in 64GB for $929, 256GB for $1,029, and 512GB for $1,229.

» **iPad:** Wi-Fi models come in 32GB for $329 and 128GB for $429; Wi-Fi + Cellular models come in 32GB for $459 and 128GB for $559.

» **iPad mini 4:** The Wi-Fi model comes in 128GB for $399, and the Wi-Fi + Cellular model comes in 128GB for $529.

Finally, the iPad models vary in screen quality and resolution, camera quality, and so on. Logically, the bigger the iPad, the bigger the price and higher the quality.

Decide How Much Storage Is Enough

Storage is a measure of how much information — for example, movies, photos, and software applications (apps) — you can store on a computing device. Storage can also affect your iPad's performance when handling such tasks as streaming favorite TV shows from the World Wide Web or downloading music.

TIP

Streaming refers to playing video or music content from the web (or from other devices) rather than playing a file stored on your iPad. You can enjoy a lot of material online without ever downloading its full content to your iPad.

Your storage options with the various iPad models range from 32 to 512GB. You must choose the right amount of storage because you can't open the unit and add more as you usually can with a desktop computer. However, Apple has thoughtfully provided iCloud, a service you can use to back up content to the Internet. (You can read more about iCloud in Chapter 3).

How much storage is enough for your iPad? Here's a guideline:

» If you like lots of media, such as movies or TV shows, you may need at least 256GB.

» For most people who manage a reasonable number of photos, download some music, and watch heavy-duty media, such as movies online, 128GB is probably sufficient.

» If you simply want to check email, browse the web, and write short notes to yourself, 32GB likely is plenty.

HOW BIG IS A GIGABYTE?

Do you know how big a gigabyte (GB) is? Technically, it's a billion bytes where a byte is the standard unit for digital information. A byte is typically 8 bits long where each bit is an on/off, yes/no, or 0/1 value. (Those terms are interchangeable in this context.)

A gigabyte can contain 60 minutes of standard TV video running at 2.2 megabits per second (2.2 Mbit/s). A gigabyte can also contain 7 minutes of high definition TV (HDTV) running at 19.39 Mbit/s. The difference between HDTV and SDTV has to do with the size of the image, but the storage also depends on the speed with which it runs: A faster speed makes for a smoother playback, and a larger image size makes for clearer images. Both the speed and the image size together determine how good the video looks.

When downloading or playing video on any computer, if you have a choice of HDTV or SDTV, pick the version that gives you the best results. In the best case, choose HDTV, but because the files are going to be larger than SDTV, if you're running out of storage space, you may want to opt for SDTV.

If you're downloading video to view later (as opposed to viewing it now), you may want to do the download at an off-peak time and watch it in the best quality once it's downloaded.

Don't forget that downloading large files also costs you more if you're not using a Wi-Fi connection. So the choice is yours based on how much storage space you have, how long you have to download the file, and how much — if anything — you have to pay for the download itself.

Consider this: Just about any computer you buy today comes with a minimum of 250GB to 500GB of storage. Computers have to tackle larger tasks than iPads do, so that amount makes sense. The iPad, which uses a technology called Flash for memory storage, is designed (to a great extent) to help you experience online media and email; it doesn't have to store much and in fact pulls lots of content from online sources. In the world of memory, 16GB is puny storage if you want to keep lots of content on the device.

Know What Else You May Need: Internet and Computer

Although you can use your iPad on its own without any Internet or Wi-Fi access and without a computer to pair it with, it's easier if you have Internet access and a computer that you can (occasionally) use with your iPad.

Use basic Internet access for your iPad

You need to be able to connect to the Internet to take advantage of most iPad features. If you have an Apple ID, you can have an iCloud account, Apple's online storage service, to store and share content online, and you can use a computer to download photos, music, or applications from non-Apple online sources (such as stores, sharing sites, or your local library) and transfer them to your iPad through a process called *syncing*. You can also use a computer or iCloud to register your iPad the first time you start it, although you can have the folks at the Apple Store handle registration for you if you have an Apple Store nearby. If you don't have a store nearby, the Chat feature on http://apple.com can connect you to a representative or to request a phone consultation. These services are free (but for Chat, you'll need an Internet connection).

You can set up your iPad without an Internet connection and without going to an Apple Store: The best way to find out more information is to contact http://support.apple.com through an Internet connection on another device or at a public library or Internet cafe.

Can you use your iPad without owning a computer and just use public Wi-Fi hotspots to go online (or a 3G/4G LTE connection, if you have such a model)? Yes. To go online using a Wi-Fi–only iPad and to use many of its built-in features at home, however, you need to have a home Wi-Fi network available.

Pair your iPad with a computer

For syncing with a computer, Apple's iPad User Guide recommends that you have

>> A Mac or PC with a USB 2.0 port and one of the following operating systems:

- Mac OS X version 10.9.5 or later
- Windows 10, 8, or 7

>> iTunes 12.5 or later, available at www.itunes.com/download

>> An Apple ID and iTunes Store account

>> Internet access

>> An iCloud account

Apple has set up its iTunes software and the iCloud service to give you two ways to manage content for your iPad — including movies, music, or photos you've downloaded — and specify how to sync your calendar and contact information.

There are a lot of tech terms to absorb here (iCloud, iTunes, syncing, and so on). Don't worry: Chapters 2 and 3 cover those settings in more detail.

Choose Wi-Fi Only or Wi-Fi + Cellular

You use Wi-Fi to connect to a wireless network at home or at locations such as an Internet cafe, a library, a grocery store, or a bus, train, plane, or airport that offers Wi-Fi. This type of network uses short-range radio to connect to the Internet; its range is reasonably limited, so if you leave home or walk out of the coffee shop, you can't use it anymore. (These limitations may change, however, as some towns are installing community-wide Wi-Fi networks.)

The *3G* and *4G(LTE)* cellular technologies allow an iPad to connect to the Internet via a widespread cellular-phone network. You use it in much the same way that you make calls from just about any-where with your cellphone. 4G(LTE) may not always be available in every location, but you can still connect to the Internet via 3G when 4G(LTE) service isn't available. You just won't have the advantage of the super-fast 4G technology. A Wi-Fi + Cellular iPad costs additional money when compared to the basic Wi-Fi–only model, but it also includes GPS (Global Positioning System) service, which pinpoints your location so that you can get more accurate driving directions.

Also, to use your 3G/4G network in the United States, you must pay a monthly fee. The good news is that no carrier requires a long-term contract, which you probably had to have when you bought your cell-phone and its service plan. You can pay for a connection during the month you visit your grandkids, for example, and get rid of it when you arrive home. Features, data allowance (which relates to access-ing email or downloading items from the Internet, for example), and prices vary by carrier and could change at any time, so visit each car-rier's website (see the following tip) to see what it offers. Note that if you intend to stream videos (watch them on your iPad from the Internet), you can eat through your data plan allowance quickly.

Go to these links for more information about iPad data plans: AT&T at www.att.com/shop/wireless/devices/apple/ipad.html, Verizon at www.verizonwireless.com/landingpages/ipad, T-Mobile at www.t-mobile.com, and Sprint at https://sprint.com.

How do you choose? If you want to wander around the woods or town — or take long drives with your iPad continually connected to the Internet to get step-by-step navigation info from the Maps app — get Wi-Fi + Cellular and pay the price. If you'll use your iPad mainly at home or via a Wi-Fi *hotspot* (a location where Wi-Fi access to the Internet is available, such as an Internet cafe), don't bother with 3G/4G(LTE). Frankly, you can find *lots* of hotspots at libraries, restaurants, hotels, airports, and other locations.

If you have a Wi-Fi–only iPad, you can use the hotspot feature on a smartphone, which allows the iPad to use your phone's 3G or 4G(LTE) connection to go online if you have a data-use plan that supports hotspot use with your phone service carrier. Check out the features of your phone to turn on the hotspot feature.

TIP

If you have CarPlay, chances are you have a mobile hotspot: It's called your car. Not all car dealers talk about technology in the same way that other people do; you may have to do a bit of poking around to find out what technology is behind "Super Duper Feature" in your car's advertising and documentation, but chances are you've got a mobile hotspot that you can use with your iPad. If you get a new car with a two- or three-month trial period for the built-in car Wi-Fi, use that time to monitor your usage per the instructions from your car dealer. See how much data you're using and, more important, keep track of what you've been doing.

TIP

Because 3G and 4G(LTE) iPads are also GPS devices, they know where you are and can act as a navigation system to get you from here to there. The Wi-Fi–only model uses a digital compass and triangulation method for locating your current position, which is less accurate; with no constant Internet connection, it won't help you get around town.

KNOW WHERE TO BUY YOUR IPAD

At this writing, you can buy an iPad at an Apple Store; at brick-and-mortar stores, such as Best Buy, Walmart, Sam's Club, and Target; and at online sites such as MacMall.com. You can also buy 3G/4G(LTE) models (models that require an account with a phone service provider) from Sprint, AT&T, T-Mobile, and Verizon, as well as at the Apple Store.

Apple Stores aren't on every corner, so if visiting one isn't an option (or you just prefer to go it alone), you can go to Apple's website (www.apple.com) and order an iPad to be shipped to you — even get it engraved, if you want. Typically, standard shipping is free, and if there's a problem, Apple's customer service reps will help you solve the problem or replace your iPad.

Additionally, smaller stores that sell electronics can have an Apple Specialist designation that allows them to carry and sell Apple products. Check your local stores for this.

Consider iPad Accessories

At present, Apple offers a few accessories that you may want to check out when you purchase your iPad, including

» **iPad Smart Case/Smart Cover:** Your iPad isn't cheap, and unlike a laptop computer, it has an exposed screen that can be damaged if you drop or scratch it. Investing in the iPad Smart Case or Smart Cover is a good idea if you intend to take your iPad out of your house — or if you have a cat or grandchildren. The iPad Smart Cover costs $40 to $130 from various vendors, depending on design and material.

» **Printers:** Several HP, Brother, Canon, and Epson printers support the wireless AirPrint feature. At this writing, prices range from $129 to $399, and discounts are often available.

» **Smart Keyboard:** You can buy an attachable keyboard for your iPad Pro for $169, which will make working with productivity apps much easier. This keyboard connects to your iPad to provide power and transmit data between the devices. Also, the Magic Keyboard from Apple costs $99 and uses Bluetooth to connect to your iPad, a Mac, an iPhone, or any other device that works with a Bluetooth keyboard.

» **Apple Pencil:** For $99, you can buy the highly sophisticated stylus for use with the iPad Pro. The Apple Pencil (see Figure 1-2) makes it easy to draw on your iPad screen or manage complex interactions more precisely.

» **Apple Digital AV Adapter:** To connect devices to output high-definition media, you can buy this adapter for about $40 and use it with an HDMI cable. More and more devices that use this technology are coming out, such as projectors and TVs. But remember that wireless connections such as Bluetooth and Wi-Fi are less expensive and can eliminate all those cables and cords. In some circumstances, a wired connection is faster and more effective than wireless.

» **Stands, docks, and other accessories:** These are available from Apple Stores and from many third parties.

Image courtesy of Apple, Inc.

FIGURE 1-2

TIP

Don't bother buying a wireless mouse to connect with your iPad via Bluetooth; the iPad recognizes your finger as its primary input device, and mice need not apply. You can use a stylus or Apple Pencil to tap your input, however.

Explore What's in the Box

After you fork over your hard-earned money for your iPad, you'll be holding one box. Besides your iPad and a small documentation package, here's a rundown of what you'll find when you take off the shrink wrap and open the box:

» **iPad:** Your iPad is covered in a thick plastic sleeve-film that you can take off and toss (unless you think there's a chance that you'll return the device, in which case you may want to keep all packaging for 14 days — Apple's standard return period).

- » **Documentation:** Notice, under the iPad itself, a small, white envelope about the size of a half-dozen index cards. Open it, and you'll find

  - **A single sheet titled iPad Info:** This pamphlet is essentially small print (that you mostly don't need to read) from agencies like the Federal Communications Commission (FCC).

  - **A label sheet:** This sheet has two white Apple logos on it. (Apple has provided these for years with its products as a form of cheap advertising when users place stickers on places like their computers or car rear windows.)

  - **A small card:** This card displays a picture of the iPad and callouts to its buttons on one side, and the other side contains brief instructions for setting it up and information about where to find out more.

- » **A Lightning-to-USB cable (fourth-generation iPad and later and all iPad mini models) or Dock Connector-to-USB cable (all earlier iPad models):** Use this cord to connect the iPad to your computer or use it with the last item in the box: the USB power adapter.

- » **USB power adapter:** The power adapter attaches to the Lightning-to-USB cable so that you can plug it into the wall and charge the battery.

That's it. That's all you'll find in the box. It's kind of a study in Zen–like simplicity.

Take a First Look at the Gadget

The little card contained in the documentation that comes with your iPad gives you a picture of the iPad with callouts to the buttons you'll find on it. In this task, I give you a bit more information about those buttons and other physical features of the iPad. Figure 1-3 shows you where each of these items is located on an iPad. The Pro model also has a Smart Connector slot in addition to items shown here.

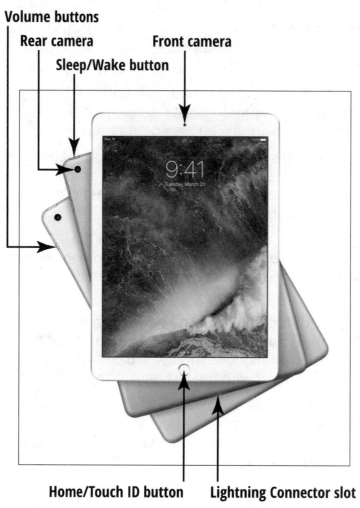

Volume buttons

Rear camera　　**Front camera**

Sleep/Wake button

9:41

Tuesday, March 21

Home/Touch ID button　　**Lightning Connector slot**

Image courtesy of Apple, Inc.

FIGURE 1-3

Here's the rundown on what the various hardware features are and what they do:

» **(The all-important) Home/Touch ID button:** On the iPad, press this button to go back to the Home screen to find just about anything. The Home screen displays all your installed and preinstalled apps and gives you access to your iPad settings. No matter where you are or what you're doing, press the Home button, and you're back at home base. You can also double-press the Home button to pull up a scrolling list of apps so that you can quickly move from one app to another. (Apple refers to this as multitasking.) If you press and hold the Home button, you open Siri, the iPhone voice assistant. Finally, on the newest iPads, the Home button contains a fingerprint reader used with the Touch ID feature.

» **Sleep/Wake button:** You can use this button (whose functionality I cover in more detail in Chapter 2) to power up your iPad, put it in Sleep mode, wake it up, or power it down.

» **Lightning Connector slot:** Plug in the Lightning connector at the USB end to the power adapter to charge your battery or use it without the power adapter to sync your iPad with your computer (which you find out more about in Chapter 3).

» **Cameras:** iPads (except for the original iPad) offer front- and rear-facing cameras, which you can use to shoot photos or video. The rear one is on the top-right corner (if you're looking at the front of the iPad), and you need to be careful not to put your thumb over it when taking shots. (I have several very nice photos of my fingers already.)

» **(Tiny, mighty) speakers:** One nice surprise when I first got my iPad was hearing what a great little stereo sound system it has and how much sound can come from these tiny speakers. The speakers are located along one side of the iPad Air 2 and iPad mini 4. With iPad Pro, you get four speakers, two on either side, which provide the best sound of all the models.

» **Volume:** Tap the volume switch, called a *rocker,* up for more volume and down for less. You can use this rocker as a camera shutter button when the camera is activated.

» **Headphone jack and microphone:** If you want to listen to your music in private, you can plug in a 3.5mm mini-jack headphone (including an iPhone headset, if you have one, which gives you bidirectional sound). A tiny microphone makes it possible to speak into your iPad to deliver commands or enter content using the Siri personal-assistant feature. Using Siri, you can do things such as make phone calls using the Internet, use video-calling services, dictate your keyboard input, or work with other apps that accept audio input.

Chapter **2**

Exploring Your iPad

Good news! Getting anything done on the iPad is simple, when you know the ropes. In fact, using your fingers to do things is a very intuitive way to communicate with your computing device, which is just what iPad is.

In this chapter, you turn on your iPad and then take your first look at the Home screen. You also practice using the onscreen keyboard, see how to interact with the touchscreen in various ways, get pointers on working with cameras, get an overview of built-in applications (more commonly referred to as apps), and more.

See What You Need to Use iPad

You need to be able, at a minimum, to connect to the Internet to take advantage of most iPad features, which you can do using a Wi-Fi network (a network that you set up in your own home or access in a public place such as a library) or a 3G/4G (LTE) connection from your cellular provider (if your iPad model supports cellular data).

You may want to have a computer so that you can connect your iPad to it to download photos, videos, music, or applications and transfer them to or from your iPad through a process called *syncing* (see Chapter 3 for more about syncing). An Apple service called iCloud syncs content from all your Apple iOS devices (such as the iPad or iPhone), so anything you buy on your iPhone that can be run on an iPad, for example, will automatically be pushed to your iPad. In addition, you can sync without connecting a cable to a computer using a wireless Wi-Fi connection to your computer.

Your iPad will probably arrive registered and activated, or if you buy it in a store, the person helping you can handle that procedure.

For an iPad Pro, iPad, or iPad mini 4, Apple recommends that you have

» A Mac or PC with a USB 2.0 or 3.0 port and one of these operating systems:

  • Mac: macOS version 10.9.5 (Mavericks) or newer

  • PC: Windows 7 or newer

» iTunes 12.5 or newer, available at www.apple.com/itunes/download

» An Apple ID

» A data contract with a cellular provider (if your iPad supports cellular data)

» Internet access

Turn On iPad for the First Time

When you're ready to get going with your new toy, be sure you're within range of a Wi-Fi network that you can connect with and then hold the iPad with one hand on either side, oriented like a pad of paper. Plug the Lightning-to-USB cable that came with your device into your iPad and plug the other end into a USB port on your computer just in case you lose your battery charge during the setup process.

Now follow these steps to set up and register your iPad:

1. Press and hold the Sleep/Wake button on the top of your iPad until the Apple logo appears. In another moment, a screen appears with a cheery Hello on it.

2. Slide your finger to the right on the screen where it says Slide to Set Up.

3. Follow the series of prompts to make choices about your language and location, using iCloud (Apple's online sharing service), and so on.

4. After you deal with all the setup screens, a Welcome to iPad screen appears; tap Get Started to display the Home screen.

If you set up iCloud when registering or after registering (see Chapter 3), updates to your operating system will be downloaded to your iPad without plugging it into a computer running iTunes. Apple refers to this feature as *PC Free*, simply meaning that your device has been liberated from having to use a physical connection to a computer to get upgrades.

You can choose to have personal items transferred to your iPad from your computer when you sync the two devices using iTunes, including music, videos, downloaded apps, audiobooks, e-books, podcasts, and browser bookmarks. Contacts and Calendars are downloaded via iCloud, or (if you're moving to iPad from an Android phone) you can download an app from the Google Play Store called Move to iOS (developed by Apple) to copy your current Android settings to your iPad (see this support article from Apple for more info: https://support.apple.com/en-us/HT201196). You can also transfer to your computer any content you download directly to your iPad by using iTunes, the App Store, or non-Apple stores.

Meet the Multitouch Screen

When the iPad Home screen appears (see Figure 2-1), you see a pretty background and two sets of icons.

FIGURE 2-1

One set of icons appears in the Dock, along the bottom of the screen. The *Dock* contains the Messages, Safari, Mail, Music, and File app icons by default, though you can swap out one app for another. The Dock appears on every Home screen and can even be accessed from within apps. You can add new apps to your iPad to populate as many as 10 additional Home screens for a total of 11 Home screens.

Other icons appear above the Dock and are closer to the top of the screen. I cover all these icons in the "Take Inventory of Preinstalled Apps" task, later in this chapter. Different icons appear in this area on each Home screen. You can also nest apps in folders, which almost gives you the possibility of storing limitless apps on your iPad. You are, in fact, limited — but only by your iPad's memory.

TIP

Treat the iPad screen carefully. It's made of glass and it will break if an unreasonable amount of force is applied, if dropped, or if your grandkids throw it against the wall.

The iPad uses *touchscreen technology:* When you swipe your finger across the screen or tap it, you're providing input to the device just as you do to a computer using a mouse or keyboard. You hear more about the touchscreen in the next task, but for now, go ahead and play with it for a few minutes — really, you can't hurt anything. Use the pads of your fingertips (not your fingernails) and try these tasks:

>> **Tap the Settings icon.** The various settings (which you read more about throughout this book) appear, as shown in Figure 2-2.

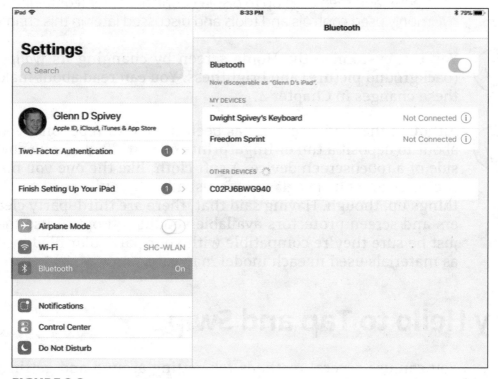

FIGURE 2-2

To return to the Home screen, press the Home button.

» **Swipe a finger from right to left on the Home screen.** This action moves you to the next Home screen.

The little white dots at the bottom of the screen, above the Dock icons, indicate which Home screen is displayed.

» **To experience the screen rotation feature, hold the iPad firmly while turning it sideways.** The screen flips to the horizontal orientation, if the app you're in supports it.

To flip the screen back, just turn the device so that it's oriented like a pad of paper again. (Some apps force iPad to stay in one orientation or the other.)

» **Drag your finger down from the very top edge of the screen to reveal the Notification Center items, such as reminders and calendar entries.** (Notification Center is covered in Chapter 17.) Drag up from the very bottom edge of the Home screen to hide Notification Center and then drag up to display Control Center (containing commonly used controls and tools and discussed later in this chapter).

You can customize the Home screen by changing its *wallpaper* (background picture) and brightness. You can read about making these changes in Chapter 4.

Although the iPad's screen has been treated to repel oils, you're about to deposit a ton of fingerprints on your iPad — one downside of a touchscreen device. A soft cloth, like the one you might use to clean your eyeglasses, is usually all you'll need to clean things up, though. Having said that, there are third-party cleaners and screen protectors available should you opt to use them; just be sure they're compatible with your particular iPad model, as materials used in each model may vary.

Say Hello to Tap and Swipe

You can use several methods for getting around and getting things done in iPad using its multitouch screen, including

» **Tap once.** To open an app, choose a field (such as a search box), choose an item in a list, use an arrow to move back or forward one screen, or follow an online link, simply tap the item once with your finger.

» **Tap twice.** Use this method to enlarge or reduce the display of a web page (see Chapter 9 for more about using the Safari web browser) or to zoom in or out in the Maps app.

» **Pinch.** As an alternative to the tap-twice method, you can pinch your fingers together or move them apart on the screen (see Figure 2-3) when you're looking at photos, maps, web pages, or email messages to quickly reduce or enlarge them, respectively. This method allows you to grow or contract the screen to a variety of sizes rather than a fixed size, as with the double-tap method.

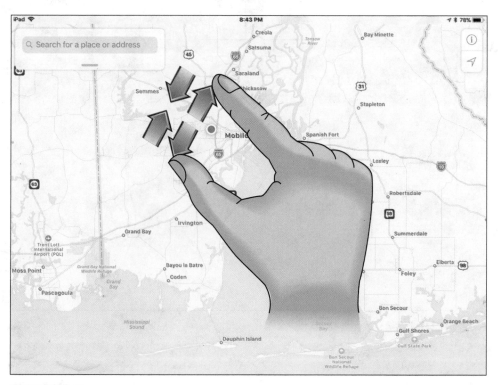

FIGURE 2-3

TIP

You can use the three-finger tap to zoom your screen to be even larger or use multitasking gestures to swipe with four or five fingers. This method is handy if you have vision challenges. Go to Chapter 4 to discover how to turn on this feature using Accessibility settings.

» **Drag to scroll (known as *swiping*).** When you touch your finger to the screen and drag to the right or left, the screen moves (see Figure 2-4). Swiping to the left on the Home screen, for example, moves you to the next Home screen. Swiping down while reading an online newspaper moves you down the page; swiping up moves you back up the page.

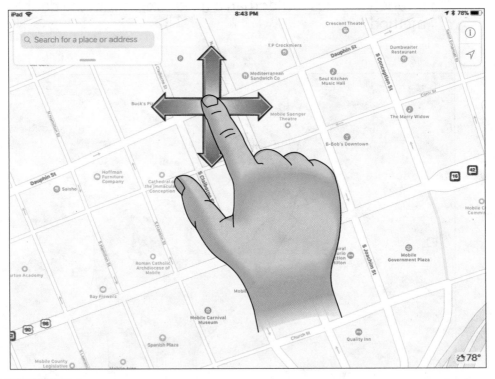

FIGURE 2-4

» **Flick.** To scroll more quickly on a page, quickly flick your finger on the screen in the direction you want to move.

» **Tap the Status bar.** To move quickly to the top of a list, web page, or email message, tap the Status bar at the top of the iPad screen. (For some sites, you have to tap the Status bar twice to get this to work.)

» **Press and hold.** If you're using Notes or Mail or any other application that lets you select text, or if you're on a web page, pressing and holding text selects a word and displays editing tools that you can use to select, cut, or copy and paste the text.

When you rock your iPad backward or forward, the background moves as well (a feature called *parallax)*. You can disable this feature if it makes you seasick. From the Home screen, tap Settings⇨General⇨Accessibility and then tap and turn on the Reduce Motion setting by tapping the toggle switch (it turns green when the option is enabled).

You can try these methods now:

» Tap the Safari button in the Dock at the bottom of any iPad Home screen to display the web browser.

» Tap a link to move to another page.

» Double-tap the page to enlarge it; then pinch your fingers together on the screen to reduce its size.

» Drag one finger up and down the page to scroll.

» Flick your finger quickly up or down on the page to scroll more quickly.

» Press and hold your finger on a word that isn't a link (links take you to another location on the web).

    The word is selected, and the Copy/Look Up/Share tool is displayed, as shown in Figure 2-5. (You can use this tool to either get a definition of a word or copy it.)

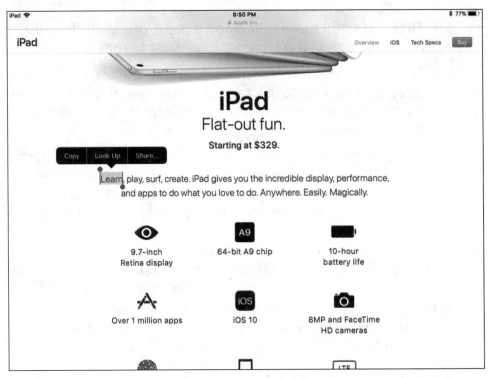

FIGURE 2-5

» Press and hold your finger on a link or an image.

A menu appears (shown in Figure 2-6) with commands that you select to open the link or picture, open it in a new tab, open it in split view, add it to your Reading List, or copy it. If you press and hold an image, the menu also offers the Save Image command.

Tap outside of the menu to close it without making a selection.

» Position your fingers slightly apart on the screen and then pinch your fingers together to reduce the page; with your fingers already pinched together on the screen, move them apart to enlarge the page.

» Press the Home button to go back to the Home screen.

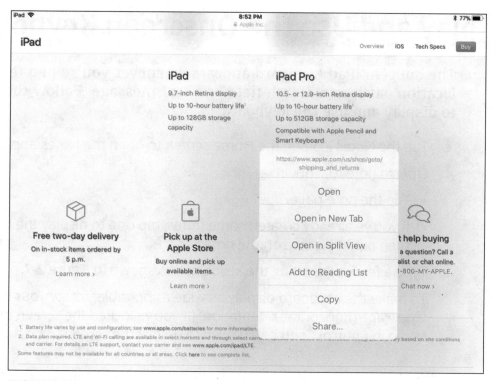

FIGURE 2-6

The Dock

The Dock at the bottom of your iPad's screen houses apps you use most often. You can remove or add apps from it simply by dragging-and-dropping their icons in or out of the Dock. You can also reorder icons within the dock using the same drag-and-drop method. To drag-and-drop, tap and hold an app icon until it pulsates (essentially tagging it to your finger) and then drag to a new location and drop it by removing your finger from the screen.

You'll note the Dock is divided between left and right sides by a thin gray line. The icons on the right side of the Dock are for those you use often, but don't keep in the Dock at all times. This makes it easier to access these apps while you're using them more heavily. You can enable or disable this behavior by opening the Settings app and going to General ⇨ Multitasking & Dock and toggling the Show Suggested and Recent Apps switch On (green) or Off.

Display and Use the Onscreen Keyboard

The built-in iPad keyboard appears whenever you're in a text-entry location, such as a search field or a text message. Follow these steps to display and use the keyboard:

1. Tap the Notes icon on the Home screen to open the Notes app.

2. Open a note to work in:

- Tap the note page.
- If you've already created some notes, tap one to display the page, then tap anywhere on the note.

3. Type a few words using the keyboard, as shown in Figure 2-7.

TIP

To make the keyboard display as wide as possible, rotate your iPad to landscape (horizontal) orientation. (If you've locked the screen orientation in Control Center, you have to unlock the screen to do this.)

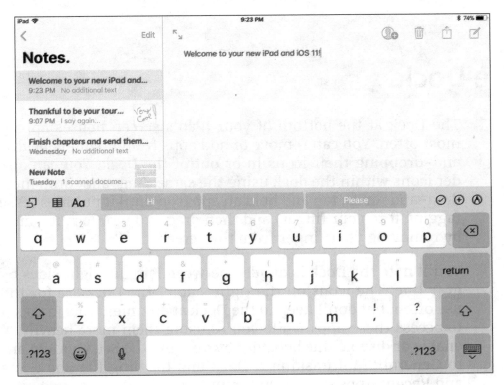

FIGURE 2-7

QuickType provides suggestions above the keyboard as you type. You can turn this feature off or on by tapping and holding either the Emoji (the smiley face) or International icon (looks like a globe) on the keyboard to display a menu. Tap Keyboard Settings and toggle the Predictive switch to turn the feature Off or On (green). To quickly return to Notes from Keyboard Settings, tap the word Notes in the upper-left of your screen.

After you open the keyboard, you're ready to use it for editing text.

You'll find a number of shortcuts for editing text:

» If you make a mistake while using the keyboard — and you will, especially when you first use it — tap the Delete key (it's near the *p* key, with the little *x* on it) to delete text to the left of the insertion point.

To type a period and space, just double-tap the spacebar.

» To create a new paragraph, tap the Return button (just like a computer keyboard).

» To type numbers and symbols, tap the number key (labeled .?123) on the left side of the spacebar (refer to Figure 2-7). The characters on the keyboard change (see Figure 2-8).

If you type a number and then tap the spacebar, the keyboard returns to the letter keyboard automatically. To return to the letter keyboard at any time, simply tap the key labeled ABC on the left side of the spacebar.

You can easily access an alternate character on a key by tapping-and-dragging down on the key. For example, if you need an exclamation mark (!), simply tap-and-drag the comma (,) key downward, and an exclamation mark will be inserted (since it's the alternate character on the comma key).

» Use the Shift button (it's a wide, upward-facing arrow in the lower-left corner of the keyboard) to type capital letters:

• Tapping the Shift button once causes only the next letter you type to be capitalized.

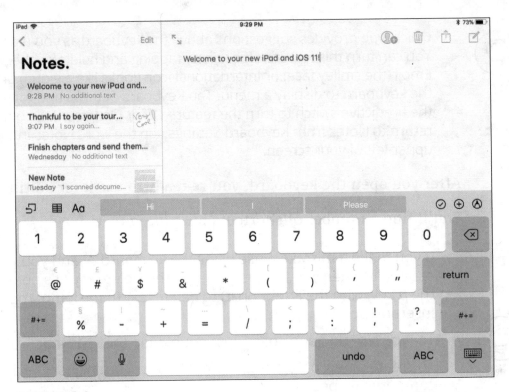

FIGURE 2-8

- Double-tap (rapidly tap twice) the Shift key to turn on the Caps Lock feature so that all letters you type are capitalized until you turn the feature off.

- Tap the Shift key once to turn off Caps Lock.

  You can control whether Caps Lock is enabled by opening the Settings app, tapping General and then Keyboard, and toggling the switch called Enable Caps Lock.

» To type a variation on a symbol or letter (for example, to see alternative presentations for the letter *A* when you press the A button on the keyboard), hold down the key; a set of alternative letters/symbols appears (see Figure 2-9).

  This trick works with only certain letters and symbols.

TECHNICAL STUFF

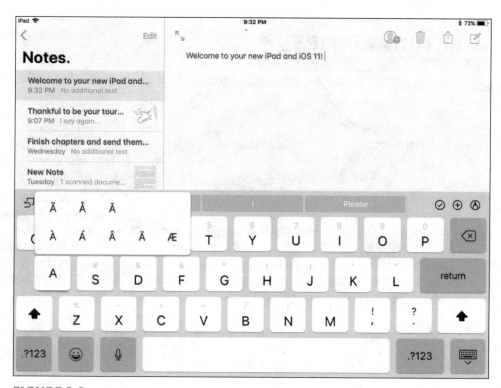

FIGURE 2-9

» Tap the smiley-faced Emoji button to display the Emoji keyboard containing symbols that you can insert, including numerical, symbol, and arrow keys, as well as a row of symbol sets along the bottom of the screen.

Tapping one of these displays a portfolio of icons from smiley faces and hearts to pumpkins, cats, and more. Tap the ABC button to close the Emoji keyboard and return to the letter keyboard.

TIP

A small globe symbol will appear instead of the Emoji button on the keyboard if you've enabled multilanguage functionality in iPad settings.

» Press the Home button to return to the Home screen.

KEYBOARD TIPS

Here are some tips to help you get the most out of the onscreen keyboard:

- You can undock the keyboard to move it around the screen. To do this, press and hold the Keyboard key (found in the lower-right of the keyboard); then, from the pop-up menu that appears, choose Undock. Now, by dragging the Keyboard key up or down, you can move the keyboard up and down on the screen. To dock the keyboard at the bottom of the screen again, press and hold the Keyboard key and choose Dock from the pop-up menu.

- In the Notes app, you can display a shortcut keyboard by using the General/ Keyboard settings. This keyboard allows you to create a checklist, choose a font style, insert a photo, or create a drawing within a note. The onscreen keyboard also uses a feature called QuickType to provide suggestions above the keyboard as you type. See Chapter 19 for more about using the Notes app.

- To type a period and space, double-tap the spacebar. If you want to add punctuation, such as a comma, and then return immediately to the letter keyboard, simply tap the .?123 key and then drag up to the punctuation symbol you want to use.

TIP

You can buy a Smart Keyboard to go with an iPad Pro for $169. This physical keyboard from Apple attaches to your iPad and allows both power and data exchange. The connection for your keyboard is magnetic, so it's a snap to put it and the iPad together.

Use the Split Keyboard

The *split keyboard* feature allows you to split the keyboard so that each side appears nearer the edge of the iPad screen. For those who are into texting or typing with thumbs, this feature makes it easier to reach all the keys from the sides of the device — useful if you're holding your iPad with both hands. Open an application such as Notes in which you can use the onscreen keyboard and then follow these steps:

1. Tap an entry field or page to display the onscreen keyboard.

2. Place one finger on each side of the keyboard and drag them apart. (I put one finger on *S* and the other on *K*.) The keyboard splits, as shown in Figure 2-10. (This feature can be finicky, so you may have to try it a few times.)

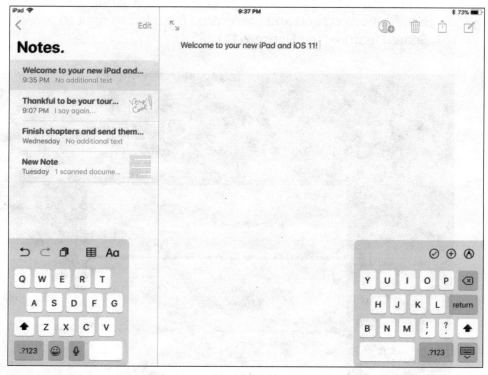

FIGURE 2-10

3. Now hold the iPad with a hand on either side and practice using your thumbs to enter text.

4. To rejoin the keyboard, drag the two parts together. You can dock or undock the keyboard to or from the bottom of the screen; you can also split or merge it.

TIP

When the keyboard is docked and merged at the bottom of your screen, you can simply drag the Keyboard key upward to undock and split the keyboard. To reverse this action, drag the Keyboard key downward. The keyboard is docked and merged.

Flick to Search

The Spotlight Search feature in iPad helps you find suggestions from the web, Music, iTunes, and the App Store as well as suggestions for nearby locations and more. Here's how to use Spotlight Search:

1. Swipe down from the top edge of any Home screen to see the Notifications screen and then swipe from left to right to reveal the Search feature (see Figure 2-11).

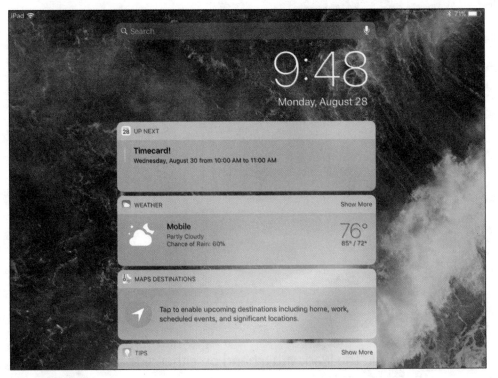

FIGURE 2-11

2. Begin entering a search term.

    In the example in Figure 2-12, after I typed the word "grocery," the Search feature displayed maps and other search results. As you continue to type a search term or phrase, the results narrow to match it.

3. Scroll down to view more results.

4. Tap an item in the search results to open it in its appropriate app or player.

FIGURE 2-12

Easily Switch Between Apps

iOS 11 lets you easily switch from one app to another without closing the first one and returning to the Home screen. With iOS 11, you
accomplish this task by previewing all open apps and jumping from
one to another; you quit an app by simply swiping upward. To find
out the ropes of basic app switching, follow these steps:

1. Open the app switcher by doing one of the following:

- Press the Home button twice.

- Swipe up from the bottom of the screen.

- Swipe up on any screen with four fingers.

2. The app switcher and Control Center appears (see Figure 2-13).

FIGURE 2-13

3. To locate another app that you want to switch to, flick to scroll to the left or right.

4. Tap an app to open it.

Press the Home button once to return to the app that you were working in.

TIP

Use Slide Over and Split View

iOS 11 allows you to be more productive than ever before with your iPad with features like Slide Over and Split View.

Slide Over lets you view one app in a floating panel, while viewing and working with other apps behind it. Split View allows two apps to share the screen between them, splitting the screen so that one app is on the left and the other is on the right. You can even adjust the amount of space each app is allocated by dragging a divider between them.

Starting with Slide Over

To use the Slide Over feature, follow these steps:

1. From the Home screen, tap and drag the app you want to view in Slide Over mode (even slightly wiggling it to keep it active).

   If all the icons on the Home screen begin jiggling, you've held down the app's icon too long. Simply press the Home button once to end this jiggling and try Step 1 again.

2. With another finger, tap the other app you want to use to open it in the background, all the while continuing to hold your finger on the screen for the first app.

3. The first app will open "floating" above the second app; it's now in Slide Over mode, as illustrated with Notes and News in Figure 2-14.

4. Simply tap the Home button to close Slide Over.

Moving to Split View

If you want to use both apps at the same time, you can move on to Split View. With Slide Over open, tap and drag the small gray handle at the top of the Slide Over window toward the center of the screen to open Split View, as shown in Figure 2-15. Simply tap the Home button to exit Split View.

While you're in Split View, you can drag the heavy black divider (see Figure 2-16) left or right to change the sizes of the panes, or you can have equal space for both apps. Both apps are fully functional, although in some special cases, the app may not show certain noncritical elements to adjust to the narrower width of the split view when compared to the full screen.

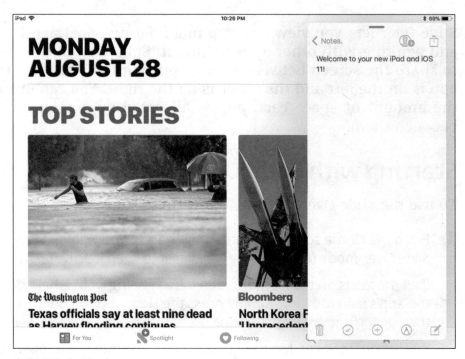

FIGURE 2-14

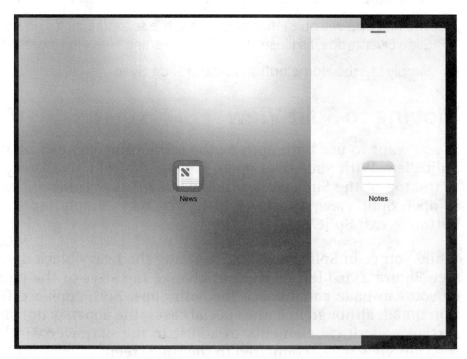

FIGURE 2-15

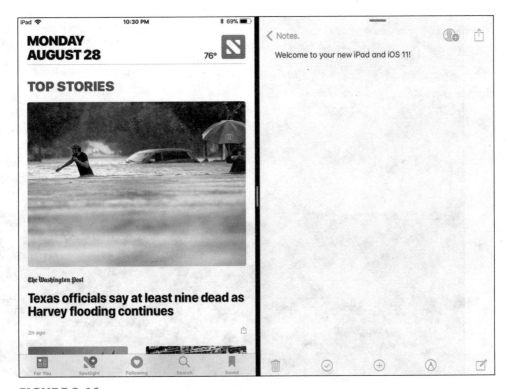

FIGURE 2-16

TIP

You can drag-and-drop items between apps in Slide Over and Split View. For example, with Photos and Notes open, drag-and-drop a picture from Photos into a note in the Notes window. Another example might be dragging a link from a text document into the Safari web browser to open it.

Examine the iPad Cameras

iPads have front- and back-facing cameras. You can use the cameras to take still photos (covered in more detail in Chapter 14) or shoot videos (covered in Chapter 15).

For now, take a quick look at your camera by tapping the Camera app icon on the Home screen. The app opens, as shown in Figure 2-17.

FIGURE 2-17

You can use the controls on the screen to

» Switch between the front and rear cameras.

» Change from still-camera to video-camera operation by using the slider at the bottom of the screen.

» Take a picture or start recording a video.

» Tap the Live button at the top of the settings (upper-right side of the screen) to capture a live photo (if your iPad models supports this feature). Tap the Live button again to disable it; when disabled, the icon will display with an overlaying slash.

» Choose a 3- or 10-second delay with the Timed Photos button.

» Turn HDR (high dynamic range for better contrast) on or off.

» Tap the Flash button to set flash to On, Off, or Auto.

» Take a "burst" of photos by tapping and holding the Camera's button. A small photo count will display above the button to show you how many photos you've taken.

» Open previously captured images or videos.

When you view a photo or video, you can use an iPad sharing feature to send the image by AirDrop, Message, Notes, Mail, and other options (depending on which apps you've installed). You can also share through iCloud Photo Sharing, a tweet, Facebook, or Flickr.

More things that you can do with images are to print them, use a still photo as wallpaper (that is, as your Home or lock screen background image) or assign it to represent a contact, and run a slideshow. See Chapters 14 and 15 for more detail about using the iPad cameras.

Discover Control Center

Control Center is a one-stop screen for common features and settings, such as connecting to a network, increasing screen brightness or volume, and more. Here's how to use it:

1. To display Control Center, swipe up from the very bottom of the screen. The Control Center screen appears to the right of the app switcher.

2. In the Control Center (highlighted in Figure 2-18), tap a button or tap and drag a slider to access or adjust a setting.

3. After you make a change, press the Home button once to exit Control Center.

Some options in Control Center are hidden from initial view but may be accessed using 3D Touch, which basically means tapping and holding a button in Control Center. For example, use 3D Touch (tap and hold) on the Brightness slider to reveal the Night Shift button (as shown in Figure 2-19).

FIGURE 2-18

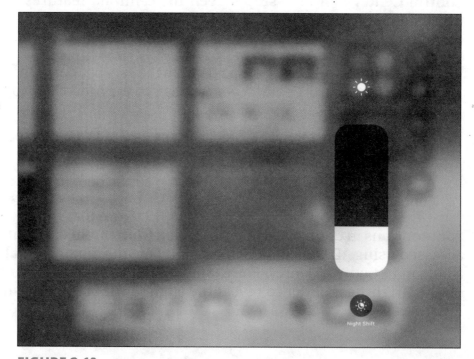

FIGURE 2-19

TIP

Try 3D Touching other buttons in Control Center to see what other options are waiting for you to discover. If you 3D Touch an item and its icon just bounces, no further options are available for the item.

iOS 11 allows you to customize Control Center (one of my favorite of the new features):

1. Tap Settings.

2. Tap Control Center and then tap Customize Controls to open the Customize screen (shown in Figure 2-20).

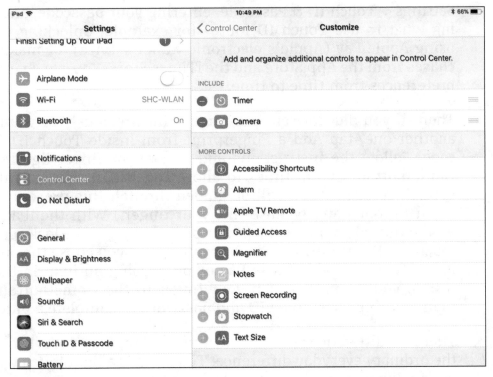

FIGURE 2-20

3. Remove items from Control Center by tapping the – to the left, and then tap the Remove button that appears to the right.

4. To add an item to Control Center, tap the + to the left. You'll see the item in Control Center the next time you visit it. Don't forget to use 3D Touch to find any extras the item may afford.

Understand Touch ID

In previous versions of the iPad, you had to set a password to protect the contents of your iPad and input that password to wake the device again every time it went to sleep. More-recent iPads sport a feature called Touch ID, which allows you to unlock your phone by touching the redesigned Home button. That button now contains a sophisticated fingerprint sensor. Because your fingerprint is unique, this feature is one of the most foolproof ways to protect your data.

If you're going to use Touch ID (it's optional), you must educate the iPad about your fingerprint on your finger of choice by tapping Settings ⇨ Touch ID & Passcode, entering your passcode, and choosing what to use Touch ID for — for example, unlocking the iPad, using Apple Pay (Apple's electronic wallet service), or making purchases from the App Store and the iTunes Store. You can change these preferences from time to time.

Then, if you did not set up a fingerprint previously or want to add another one, tap Add a Fingerprint from inside Touch ID & Passcode. Follow the instructions and press your finger lightly on the Home button several times to allow Touch ID to sense and record your fingerprint. (You will be guided through this process and told when to touch and when to lift your finger.) With the iPad Unlock option turned on, press the power button to go to the lock screen and touch the Home button. The iPad unlocks. If you chose the option for using Touch ID with Apple Pay or purchasing an item in the Apple stores, you'll simply touch your finger to the Home button rather than entering your Apple ID and password to complete a purchase.

TIP

There's a difference between touching and tapping your iPad. It's the ordinary everyday difference: Touching is a light touch without applying pressure. Tapping means you apply pressure — the same amount you would use in tapping people on their shoulder to get their attention.

Lock Screen Rotation

Sometimes you don't want your screen orientation to flip when you move your iPad around. Use these steps to lock the iPad into portrait orientation (narrow and tall, not low and wide):

1. Swipe up from the bottom of any screen to open Control Center.

2. Tap the Lock Screen button. (It's the button in the top-right corner of Control Center.)

3. Press the Home button once to exit Control Center.

Perform the steps again to unlock the screen, if desired.

Explore the Status Bar

Across the top of the iPad screen is the Status bar. Tiny icons in this area can provide useful information, such as the time, battery level, and wireless-connection status. Table 2-1 lists some of the most common items you find on the Status bar.

TABLE 2-1   Common Status Bar Icons

Icon	Name	What It Indicates
	Wi-Fi	You're connected to a Wi-Fi network.
	Activity	A task is in progress — a web page is loading, for example.
2:30 PM	Time	You guessed it: You see the time.
	Screen Rotation Lock	The screen is locked in portrait orientation and doesn't rotate when you turn the iPad.
	Battery Life	This shows the charge percentage remaining in the battery. The indicator changes to a lightning bolt when the battery is charging.

TIP

If you have GPS, 3G/4G (LTE) cellular (if your iPad supports it), Bluetooth service, or a connection to a virtual private network (VPN), a corresponding symbol appears on the Status bar whenever a feature is active. (If you don't already know what a virtual private network is, there's no need to worry about it.)

Take Inventory of Preinstalled Apps

The iPad comes with certain functionality and applications — or apps, for short — built in. When you look at the Home screen, you see icons for each app. This task gives you an overview of what each app does. (You can find out more about every one of them as you read different chapters in this book.)

By default, the following icons appear in the Dock at the bottom of every Home screen (refer to Figure 2-1), from left to right:

» **Messages:** For those who love to instant message, the Messages app comes to the rescue. The Messages app has been in iPad for quite some time. Now you can engage in live text- and image-based conversations with others on their phones or other devices that use email. You can also send video or audio messages.

» **Safari:** You use the Safari web browser (see Figure 2-21) to navigate on the Internet, create and save bookmarks of favorite sites, and add web clips to your Home screen so that you can quickly visit favorite sites from there. You may have used this web browser (or another, such as Google Chrome) on your desktop computer.

» **Mail:** Use this application to access email accounts that you have set up in iPad. Your email is then displayed without you having to browse to the site or sign in. You can use tools to move among a few preset mail folders, read and reply to email, and download attached photos to your iPad. Read more about email accounts in Chapter 10.

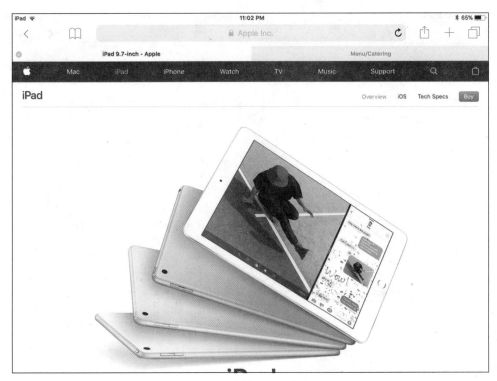

FIGURE 2-21

» **Music:** Music is the name of your media player. Though its main function is to play music, you can use it to play audio podcasts and audiobooks as well.

» **Files:** New to iOS 11, this app allows you to browse files that are stored not only on your iPad (it's about time!), but also files you may have stored on other services, such as iCloud Drive, Google Drive, Dropbox, and the like.

Apps with icons above the Dock on the Home screen include

» **Calendar:** Use this handy onscreen daybook (see Figure 2-22) to set up appointments and send alerts to remind you about them.

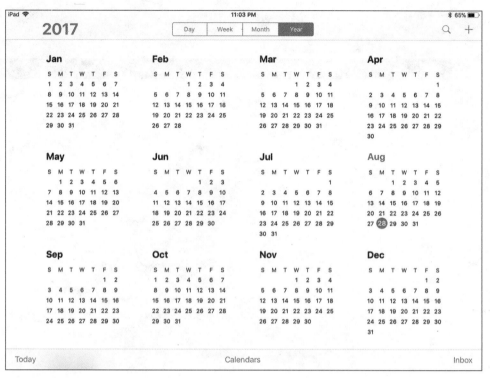

FIGURE 2-22

» **Photos:** The Photos app in iPad helps you organize pictures in folders, send photos in email, use a photo as your iPad wallpaper, and assign pictures to contact records. You can also run slideshows of your photos, open albums, pinch or unpinch to shrink or expand photos, and scroll photos with a simple swipe.

» **FaceTime:** Use FaceTime to place phone calls using video of the sender and receiver to have a more personal conversation.

» **Camera:** The Camera app is Control Center for the still and video cameras built into the iPad.

» **Clock:** This app allows you to display clocks from around the world, set alarms, and use timer and stopwatch features.

» **Maps:** With this iPad mapping app, you can view classic maps or aerial views of addresses and find directions from one place to another whether traveling by car, foot, or public transportation (which requires installing a third-party app). You can even get your directions read aloud by a spoken narration feature.

» **TV:** This media player is similar to Music but specializes in playing videos and offers a few features specific to this type of media, such as chapter breakdowns and information about a movie's plot and cast.

» **Notes:** Enter text, format text, or cut and paste text and objects (such as images) from a website into this simple notepad app.

» **Contacts:** In this address-book feature, you can enter contact information (including photos, if you like, from your Photos or Cameras app) and share contact information by email. You can also use the search feature to find your contacts easily.

» **Reminders:** This useful app centralizes all your calendar entries, alerts to keep you on schedule, and allows you to create to-do lists.

» **News:** News is a customizable aggregator for stories from your favorite news sources.

» **iTunes Store:** Tapping this icon takes you to the iTunes store, where you can shop 'til you drop (or until your iPad battery runs out of juice) for music, movies, TV shows, and audiobooks and then download them directly to your iPad. (See Chapter 11 for more about how the iTunes Store works.)

» **App Store**: Here you can buy and download applications that do everything from enabling you to play games to building business presentations. Many of these apps and games are free!

» **iBooks**: The iBooks app is now bundled with the iPad out of the box. Because the iPad has been touted as being a good small screen e-reader — a device that enables you to read books on an electronic device, similar to the Amazon Kindle Fire HD — you should definitely check this one out. (To work with the iBooks e-reader application itself, go to Chapter 12.)

» **Home**: Home helps you control most (if not all) of your home automation devices in one convenient app.

» **Settings**: Settings is the central location on the iPad where you can specify settings for various functions and do administrative tasks, such as set up email accounts or create a password.

Some preinstalled apps are located on the second Home screen by default, including Tips, Podcasts, Photo Booth (fun for the grand-kids!), Find Friends (fun for the grandparents!), and Find iPhone (which functions to find any of your Apple devices, such as iPad, iPhone, or Apple Watch).

Several useful apps are free for you to download from the App Store, if they're not already preloaded on your iPad. These include iMovie and GarageBand, as well as the Pages, Keynote, and Numbers apps of the iWork suite.

Lock iPad, Turn It Off, or Unlock It

Sleep is a state in which the screen goes black, though you can quickly wake up the iPad. You can also turn off the power to give your new toy a rest.

Here are the procedures you use to put the iPad to sleep or turn it off:

» **Sleep:** Press the Sleep/Wake button, and the iPad goes to sleep. The screen goes black and is locked.

The iPad automatically enters Sleep mode after a brief period of inactivity. You can change the time interval at which it sleeps by adjusting the Auto-Lock feature in Settings ⇨ Display & Brightness.

» **Power Off:** From any app or Home screen, press and hold the Sleep/Wake button until the Slide to Power Off bar appears at the top of the screen, and then swipe the bar. You've just turned off your iPad.

» **Force Off:** If the iPad becomes unresponsive, hold the Power and Home buttons simultaneously until the iPad shuts itself off.

To wake the iPad up from Sleep mode, simply press the Home button once.

TIP

If you have the Passcode feature enabled, you'll need to enter your Passcode before proceeding to unlock your screen after pressing the Home button. However, if you have Touch ID enabled, you need to press the Home button only once and rest your finger on it for it to scan your fingerprints; the iPad will automatically unlock.

TIP

Want a way to shut down your iPad without having to press buttons? Go to Settings ⇨ General and scroll all the way to the bottom of the screen. Tap the Shut Down button, slide the Power Off slider, and your iPad will go off.

Chapter **3**

Beyond the Basics

I n this chapter, I look at updating your iOS version (the operating system that your iPad uses) and making sure that your iPad's battery is charged.

Next, if you want to find free or paid content for your iPad from Apple, from movies to music to e-books to audiobooks, you'll need to have an iTunes account.

You can also use the wireless sync feature to exchange content between your computer and iPad over a wireless network.

Another feature you might take advantage of is the iCloud service from Apple to store and push all kinds of content and data to all your Apple devices — wirelessly. You can pick up where you left off from one device to another through iCloud Drive, an online storage service that enables sharing content among devices so that edits that you make to documents in iCloud are reflected in all iOS devices and Macs running OS X Yosemite or later.

Update the Operating System to iOS 11

This book is based on the latest version of the iPad operating system at the time: iOS 11. To be sure that you have the latest and greatest features, update your iPad to the latest iOS now (and do so periodically to receive minor upgrades to iOS 11 or future versions of iOS). If you've set up an iCloud account on your iPad, you'll receive an alert and can choose to install the update or not, or you can update manually:

1. Tap Settings. (Be sure you have Wi-Fi enabled and that you're connected to a Wi-Fi network to perform these steps.)

2. Tap General.

3. Tap Software Update.

   Your iPad checks to find the latest iOS version and walks you through the updating procedure if an update is available.

Charge the Battery

My iPad showed up in the box fully charged, and I hope yours did, too. Because all batteries run down eventually, one of your first priorities is to know how to recharge your iPad battery.

Gather your iPad and its Lightning-to-USB cable (earlier models have the Dock cable) and the Apple USB power adapter.

Here's how to charge your iPad:

1. Gently plug the Lightning connector end (the smaller of the two connectors) of the Lightning-to-USB cable into the iPad.

TIP
If you have a hard case for your iPad and you're charging for more than several hours, you should remove the iPad from it because these cases retain heat, which is bad for the iPad and the case.

2. Plug the USB end of the Lightning-to-USB cable into the Apple USB power adapter (see Figure 3-1).

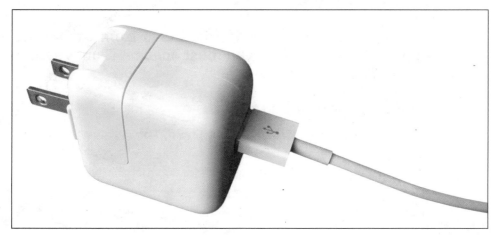

FIGURE 3-1

3. Plug the adapter into an electric outlet.

 TIP
If you're moving from an Android tablet to an iPad, consider downloading the Move to iOS app (which was developed by Apple). This app allows you to wirelessly transfer key content, such as contacts, message history, videos, mail accounts, photos, and more from your old tablet to your new iPad. If you had free apps on your Android device, iPad will suggest you download them from the App Store. Any paid apps will be added to your iTunes Wish List. By the way, when you download the app from the Google Play Store you'll be well-served not to bother reading some of the viciously negative comments made by some Android users who harbor a true hatred of all things Apple.

Sign into an iTunes Account for Music, Movies, and More

The terms iTunes Account and Apple ID are interchangeable: Your Apple ID is your iTunes Account, but you'll need to be signed into iTunes with your Apple ID to download items from the iTunes Store.

To be able to buy or download free items from the iTunes Store or the App Store on your iPad, you must open an iTunes account. Here's how to sign in to an account:

1. Tap Settings on your iPad.
2. Scroll down and tap iTunes & App Store. The screen shown in Figure 3-2 appears.

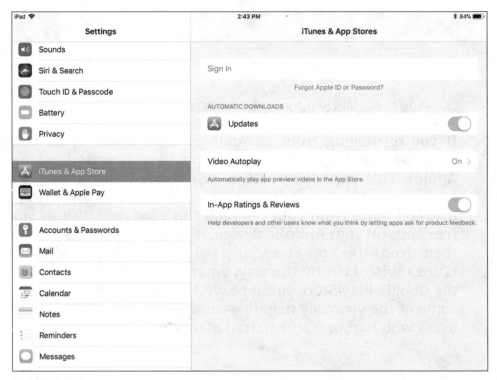

FIGURE 3-2

3. Tap Sign In (see Figure 3-3), enter your Apple ID and password, and then tap the Sign In button.

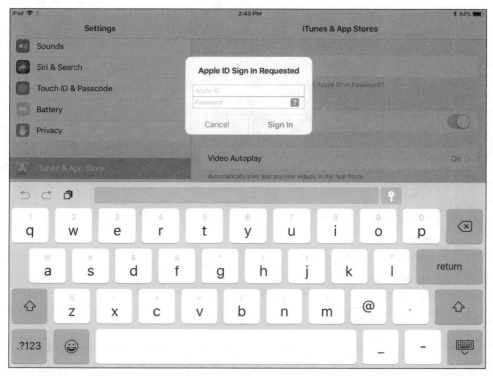

FIGURE 3-3

4. Tap Password Settings in the iTunes & App Store screen to bring up the screen shown in Figure 3-4.

5. Select whether you'd like your password to be requested every time a download is attempted (recommended) or to allow downloads for up to 15 minutes after the password has been entered without having to reenter it. Also, toggle the switch to On or Off (depending on whether you require your password to be entered when downloading free items). I recommend setting it to On; even if an app is free, there may be some items that you just don't want loaded onto your iPad without your permission.

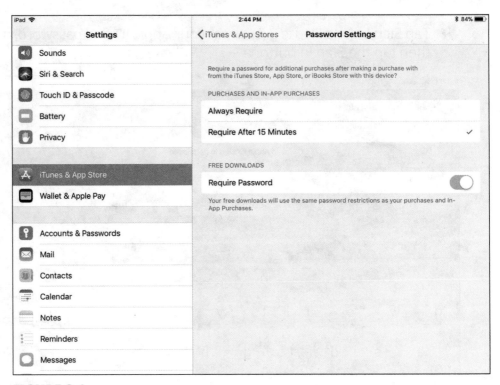

FIGURE 3-4

TIP

If you prefer not to leave your credit card info with Apple, one option is to buy an iTunes gift card and provide that as your payment information. You can replenish the card periodically through the Apple Store.

Sync Wirelessly

You can connect your iPad to a computer and use the tools there to sync content on your computer to your iPad. Also, with Wi-Fi turned on in Settings, use the iTunes Wi-Fi Sync setting to allow cordless syncing if you're within range of a Wi-Fi network that has a computer connected to it with iTunes installed and open.

There are a few steps you have to take with your iPad connected to your computer before you can perform a wireless sync with iTunes:

1. If you're charging with an electrical outlet, remove the power adapter.

2. Use the Lightning-to-USB cable to connect your iPad to your computer.

3. Open iTunes and then click the icon of an iPad that appears in the tools in the left corner of the screen (see Figure 3-5).

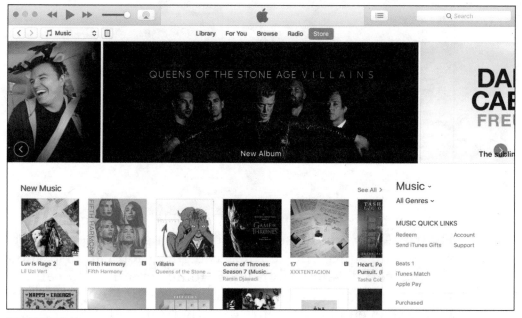

FIGURE 3-5

4. Click the check box labeled Sync with this iPad over Wi-Fi (as seen in Figure 3-6).

TIP

You may need to scroll down a bit to see the Sync with this iPad over Wi-Fi option.

5. Click Apply in the lower-right corner of the iTunes window.

6. Disconnect your iPad from your computer.

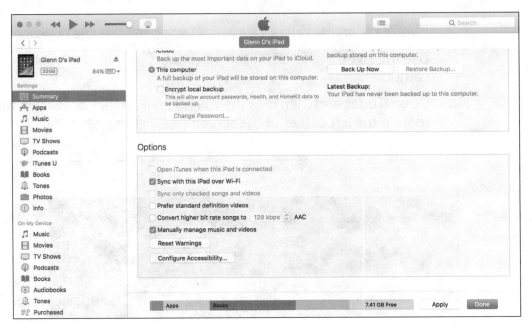

FIGURE 3-6

TIP

You can click any item on the left side of the screen shown in Figure 3-6 to handle settings for syncing such items as Movies, Music, and Apps. In the Apps category, you can also choose to remove certain apps from your Home screens. You can also tap the list of items in the On My Device section on the left side to view and even play contents directly from your iPad.

After you complete the preceding steps, you'll be able to wirelessly sync your iPad with your computer. Follow these steps:

TIP

1. Back up your iPad.

   Chapter 20 shows how to back up your iPad.

2. On the iPad, tap Settings ⇨ General ⇨ iTunes Wi-Fi Sync. The iTunes Wi-Fi Sync settings appear.

3. In the iTunes Wi-Fi Sync settings, tap Sync Now to sync with a computer connected to the same Wi-Fi network.

4. If you need to connect your iPad to a network, tap Settings ⇨ Wi-Fi and then tap a network to join.

TIP

If you have your iPad set up to sync wirelessly to your Mac or PC and both are within range of the same Wi-Fi network, iPad will appear in your iTunes Devices list. This setup allows you to sync and manage syncing from within iTunes.

Your iPad will automatically sync with iTunes once a day if both are on the same Wi-Fi network, iTunes is running, and your iPad is charging.

Understand iCloud

There's an alternative to syncing content by using iTunes. iCloud is a service offered by Apple that allows you to back up most of your content to online storage. That content is then pushed automatically to all your Apple devices through a wireless connection.

All you need to do is get an iCloud account, which is free (again, this is simply using your Apple ID), and make settings on your devices and in iTunes for which types of content you want pushed to each device. After you've done that, content that you create or purchase on one device — such as music, apps, and TV shows, as well as documents created in Apple's iWork apps (Pages, Keynote, and Numbers), photos, and so on — is synced among your devices automatically.

TIP

See Chapter 11 for more about using the Family Sharing feature to share content that you buy online and more with family members through iCloud.

You can stick with iCloud's default storage capacity, or you can increase it if you need more capacity:

> » Your iCloud account includes 5GB of free storage. You may be fine with the free 5GB of storage.

Content that you purchase from Apple (such as apps, books, music, iTunes Match content, Photo Sharing contents, and TV shows) isn't counted against your storage.

» If you want additional storage, you can buy an upgrade. Currently, 50GB costs only $0.99 per month.

To upgrade your storage, go to Settings, tap your Apple ID at the top of the screen, go to iCloud ⇨ Manage Storage, and then tap Change Storage Plan next to iCloud Storage. On the next screen, tap the amount you need and then tap Buy (in the upper-right corner), as shown in Figure 3-7.

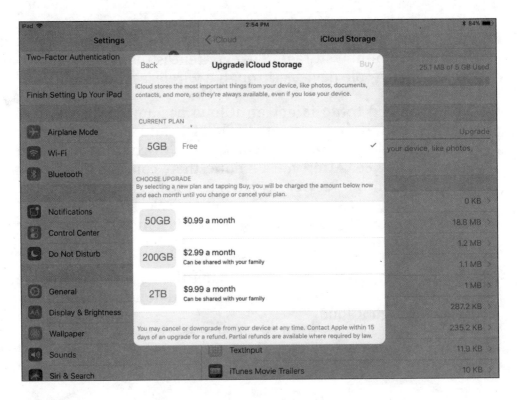

FIGURE 3-7

If you change your mind, you can get in touch with Apple within 15 days to cancel your upgrade.

Turn on iCloud Drive

iCloud Drive is the online storage space that comes free with iCloud (as covered in the preceding section).

Before you can use iCloud Drive, you need to be sure that iCloud Drive is turned on. Here's how to turn on iCloud Drive:

1. Tap Settings and then tap your Apple ID at the top of the screen.
2. Tap iCloud to open the iCloud screen.
3. Scroll down in the iCloud screen and tap iCloud Drive.
4. Tap the On/Off switch to turn on (green) iCloud Drive (see Figure 3-8).

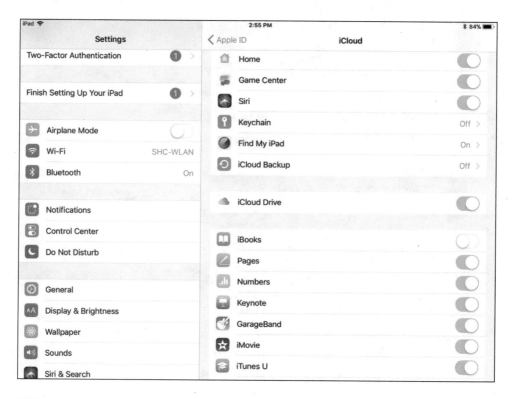

FIGURE 3-8

Make iCloud Sync Settings

When you have an iCloud account up and running, you have to specify which type of content should be synced with your iPad by iCloud.
Follow these steps:

1. Tap Settings, tap your Apple ID at the top of the screen, and then tap
iCloud.

2. In the iCloud settings shown in Figure 3-9, tap the On/Off switch for
any item that's turned off that you want to turn on (or vice versa). You
can sync Photos, Mail, Contacts, Calendars, Reminders, Safari, Notes,
News, Wallet, Keychain (an app that stores all your passwords and
even credit card numbers across all Apple devices), and more. The
listing of apps on this screen isn't alphabetical, so scroll down if at first
you don't see what you're looking for.

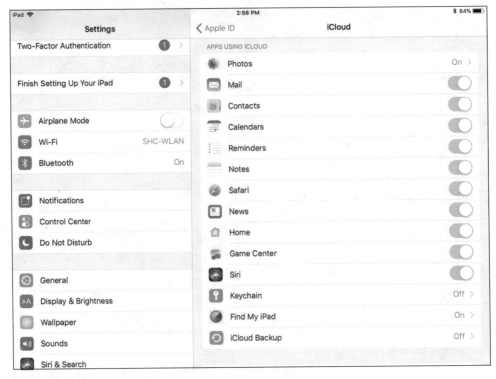

FIGURE 3-9

TIP

If you want to allow iCloud to provide a service for locating a lost or stolen iPad, toggle the On/Off switch in the Find My iPad field to On (green) to activate it. This service helps you locate, send a message to, or delete content from your iPad if it falls into other hands. See Chapter 22 for more information.

3. To enable automatic downloads of iTunes-purchased music, apps, and books, return to the main Settings screen and then tap iTunes & App Store.

4. Tap the On/Off switch for Music, Apps, Books & Audiobooks, or Updates to set up automatic downloads of any of this content to your iPad by iCloud.

TIP

Consider turning off the Cellular Data option (if your iPad supports it), which you find in the Cellular section of Settings, to avoid having these downloads occur over your cellular connection, which can use up your data allowance. Wait until you're on a Wi-Fi connection to have iPad perform the updates.

Browse Your iPad's Files

Long-time iPad users have pined for a way to browse files stored on their devices, as opposed to being limited to finding documents and other files only within the apps they're intended for or created by. Finally, iOS 11 introduces us to a new app called Files, which will allow you to browse not only for files stored on your iPad, but also see the stuff that you've stored on other online (cloud) services, such as Google Drive, Dropbox, and others.

You'll find the Files app in the Dock at the bottom of your screen, by default.

1. Tap the Files icon to open the app.

2. On the Browse screen (shown in Figure 3-10):

   • Tap the Search field to search for items by title.

   • Tap a source in the Locations or Favorites sections to browse a particular service or your iPad.

FIGURE 3-10

- Tap colors under Tags to search for files you've tagged according to categories.

3. Once in a source (see Figure 3-11), you may tap files to open or preview them, and you may tap folders to open them and view their contents.

4. Tap Select in the upper-right corner of the screen and then tap items to select them for an action. Available actions, found at the bottom of the screen, include

- **Duplicating files:** Make copies of selected items.

- **Moving files:** Move files to other sources.

- **Sharing files:** Share files with other people in a variety of ways (Messages and Mail, for example), and you can even invite them to make edits, if you like.

- **Deleting files:** Trash files you no longer need.

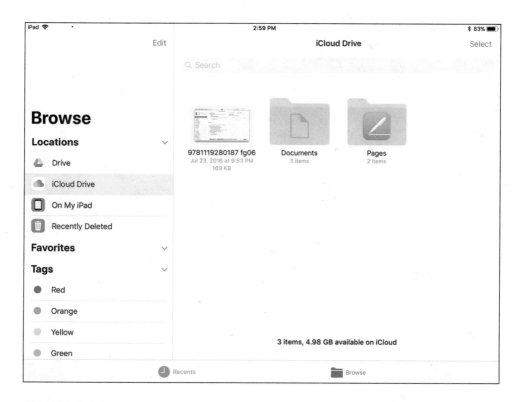

FIGURE 3-11

TIP

Should you like to retrieve a file you've deleted, go the Browse screen (tap Browse at the bottom of the screen if you're not already there) and tap Recently Deleted in the left toolbar. Tap Select in the upper-right corner, tap the file you'd like to retrieve, and tap the Recover button at the bottom of the screen. The file will be placed back in the location it was originally deleted from. Please note that some services may not allow you to retrieve a file you've deleted, so if you don't see the file you're looking for, contact that particular service.

2
Beginning to Use Your iPad

IN THIS PART . . .

Understanding accessibility features

Getting to know Siri, the iPad's built-in virtual assistant

Discovering new apps

Reaching out with FaceTime and Messages

Using social media and the Internet

Working with email

Chapter **4**

Making Your iPad More Accessible

iPad users are all different, and some face visual, motor, or hearing challenges. If you're one of these folks, you'll be glad to hear that iPad offers some handy accessibility features.

To make your screen easier to read, you can use the Magnifier, adjust the brightness, or change wallpaper. You can also set up the VoiceOver feature to read onscreen elements out loud. Then you can turn a slew of features on or off, including Zoom, Invert Colors, Speak Selection, Large Type, and more.

If hearing is your challenge, you can do the obvious thing and adjust the system volume. The iPad also allows you to use mono audio (useful when you're wearing headphones) and an LED flash when an alert sounds.

Features that help you deal with physical and motor challenges include an AssistiveTouch feature if you have difficulty using the iPad touchscreen, Switch Control for working with adaptive accessories, and the Home Button and Call Audio Routing settings that allow you to adjust how quickly you have to tap the iPad screen to work with features and whether you can use a headset or speaker to answer calls.

Finally, the Guided Access feature helps if you have difficulty focusing on one task. It also provides a handy mode for showing presentations of content in settings where you don't want users to flit off to other apps, as in school or a public kiosk.

Use Magnifier

The Magnifier feature uses your iPad's camera to help you magnify objects. Magnifier is considered an accessibility feature, but almost everyone needs a magnifier at one time or another. To access Magnifier:

1. Tap Settings ➪ General ➪ Accessibility, as shown in Figure 4-1.

2. Tap Magnifier and then toggle the Magnifier switch to On (green).

3. Press the Home button three times to turn Magnifier on. (I find it easiest to do that with my thumb while I'm holding the iPad.)

When Magnifier is on, you can use the back camera of your iPad just like a magnifying glass. In fact, it's like an illuminated magnifying glass. You see the magnified image on your screen. A slider lets you set the degree of magnification, as shown in Figure 4-2. You can also turn on a light by tapping the lightning bolt icon in the lower-left corner (if your iPad includes one) and lock the magnification level (also at the left). At the right, the three circles let you change the colors. Use the round button (like a camera shutter) to have the iPad adjust its focus for what you're pointing at.

FIGURE 4-1

in matter when the proper dispositions cease to exist. In this way, when the heat, natural humidity, and the like, are removed from the body, the union of soul and body is destroyed, because the body is disposed to receive the soul by means of these things. Hence things of this kind intervene as dispositions between the soul and the body. The explanation of this was given above.

17. Dimensions can be considered to exist in matter only so far as matter is given substantial corporeal existence through a substantial form. In man this kind of existence is not bestowed by any other form than the soul, as has been explained. Consequently these dimensions are not understood actually to precede the existence of the soul in matter absolutely, but relative to the highest grades of perfection, as was explained above.

18. The soul and the body do not differ from each other as things of different genera and species do, because neither of them exists in a genus or a species, but only the composite of which they are parts, as we have shown in the preceding questions. However, the soul by its very essence is the form of the body giving it its act of existing. Hence it is united to the body essentially and directly.

19. The human body has something in common with a celestial body; not inasmuch as something characteristic of a celestial body, such as light, intervenes as a medium between the soul and the body, but inasmuch as the human body is given a certain tempered combination lacking contrariety, as was shown in preceding questions.[14]

[14] See op. LIX, De pluralitate formarum.

ades of perfection, as

body do not differ from

a and species do, beca

a species, but only th

e have shown in the p

by its very essence is t

existing. Hence it is

tly

FIGURE 4-2

You can combine magnification with your iPad's portability so that you can reach up to (or behind) an object and magnify something that would not only be too small to see otherwise but would be out of view entirely.

Set Brightness and Night Shift

Especially when using iPad as an e-reader, you may find that a slightly less bright screen reduces strain on your eyes. To adjust screen brightness, follow these steps:

1. Tap the Settings icon on the Home screen.

   If glare from the screen is a problem for you, consider getting a screen protector. This thin film both protects your screen from damage and reduces glare. You can easily find them on Amazon, and just about any cellphone dealer carries them.

2. In Settings, tap Display & Brightness.

3. To control brightness manually, tap and drag the Brightness slider (see Figure 4-3) to the right to make the screen brighter or to the left to make it dimmer.

4. Press the Home button to close Settings.

By default, your iPad automatically adjusts brightness according to the amount of light detected in your current environment. To disable this feature, go to General⇨ Accessibility⇨ Display Accommodations and tap the Auto-Brightness switch to Off.

In the iBooks e-reader app, you can set a sepia tone for the page, which may be easier on your eyes. See Chapter 12 for more about using iBooks.

Night Shift is another option in Display & Brightness that you can use during hours of darkness. It changes the screen colors to reduce the amount of blue in the images on your iPad. Bright blue light seems to interfere with sleep in some people, so turning on Night Shift if you read before bed (or in bed) may help you sleep better.

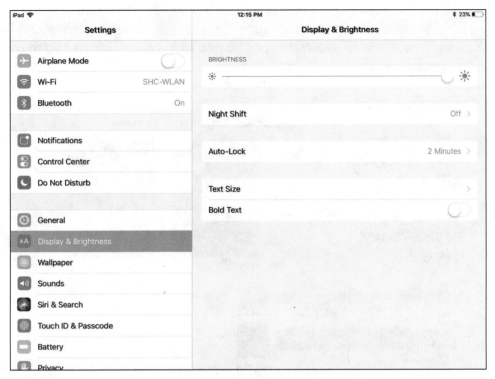

FIGURE 4-3

Change the Wallpaper

The default iPad background image on your iPad may be pretty, but it may not be the one that works best for you. Choosing different wallpaper may help you see all the icons on your Home screen. Follow these steps:

1. Tap the Settings icon on the Home screen.

2. In Settings, tap Wallpaper.

3. In the Wallpaper settings, tap Choose a New Wallpaper.

4. Tap a wallpaper category, as shown in Figure 4-4, to view choices.

5. Tap a sample to select it.

TIP

If you prefer to use a picture that's on your iPad, tap an album in the lower part of the Wallpaper screen to locate a picture; tap to use it as your wallpaper.

FIGURE 4-4

6. In the preview that appears (see Figure 4-5), tap your choice of

- Set Lock Screen (the screen that appears when you lock the iPad by tapping the power button)

- Set Home Screen

- Set Both

TECHNICAL STUFF

Some wallpaper may allow you to select either

- Still (the picture is static)

- Perspective (the picture seems to move when you move your iPad)

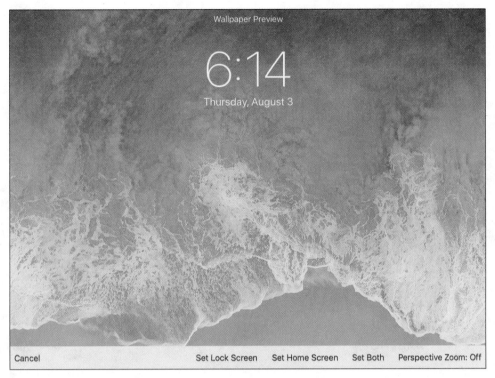

Wallpaper Preview

6:14

Thursday, August 3

Cancel   Set Lock Screen   Set Home Screen   Set Both   Perspective Zoom: Off

FIGURE 4-5

7. Press the Home button.

You return to your Home screen with the new wallpaper set as the background.

Set Up VoiceOver

VoiceOver reads the names of screen elements and settings to you, but it also changes the way you provide input to the iPad. In Notes, for example, you can have VoiceOver read the name of the Notes buttons to you, and when you enter notes, it reads words or characters that you've entered. It can also tell you whether such features as Auto-Correction are on.

To turn on VoiceOver, follow these steps:

1. Tap the Settings icon on the Home screen.

2. In Settings, tap General and then tap Accessibility.

3. In the Accessibility pane, shown in Figure 4-6, tap VoiceOver.

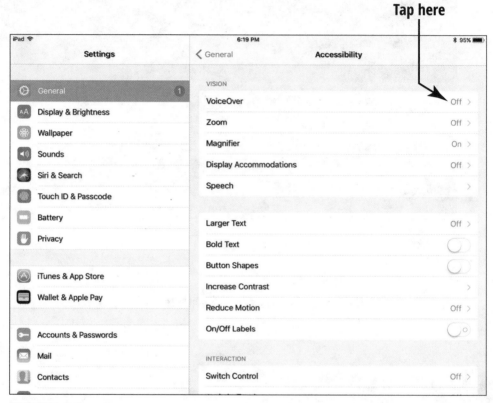

FIGURE 4-6

4. In the VoiceOver pane, shown in Figure 4-7, tap the VoiceOver On/Off switch to turn on this feature. With VoiceOver on, you must first single-tap to select an item such as a button, which causes VoiceOver to read the name of the button to you. Then you double-tap the button to activate its function.

Tap here

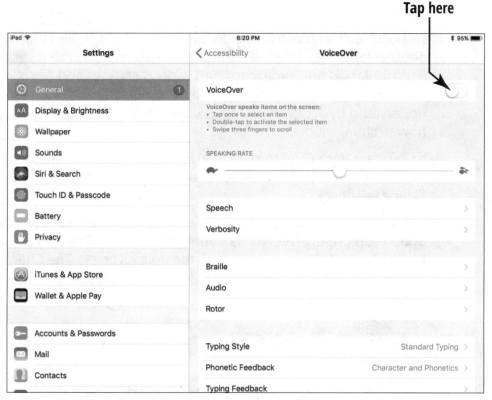

FIGURE 4-7

5. Tap the VoiceOver Practice button to select it and then double-tap the button to open VoiceOver Practice. (This is the new method of tapping that VoiceOver activates.) Practice using gestures (such as pinching or flicking left), and VoiceOver tells you what action each gesture initiates.

6. Tap the Done button and then double-tap the same button to return to the VoiceOver dialog.

7. Tap the Verbosity button once and then double-tap to open its options:

- Tap the Speak Hints On/Off switch and then double-tap the switch to turn the feature on (or off). VoiceOver speaks the name of each tapped item.

- Tap once and then double-tap the VoiceOver button in the upper-left corner to go back to the VoiceOver screen.

TIP

You can change the language that VoiceOver speaks. In General settings, tap Language & Region, tap iPad Language, and then select another language. However, this action also changes the language used for labels on Home icons and various settings and fields in iPad. Be careful with this setting, lest you choose a language you don't understand by accident and have a very difficult time figuring out how to change it back.

8. If you want VoiceOver to read words or characters to you (for example, in the Notes app), scroll down and then tap and double-tap Typing Feedback.

9. In the Typing Feedback dialog, tap and then double-tap to select the option you prefer. The Words option causes VoiceOver to read words to you, but not characters, such as the dollar sign ($). The Characters and Words option causes VoiceOver to read both and so on.

10. Press the Home button to return to the Home screen.

The following section shows how to navigate your iPad after you've turned on VoiceOver.

TIP

You can use the Accessibility Shortcut setting to help you more quickly turn the VoiceOver, Zoom, Switch Control, Assistive-Touch, Grayscale, or Invert Colors features on and off:

1. In the Accessibility screen, tap Accessibility Shortcut (at the very bottom of the screen).

2. In the screen that appears, choose what you want three presses of the Home button to activate. Now three presses with a single finger on the Home button provide you with the option you selected wherever you go in iPad.

Use VoiceOver

After VoiceOver is turned on (see preceding section), you need to figure out how to use it. I won't kid you — using it is awkward at first, but you'll get the hang of it!

Here are the main onscreen gestures you should know how to use:

» **Tap an item to select it.** VoiceOver then speaks its name.

» **Double-tap the selected item.** This action activates the item.

» **Flick three fingers.** It takes three fingers to scroll around a page with VoiceOver turned on.

TIP

If tapping with two or three fingers seems difficult for you, try tapping with one finger from one hand and one or two from the other. When double- or triple-tapping, you have to perform these gestures as quickly as you can for them to work.

Table 4-1 provides additional gestures to help you use VoiceOver. If you want to use this feature often, I recommend the VoiceOver section of the iPad online User Guide, which goes into great detail about using VoiceOver. You'll find the User Guide at `https://support.apple.com/manuals/iPad`. When there, just click on the model of iPad or the version of iOS you have to read its manual. You can also get an iBooks version of the manual through that app in the iBooks Store.

TABLE 4-1 **VoiceOver Gestures**

Gesture	Effect
Flick right or left	Select the next or preceding item
Tap with two fingers	Stop speaking the current item
Flick two fingers up	Read everything from the top of the screen
Flick two fingers down	Read everything from the current position
Flick three fingers up or down	Scroll one page at a time
Flick three fingers right or left	Go to the next or preceding page
Tap three fingers	Speak the scroll status (for example, line 20 of 100)
Flick four fingers up or down	Go to the first or last element on a page
Flick four fingers right or left	Go to the next or preceding section (as on a web page)

TIP Check out some of the settings for VoiceOver, including a choice for Braille, Language Rotor for making language choices, the ability to navigate images, and a setting to have iPad speak notifications.

Make Additional Vision Settings

Several Vision features are simple on/off settings that you can turn on or off after you tap Settings ⇨ General ⇨ Accessibility:

» **Zoom:** The Zoom feature enlarges the contents displayed on the iPad screen when you double-tap the screen with three fingers. The Zoom feature works almost everywhere in iPad: in Photos, on web pages, on your Home screens, in your Mail, in Music, and in Videos. Give it a try!

» **Magnifier:** Enable Magnifier to use your iPad's built-in camera as a magnifying glass. Just triple-click the Home button to activate it (after you've turned the feature on, of course).

» **Display Accommodations:** Includes such features as

- Color Filters (aids in case of color blindness)
- Reduce White Point (helps reduce the intensity of bright colors)
- Invert Colors (which reverses colors on your screen so that white backgrounds are black and black text is white)

TIP The Invert Colors feature works well in some places and not so well in others. For example, in the Photos application, pictures appear almost as photo negatives (which is a really cool trick to try). Your Home screen image will likewise look a bit strange. And don't even think of playing a video with this feature turned on! However, if you need help reading text, White on Black can be useful in several apps.

» **Speech:** Options here include the ability to have your iPad speak items you've selected or hear the content of an entire screen, highlight content as it's spoken, and more.

» **Larger Text**: If having larger text in such apps as Contacts, Mail, and Notes would be helpful to you, you can turn on the Larger Text feature and choose the text size that works best for you.

» **Bold Text:** Turning on this setting restarts your iPad (after asking you for permission to do so) and then causes text in various apps and in Settings to be bold.

» **Button Shapes:** This setting applies shapes to buttons so that they're more easily distinguishable. For an example, check out the General button in the upper-left corner of the screen after you enable Button Shapes by toggling its switch to On. Turn it back off and notice the difference (shown in Figure 4-8).

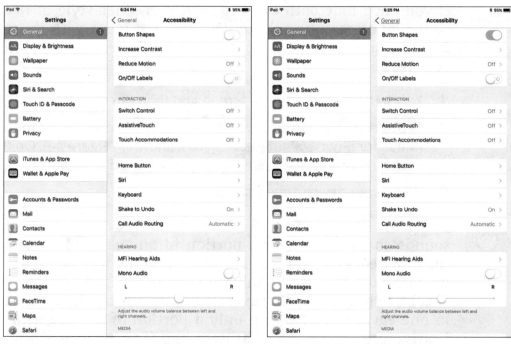

FIGURE 4-8

» **Increase Contrast:** Use this setting to set up backgrounds in some areas of iPad and apps with greater contrast, which should improve visibility.

- » **Reduce Motion:** Tap this accessibility feature and then tap the On/Off setting to turn off the parallax effect, which causes the background of your Home screens to appear to float as you move the iPad around.

- » **On/Off Labels:** If you have trouble making out colors and therefore find it hard to tell when an On/Off setting is On (green) or Off (white), use this setting to add a circle to the right of a setting when it's off and a white vertical line to a setting when it's on.

Use iPad with Hearing Aids

If you have Bluetooth enabled or use another style of hearing aid, your iPhone may be able to detect it and work with its settings to improve sound. Follow these steps to connect your hearing aid to your iPad.

1. Tap Settings on the Home screen and then tap General.

2. Tap Accessibility, scroll down to the Hearing section, and tap MFi (Made for iPhone/iPad) Hearing Aids, shown in Figure 4-9. On the next screen, your iPad searches for hearing aid devices.

3. When your device appears, tap it.

TIP

Using the stereo effect in headphones or a headset breaks up sounds so that you hear a portion in one ear and a portion in the other ear. The purpose is to simulate the way your ears process sounds. If there is only one channel of sound, that sound is sent to both ears. However, if you're hard of hearing or deaf in one ear, you're hearing only a portion of the sound in your hearing ear, which can be frustrating. If you have such hearing challenges and want to use iPad with a headset connected, you should turn on Mono Audio in the Hearing section of the Accessibility options. When it's turned on, all sound is combined and distributed to both ears. You can use the slider below Mono Audio to direct more sound to the ear you hear best with.

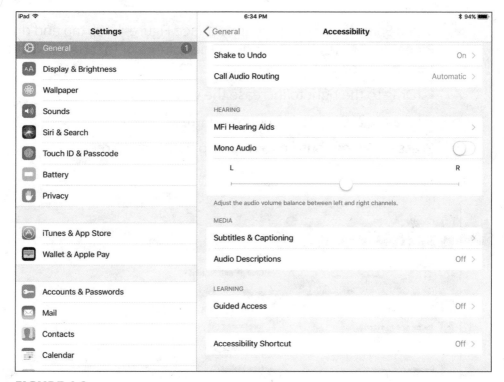

FIGURE 4-9

TIP

If you have a non-MFi hearing aid, add your hearing aid in Bluetooth settings. To do so, go to Settings ⇨ Bluetooth, make sure the Bluetooth toggle switch is On (green), and select your hearing aid in the list of devices.

Adjust the Volume

Though individual apps (such as Music and TV) have their own volume settings, you can set your iPad system volume for your ringer and alerts as well to help you better hear what's going on. Follow these steps:

1. Tap Settings on the Home screen and then tap Sounds.

TIP

In the Sounds settings, you can turn on or off the sounds that iPad makes when certain events occur (such as receiving new Mail or Calendar alerts). These sounds are turned on by default.

2. In the Sounds settings that appear (see Figure 4-10), tap and drag the Ringer and Alerts slider to adjust the volume of these audible attention grabbers:

- Drag to the right to increase the volume.
- Drag to the left to lower the volume.

3. Press the Home button to return to the Home screen.

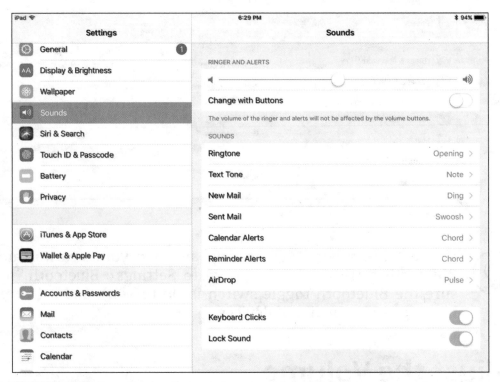

FIGURE 4-10

Set Up Subtitles and Captioning

Closed captioning and subtitles help folks with hearing challenges enjoy entertainment and educational content. Follow these steps:

1. Tap Settings on the Home screen, tap General, and then tap Accessibility.

TIP

2. Scroll down to the Media section and tap Subtitles & Captioning.

3. On the following screen, shown in Figure 4-11, tap the On/Off switch to turn on Closed Captions + SDH (Subtitles for the Deaf and Hard of Hearing).

   You can also tap Style and choose a text style for the captions. A neat video helps show you what your style will look like when the feature is in use.

4. Press the Home button to return to the Home screen.

Tap here

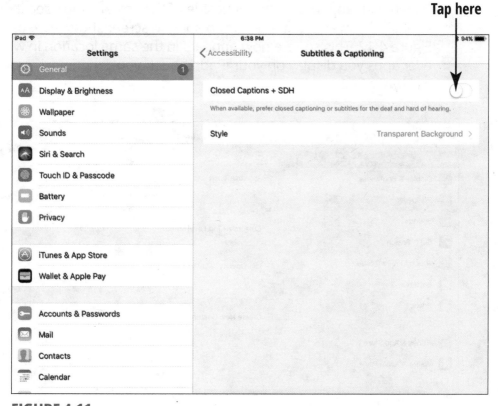

FIGURE 4-11

Turn On and Work with AssistiveTouch

If you have difficulty using buttons, the AssistiveTouch Control Panel aids input using the touchscreen.

1. To turn on AssistiveTouch, tap Settings on the Home screen and then tap General and Accessibility.

2. In the Accessibility pane, scroll down and tap AssistiveTouch. In the pane that appears, tap the On/Off switch for AssistiveTouch to turn it on (see Figure 4-12). A gray square (called the AssistiveTouch Control Panel) then appears on the right side of the screen; you'll see it on your iPad's screen, but it doesn't display in screenshots, such as Figure 4-12. This square now appears in the same location in whatever apps you display on your iPad, though you can move it around with your finger.

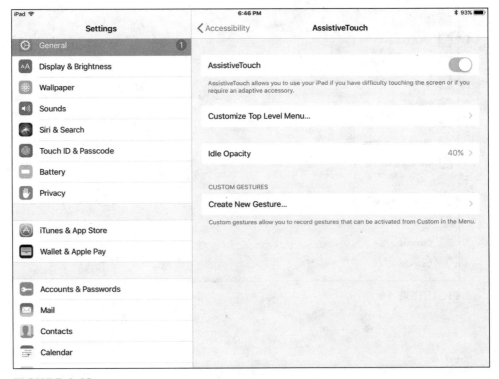

FIGURE 4-12

3. Tap the AssistiveTouch Control Panel to display options, as shown in Figure 4-13. The panel includes Notifications and Control Center options.

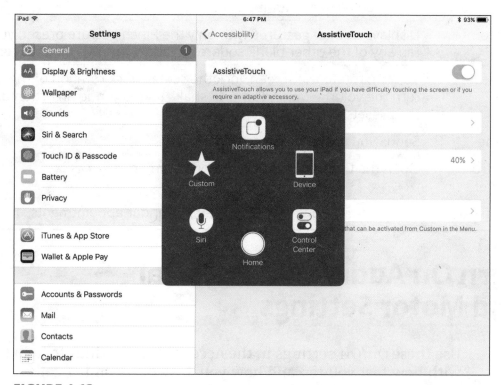

FIGURE 4-13

4. You can tap Custom or Device on the panel to see additional choices, tap Siri to activate the personal assistant feature, tap Notifications or Control Center to display those panels, or press Home to go directly to the Home screen. After you choose an option, pressing the Home button takes you back to the Home screen.

Table 4-2 shows the major options available in the AssistiveTouch Control panel and their purpose.

TABLE 4-2 **AssistiveTouch Controls**

Control	Purpose
Siri	Activates the Siri feature, which allows you to speak questions and make requests of your iPad
Custom	Displays a set of gestures with only the Pinch gesture preset; you can tap any of the other blank squares to add your own favorite gestures
Device	You can rotate the screen, lock the screen, lock rotation of the screen, turn the volume up or down, or shake iPad to undo an action using the presets in this option
Home	Sends you to the Home screen
Control Center	Open the Control Center common commands
Notifications	Open Notifications with reminders, Calendar appointments, and so on

Turn On Additional Physical and Motor Settings

Use these On/Off settings in the Accessibility settings to help you deal with how fast you tap and how you answer incoming calls:

» **Home Button:** Sometimes if you have dexterity challenges, it's hard to double-press or triple-press the Home button fast enough to make an effect. Choose the Slow or Slowest option when you tap this setting to allow you a bit more time to make that second or third tap. Also, the Rest Finger to Open feature at the bottom of the screen is helpful by allowing you to simply rest your finger on the Home button to open your iPad using Touch ID (if enabled), as opposed to needing to press the Home button.

» **Call Audio Routing:** If you prefer to use your speaker phone to receive incoming calls, or you typically use a headset with your iPad that allows you to tap a button to receive a call, tap this option and then choose Headset or Speaker. Speakers and headsets can both provide a better hearing experience for many.

TIP

If you have certain adaptive accessories that allow you to control devices with head gestures, you can use them to control your iPad, highlighting features in sequence and then selecting one. Use the Switch Control feature in the Accessibility settings to turn this mode on and make settings.

Focus Learning with Guided Access

Guided Access is a feature that you can use to limit a user's access to iPad to a single app, and even limit access in that app to certain features. This feature is useful in several settings, ranging from a classroom, for use by someone with attention deficit disorder, and even to a public setting (such as a kiosk where you don't want users to be able to open other apps).

1. Tap Settings and then tap General.

2. Tap Accessibility and then scroll down and tap Guided Access; then, on the screen that follows (see Figure 4-14), tap Guided Access to turn the feature on.

3. Tap Passcode Settings and then tap Set Guided Access Passcode to activate a passcode so that those using an app can't return to the Home screen to access other apps.

4. In the Set Passcode dialog that appears (see Figure 4-15), enter a passcode using the numeric pad. Enter the number again when prompted.

5. Press the Home button and tap an app to open it.

6. Rapidly press the Home button three times. You're presented with an Options button along the bottom of the screen; tap the button to display these options:

   • **Sleep/Wake Button:** You can put your iPad to sleep or wake it up with three presses of the Home button.

   • **Volume Buttons:** You can tap Always On or Always Off. If you don't want users to be able to adjust volume using the volume toggle on the side of the iPad, for example, use this setting.

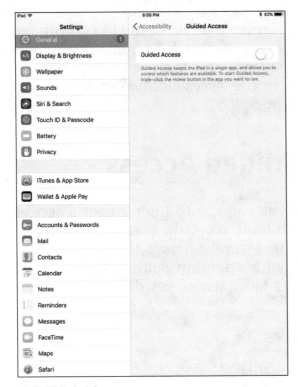

FIGURE 4-14

FIGURE 4-15

- **Motion:** Turn this setting off if you don't want users to move the iPad around — for example, to play a race car driving game.

- **Keyboards:** Use this setting to prohibit people using this app from entering text using the keyboard.

- **Touch:** If you don't want users to be able to use the touchscreen, turn this off.

- **Time Limit:** Tap this and use settings that are displayed to set a time limit for the use of the app.

7. Tap Done to hide the options.

TIP

At this point, you can also use your finger to circle areas of the screen that you want to disable, such as a Store button in the Music app.

8. Press the Start button and then press the Home button three times. Enter your passcode, if you set one, and tap End.

9. Tap the Home button again to return to the Home screen.

Chapter **5**

Conversing with Siri

One of the hottest features on iPad is Siri, a personal assistant feature that responds to the commands you speak to your iPad. With Siri, you can ask for nearby restaurants, and a list appears. You can dictate your email messages rather than type them. You can open apps with a voice command or open the App Store. Placing a FaceTime call to your mother is as simple as saying, "Call Mom." Want to know the capital of Rhode Island? Just ask. Siri checks several online sources to answer questions ranging from the result of a mathematical equation to the next scheduled flight to Rome (Italy or Georgia). You can have Siri search photos and videos and locate what you need by date, location, or album name. Ask Siri to remind you about an app you're working in, such as Safari, Mail, or Notes, at a later time so that you can pick up where you left off.

You can also have Siri perform tasks, such as returning calls and controlling Music. Finally, you can even play music or have Siri identify tagged songs (songs that contain embedded information that identifies them by categories such as artist or genre of music) for you.

Siri has gained some other improvements with its newest incarnation. For example, you can hail a ride with Uber or Lyft, watch live TV just by saying "Watch ESPN" (or, say, another app you might use, such as CBS), find tagged photos, make payments with some third-party apps, and more.

Activate Siri

When you first go through the process of registering your iPad, you see a screen similar to Figure 5-1; tap Get Started to begin making settings for your location, using iCloud, and so on, and at one point, you will see the option to activate Siri. As you begin to use your device, iPad reminds you about using Siri by displaying a message.

TIP

If you buy a car with the Car Play feature, you can interact with your car using your voice and Siri.

TIP

Siri is available on the iPad only when you have Internet access, but remember that cellular data charges may apply when Siri checks online sources if that Internet connection is via 3G/4G (LTE). In addition, Apple warns that available features may vary by area.

If you didn't activate Siri during the registration process, you can use Settings to turn Siri on by following these steps:

1. Tap the Settings icon on the Home screen.

2. Tap Siri & Search (see Figure 5-2).

3. In the Siri & Search dialog on the right, toggle the On/Off switch to On (green) to activate any or all of the following features:

FIGURE 5-1

FIGURE 5-2

- If you want to be able to activate Siri for hands-free use, toggle the Listen for "Hey Siri" switch to turn on the feature. With this feature enabled, just say "Hey, Siri," and Siri opens up, ready for a command. In addition, with streaming voice recognition, Siri displays in text what it's hearing as you speak, so you can verify that it has understood you correctly. This streaming feature makes the whole process of interacting with Siri faster.

REMEMBER

iPad models other than iPad Pro 12.9-inch (2nd generation), iPad Pro 10.5-inch, and iPad Pro (9.7-inch) must be plugged into a power source to use the "Hey Siri" feature.

- Press Home for Siri requires you to press the Home button to activate Siri.

- Allow Siri When Locked allows you to use Siri even when the iPad is locked.

4. If you want to change the language Siri uses, tap Language and choose a different language in the list that appears.

5. To change the nationality or gender of Siri's voice from American to British or Australian (for example), or from female to male, tap Siri Voice and make your selections.

6. Let Siri know about your contact information by tapping My Information and selecting yourself from your Contacts.

If you want Siri to verbally respond to your requests only when the iPad isn't in your hands, tap Voice Feedback and choose Hands-Free Only. Here's how this setting works and why you may want to use it: In general, if you're holding your iPad, you can read responses on the screen, so you might choose not to have your device talk to you out loud. But if you're cooking dinner while helping your spouse make travel plans and want to speak requests for destinations and hear the answers rather than have to read them, Hands-Free Only is a useful setting.

Understand All That Siri Can Do

Siri allows you to interact by voice with many apps on your iPad.

No matter what kind of action you want to perform, first press and hold the Home button until Siri opens.

You can pose questions or ask to do something like make a Face-Time call or add an appointment to your calendar, for example. Siri can also search the Internet or use an informational service called Wolfram|Alpha to provide information on just about any topic.

To see examples of what Siri can do for you, engage Siri but don't say anything. In a few seconds, Siri will display a list like the one in Figure 5-3.

Siri also checks with Wikipedia and Twitter to get you the information you ask for. In addition, you can use Siri to tell iPad to return a call, play your voice mail, open and search the App Store, or control Music playback.

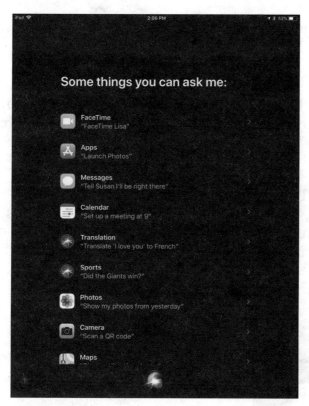

FIGURE 5-3

Siri knows what app you're using, though you don't have to have that app open to make a request involving it. However, if you are in the Messages app, you can make a statement like "Tell Susan I'll be late," and Siri knows that you want to send a message. You can also ask Siri to remind you about what you're working on, and Siri notes what you're working on, in which app, and reminds you about it at a later time you specify.

TIP

If you want to dictate text in an app like Notes, use the Dictation key on the onscreen keyboard to do so. See the section "Use Dictation," later in this chapter, for more about this feature.

Siri requires no preset structure for your questions; you can phrase things in several ways. For example, you might say, "Where am I?" to see a map of your current location, or you could say, "What is my current location?" or "What address is this?" and get the same results.

If you ask a question about, say, the weather, Siri responds to you both verbally and with text information (see Figure 5-4) or by opening a form, as with email, or by providing a graphic display for some items, such as maps. When a result appears, you can tap it to make a choice or open a related app.

Siri works with FaceTime, the App Store, Music, Messages, Reminders, Calendar, Maps, Mail, Weather, Stocks, Clock, Contacts, Notes, social media apps (such as Twitter), and Safari (see Figure 5-5). In the following sections, I provide a quick guide to some of the most useful ways you can use Siri.

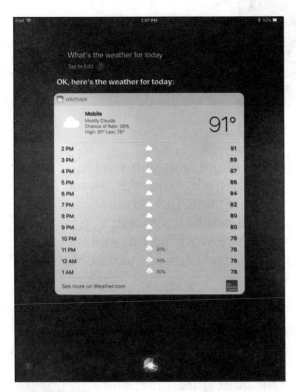

FIGURE 5-4

FIGURE 5-5

TIP

Siri now supports many different languages, so you can finally show off those language lessons you took in high school. Some languages supported include Chinese, Dutch, English, French, German, Italian, Spanish, Arabic, Danish, Finnish, Hebrew, Japanese, Korean, and more!

Get Suggestions

Siri anticipates your needs by making suggestions when you swipe from left to right on the Home screen and tap within the Search field at the top of the screen. Siri will list contacts you've communicated with recently, apps you've used, and nearby businesses, such as restaurants, gas stations, or coffee spots. If you tap on an app in the suggestions, it will open displaying the last viewed or listened to item.

Additionally, Siri lists news stories that may be of interest to you based on items you've viewed before.

Call Contacts via FaceTime

First, make sure that the person you want to call is entered in your Contacts app and include that person's phone number in his record. If you want to call somebody by stating your relationship to her, such as "Call sister," be sure to enter that relationship in the Add Related Name field in her contact record. Also make sure that the settings for Siri (refer to Figure 5-2) include your own contact name in the My Information field. (See Chapter 7 for more about creating contact records.)

To call contacts via FaceTime, follow these steps:

1. Press and hold the Home button (or say "Hey, Siri," if you're using that feature) until Siri appears.

2. Speak a command, such as "Make a FaceTime call to Cindy," or say "FaceTime Mom."

3. If you have two contacts who might match a spoken name, Siri responds with a list of possible matches (see Figure 5-6). Tap one in the list or state the correct contact's name to proceed.

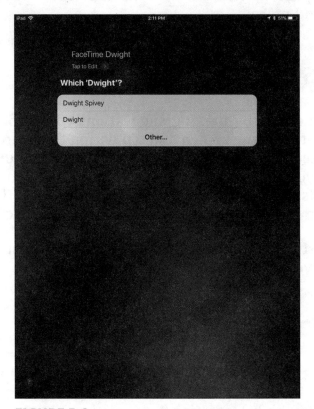

FIGURE 5-6

4. The call is placed. To end the call before it completes, press the Home button and then tap End.

TIP

To cancel any spoken request, you have three options: Say "Cancel," tap the Siri button on the Siri screen (looks like swirling bands of light), or press the Home button. If you're using a headset or Bluetooth device, tap the End button on the device.

Create Reminders and Alerts

You can also use Siri with the Reminders app:

1. To create a reminder or alert, press and hold the Home button and then speak a command, such as "Remind me to call Dad on Thursday at 10 a.m." or "Wake me up tomorrow at 6:15 a.m."

2. A preview of the reminder or alert is displayed (see Figure 5-7). Tell Siri to Cancel or Remove if you change your mind.

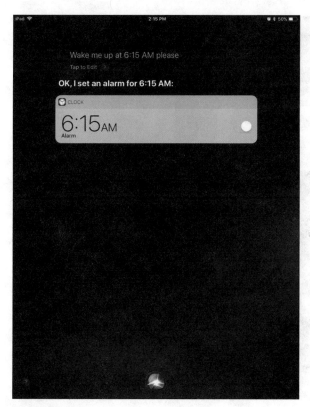

FIGURE 5-7

3. If you want a reminder ahead of the event that you created, activate Siri and speak a command, such as "Remind me tonight about the play on Thursday at 8 p.m." A second reminder is created, which you can confirm or cancel if you change your mind.

Add Tasks to Your Calendar

You can also set up events on your Calendar using Siri:

1. Press and hold the Home button and then speak a phrase, such as "Set up meeting at 3 p.m. tomorrow."

2. Siri sets up the appointment (see Figure 5-8) and asks whether you want to schedule the new appointment. You can say, "Confirm" or "Cancel" at that point or tap the Confirm or Cancel button.

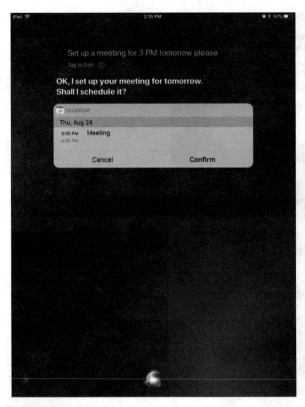

FIGURE 5-8

Play Music

You can use Siri to play music from the Music app:

1. Press and hold the Home button until Siri appears.

2. To play music, speak a command, such as "Play music" or "Play Jazz radio station" to play a specific song, album, or radio station, as seen in Figure 5-9.

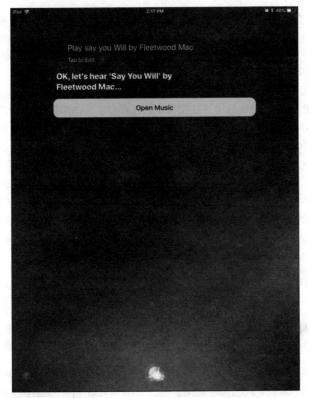

FIGURE 5-9

You can use the integration of iPad with Shazam, a music identifier app (you'll need to download it from the App Store), to identify tagged music.

1. When you're near an audio source playing music, press and hold the Home button to activate Siri.

2. Ask Siri a question, such as "What music is playing?" or "What's this song?"

3. Siri listens for a bit. If Siri recognizes the song, it shows you the song name, artist, any other available information, and the ability to purchase the music in the iTunes Store.

If you're listening to music or a podcast with earphones plugged in and stop midstream, the next time you plug in earphones, Siri recognizes that you may want to continue with the same item.

Get Directions

You can use the Maps app and Siri to find your current location, get directions, find nearby businesses (such as restaurants or a bank), or get a map of another location. Be sure to turn on Location Services to allow Siri to know your current location (go to Settings and tap Privacy ⇨ Location Services; make sure Location Services is on and that Siri & Dictation is turned on further down in these settings).

Here are some of the commands that you can try to get directions or a list of nearby businesses:

» **"Where am I?"** Displays a map of your current location.

» **"Where is Auburn, Alabama?"** Displays a map of that city, as shown in Figure 5-10.

» **"Find pizza restaurants."** Displays a list of restaurants near your current location; tap one to display a map of its location.

» **"Find Bank of America."** Displays a map with the location of the indicated business (or in some cases, several nearby locations, such as a bank branch and all ATMs).

» **"Get directions to the Empire State Building."** Loads a map with a route drawn and provides a narration of directions to the site from your current location.

After a location is displayed on a map, tap the Information button on the location's label to view its address, phone number, and website address, if available.

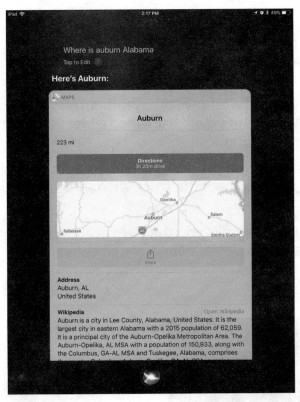

FIGURE 5-10

Ask for Facts

Wolfram|Alpha is a self-professed online computational knowledge engine. That means that it's more than a search engine because it provides specific information about a search term rather than multiple search results. If you want facts without having to spend time browsing websites to find those facts, Wolfram|Alpha is a very good resource.

Siri uses Wolfram|Alpha and such sources as Wikipedia to look up facts in response to questions, such as "What is the capital of Kansas?", "What is the square root of 2,300?", or "How large is Mars?" Just press and hold the Home button and ask your question; Siri consults its resources and returns a set of relevant facts.

You can also get information about other things, such as the weather, stocks, or the time. Just say a phrase like one of these to get what you need:

» **"What is the weather?"** Siri shows the weather report for your current location. If you want weather in another location, just specify the location in your question.

» **"What is the price of Apple stock?"** Siri tells you the current price of the stock or the price of the stock when the stock market last closed.

» **"How hot is the sun?"** Siri tells you the temperature of the sun, and even breaks it down into various unit conversions (see Figure 5-11).

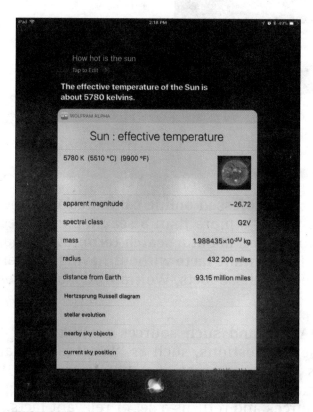

FIGURE 5-11

Search the Web

Although Siri can use its resources to respond to specific requests such as "Who is the Queen of England?", more general requests for information will cause Siri to search further on the web. Siri can also search Twitter for comments related to your search.

For example, if you speak a phrase, such as "Find a website about birds" or "Find information about the World Series," Siri can respond in a couple of ways. The app can simply display a list of search results by using the default search engine specified in your settings for Safari or by suggesting, "If you like, I can search the web for such and such." In the first instance, just tap a result to go to that website. In the second instance, you can confirm that you want to search the web or cancel.

Send Email, Messages, or Tweets

You can create an email or an instant message using Siri and existing contacts. For example, if you say "Email John Michael Bassett," a form opens that is already addressed to that stored contact. Siri asks for a subject and then a message. Speak your message contents and then say "Send" to speed your message on its way.

Siri also works with messaging apps, such as Messages. If you have the Messages app open and you say "Tell Victoria I'll call soon," Siri creates a message for you to approve and send.

TIP

Siri can also tweet, connect with Flickr and Vimeo, and post to Facebook. Go to Settings and turn on Flickr, Vimeo, Twitter, or Facebook support and provide your account information. Now you can say such things to Siri as "Post tweet" or "Post to Facebook." Siri asks what you want to say, lets you review it, and posts it.

Use Dictation

Text entry isn't Siri's strong point. Instead, you can use the Dictation key that appears with a microphone symbol on the onscreen keyboard (see Figure 5-12) to speak text rather than type it. This feature is called Dictation.

FIGURE 5-12

To use dictation:

1. Go to any app where you enter text, such as Notes or Mail, and tap in the document or form. The onscreen keyboard appears.

2. Tap the Dictation key on the keyboard and speak your text.

3. To end the dictation, tap Done.

When you finish speaking text, you can use the keyboard to make edits to the text Siri entered, although as voice recognition programs go, Dictation is pretty darn accurate. If a word sports a blue underline, which means there may be an error, you can tap to select and make edits to it.

Translate Words and Phrases

One of Siri's best new features in iOS 11 is the ability to translate English into Mandarin, French, German, Italian, or Spanish, which is great if you're on a road trip and don't speak the local language. Apple has plans to expand this feature, and its potential is exciting.

1. Activate Siri.

2. Say "translate" followed by your phrase and the language of your choice, as illustrated in Figure 5-13.

3. Siri displays the translation on your screen, as well as speaks it.

Tap the Play button to the left of the translation to hear Siri speak it again.

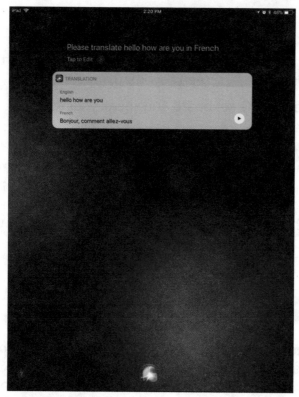

FIGURE 5-13

Type Your Commands or Questions

Type to Siri is another great addition to Siri that comes with iOS 11. This feature allows you to type commands or inquiries instead of verbalizing them. This feature is great if you have difficulty speaking or if you're in a situation where you're not able to speak.

To enable this feature:

1. Go to General ⇨ Accessibility.

2. Tap Siri and then toggle the switch for Type to Siri to On (green).

3. Now, when you activate Siri, a keyboard appears for you to enter your commands or questions (see Figure 5-14).

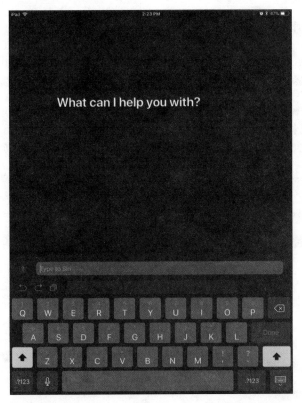

FIGURE 5-14

Get Helpful Tips

I know you're going to have a wonderful time learning the ins and outs of Siri, but before you do, here are some tips to get you going:

» **If Siri doesn't understand you:** Siri has vastly improved at recognizing voices, but it isn't perfect. When you speak a command and Siri displays what it thought you said, if it misses the mark, you have a few options. To correct a request you've made, you can tap Tap to Edit under the command Siri heard and edit the question by typing or tapping the Dictation key on the onscreen keyboard and dictating the correct information. If a word is underlined in blue, it's a possible error. Tap the word and then tap an alternative that Siri suggests. You can also simply speak to

Siri and say something like "I meant Sri Lanka" or "No, send it to Sally." If corrections aren't working, you may need to restart your iPad to reset the Siri software.

» **Headsets and earphones:** If you're using earphones or a Bluetooth headset to activate Siri, instead of pressing the Home button, press and hold the center button (the little button on the headset that starts and stops a call).

» **Using Find Friends:** The Find Friends app, in addition to allowing you to use it with keyboard input, allows you to ask Siri to locate your friends geographically.

» **Getting help:** To get help with Siri features, just press and hold the Home button and ask Siri, "What can you do?"

» **Joking around:** If you need a good laugh, ask Siri to tell you a joke. It has quite the sense of humor.

Chapter **6**

Expanding Your iPad Horizons with Apps

S ome apps (short for applications) come preinstalled on your iPad, such as Files and Music. But you can choose from a world of other apps out there for your iPad, some for free (such as USA Today) and some for a price (typically, ranging from 99 cents to about $10, though some can top out at much steeper prices).

Apps range from games to financial tools (such as loan calculators) to apps that help you when you're planning or taking a trip. Still more apps are developed for use by private entities, such as hospitals and government agencies.

In this chapter, I suggest some apps that you may want to check out and explain how to use the App Store feature of your iPad to find, purchase, and download apps.

Explore Senior-Recommended Apps

As I write this book, new iPad apps are in development, so even more apps that can fit your needs are available seemingly every day. Still, to get you exploring what's possible, I provide a quick list of apps that may whet your appetite.

Access the App Store (completely redesigned in iOS 11) by tapping the App Store icon on the Home screen. You can start by exploring the Today tab (which features special apps and articles), by Categories, or by the Top Charts (see the buttons along the bottom of the screen). Or you can tap Search and find apps on your own. Tap an app to see more information about it.

Here are some interesting apps to explore:

» **Sudoku (free):** If you like this mental logic puzzle in print, try it on your iPad. It has three lessons and several levels ranging from easiest to nightmare, making it a great way to make time fly by in a doctor's or dentist's waiting room.

» **StockWatch Portfolio Tracking and Stock Market Quotes ($2.99):** Even though Apple offers a Stocks app for the iPad, this app will help you keep track of your investments in a portfolio format. You can use the app to create a watch list and record your stock performance.

» **Goodreads (free):** If you're a reader, this is an app you won't want to be without. This app will keep you up-to-date on the latest releases, and you can browse reading lists from thousands of other users.

» **ArtStudio ($4.99):** Get creative! You can use this powerful app to draw, add color, and even create special effects.

» **Virtuoso Piano Free 4 (free):** If you love to make music, you'll love this app, which gives you a virtual piano keyboard to play and compose on the fly.

» **Travelzoo (free):** Get great deals on hotels, airfare, rental cars, entertainment, and more. This app also offers tips from travel experts.

» **Blood Pressure Monitor (free):** This app helps you keep track of your blood pressure and maintain records over extended periods of time in one convenient place — your iPad. Use the accompanying reports to give your doctor a good overview of your blood pressure.

» **Skype (free):** Make Internet calls to your friends and family for free. While your iPad comes with FaceTime, some members of your circle may not have iPads, so Skype (see Figure 6-1) would be the best way to communicate.

» **Nike+ Training Club (free):** Use this handy utility to help design personalized workouts, see step-by-step instructions to help you learn new exercises, and watch video demonstrations. The reward system in this app may just keep you going toward your workout goals.

FIGURE 6-1

TIP

Note that you can work on documents using apps in the cloud. Use Keynote, Numbers, Pages, and more apps to get your work done from any device. See Chapter 3 for more about using iCloud Drive.

Search the App Store

If you've got the time, you can find lots of happy surprises by simply browsing the App Store, but if you' re in a hurry or already know what you're looking for, a search is the best way to go.

To search the App Store:

1. Tap the App Store icon on the Home screen; by default, the first time you use App Store, it will open to the Today tab, as seen in Figure 6-2.

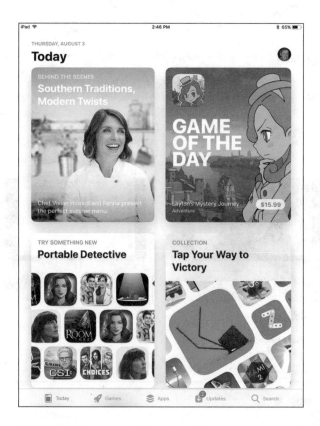

FIGURE 6-2

2. At this point, you have several options for finding apps:

- Scroll downward to view various featured apps and articles, such as The Daily List and Our Favorites.

  Tap the name of a category to see more apps.

- Tap the Apps tab at the bottom of the screen to browse by the type of app you're looking for or search by categories (tap the See All button in the Top Categories section), such as Lifestyle or Finance, as shown in Figure 6-3.

- Tap the Games tab at the bottom of the screen to see the newest releases and bestselling games. Explore by paid apps, free apps, by categories, and even by special subjects such as The Most Beautiful Games and What We're Playing.

- Tap the Search button at the bottom of the screen, then tap in the Search field, enter a search term, and tap the result you want to view.

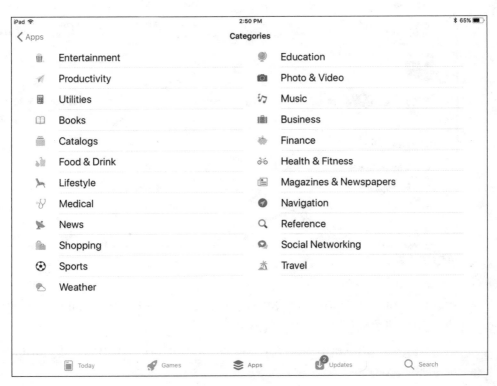

FIGURE 6-3

Get Applications from the App Store

Buying or getting free apps requires that you have an iTunes account, which I cover in Chapter 3. After you have an account, you can use the saved payment information there to buy apps or download free apps with a few simple steps:

1. With the App Store open, tap the Apps tab and then tap the See All button (blue text to the right) in the Top Free section, as shown in Figure 6-4.

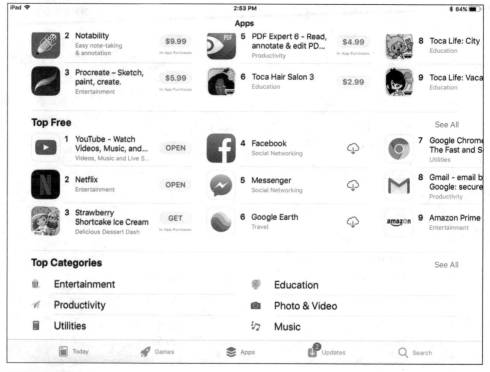

FIGURE 6-4

2. Tap the Get button for an app that appeals to you or, if you'd like more information, simply tap the app's icon.

   To get a paid app, you tap the same button, which is then labeled with a price.

TIP

If you've opened an iCloud account, you can set it up so that anything you purchase on your iPad is automatically pushed to other Apple iOS devices (such as an iPhone or another iPad) and your iTunes library, and vice versa. See Chapter 3 for more about iCloud.

3. A sheet opens on-screen listing the app and the iTunes account being used to get/purchase the app. Tap Enter Password at the bottom of the sheet, tap the Password field, and then enter the password. The Get button changes to the Installing button, which looks like a circle; the thick blue line on the circle represents the progress of the installation.

4. The app downloads, and you can find it on one of the Home screens. If you purchase an app that isn't free, your credit card or gift card balance is charged at this point for the purchase price.

TIP

Out of the box, only preinstalled apps are located on the first iPad Home screen, with a few (such as Photo Booth and Podcasts) located on the second Home screen. Apps that you download are placed on available Home screens, and you have to swipe to view and use them; this procedure is covered later in this chapter. See the next task for help in finding your newly downloaded apps using multiple Home screens.

Organize Your Applications on Home Screens

By default, the first Home screen contains preinstalled apps, and the second contains a few more preinstalled apps. Once those initial screens are fully populated with app icons, other screens are created to contain any further apps you download or sync to your iPad. At the bottom of any iPad Home screen (just above the Dock), dots indicate the number of Home screens you've filled with apps; a solid dot specifies which Home screen you're on now, as shown in Figure 6-5.

1. Press the Home button to open the last displayed Home screen.

2. Flick your finger from right to left to move to the next Home screen. To move back, flick from left to right.

**Dots indicating the
number of Home screens**   **Screen you're on**

FIGURE 6-5

3. To reorganize apps on a Home screen, press and hold any app on that page. The app icons begin to jiggle (see Figure 6-6), and many (not all) apps will sport a Delete button (a gray circle with a black X on it).

4. Press, hold, and drag an app icon to another location on the screen to move it.

TIP

To move an app from one page to another, while the apps are jiggling, you can press, hold, and drag an app to the left or right to move it to the next Home screen. You can also manage which app resides on which Home screen and change the order of the Home screens from iTunes when you've connected your iPad to iTunes on your computer via a cable or wireless sync.

5. Press the Home button to stop all those icons from jiggling!

A Delete button

FIGURE 6-6

TIP

You can use the multitasking feature for switching between apps easily. Quickly press the Home button twice to get a preview of open apps. Swipe right or left to scroll among the apps and tap the one you want to go to. You can also swipe an app upward from this preview list to close it.

Organize Apps in Folders

iPad lets you organize apps in folders so that you can find them more easily. The process is simple:

1. Tap and hold an app until all apps start jiggling.

2. Drag one app on top of another app.

The two apps appear in a box with a placeholder name in a box above them (see Figure 6-7).

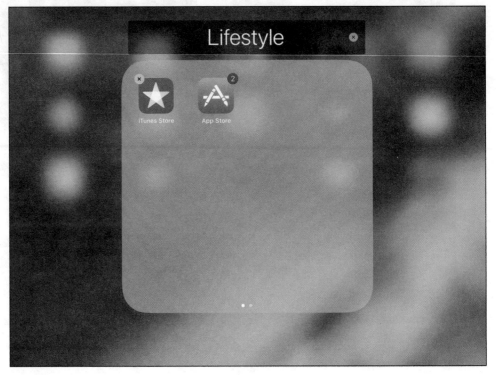

FIGURE 6-7

3. To change the name, tap in the field at the end of the placeholder name, and the keyboard appears.

4. Tap the Delete key to delete the placeholder name and type one of your own.

5. Tap Done and then tap anywhere outside the box to close it.

6. Press the Home button to stop the icons from dancing around. You see your folder on the Home screen where you began this process.

TIP

iOS 11 introduces the neat trick of allowing you to move multiple apps together at the same time:

1. Tap and hold the first app you'd like to move until the apps are jiggling.

2. Move the app just a bit so that it's no longer in its original place.

3. With your free hand, tap the other app(s) you'd like to move along with the first app. As you tap additional apps, their icons "move under" or "attach themselves" to the first app.

4. Once you've selected all your apps, move them to their new location; they'll all move together in a little app caravan.

Delete Apps You No Longer Need

When you no longer need an app you've installed, it's time to get rid of it. You can also remove most of the preinstalled apps that are native to iOS 11. If you use iCloud to push content across all Apple iOS devices, deleting an app on your iPad won't affect that app on other devices.

1. Display the Home screen that contains the app you want to delete.

   If you remove a native iOS 11 app, it's hidden, not deleted. If you need it later, you can go to the App Store, find the name of the app there, and reinstall it (or technically, just unhide it).

2. Press and hold the app until all apps begin to jiggle.

3. Tap the Delete button for the app you want to delete (refer to Figure 6-6). A confirmation like the one shown in Figure 6-8 appears.

4. Tap Delete (or Remove if the app is preinstalled by iOS 11) to proceed with the deletion.

Don't worry about wiping out several apps at one time by deleting a folder. When you delete a folder, the apps that were contained within the folder are placed back on a Home screen if space is available, and you can still find the apps using the Spotlight Search feature.

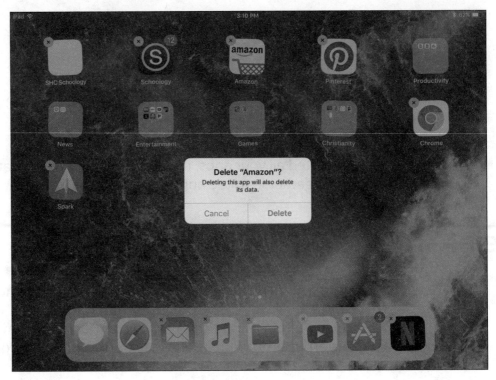

FIGURE 6-8

Offload Apps to Keep Data

When you delete an app from your iPad you're simultaneously delet-ing its data and documents. New to iOS 11 is the ability to delete an app without removing its data and documents; this feature is called Offloading. If you find later that you'd like to revisit the app, simply download it again from the App Store, and its data and settings will be retained.

1. Open Settings and go to General ➪ iPad Storage. You may need to wait a few seconds for content to load.

2. You can allow your iPad to automatically offload unused apps as storage gets low, or you can offload individual apps manually:

   - To automatically offload unused apps, scroll down the screen to the Offload Unused Apps option and tap the Enable button, shown in Figure 6-9. To disable the feature, go to Settings ➪ iTunes & App Store, scroll to the bottom of the page, and then toggle the Offload Unused Apps switch to Off (white).

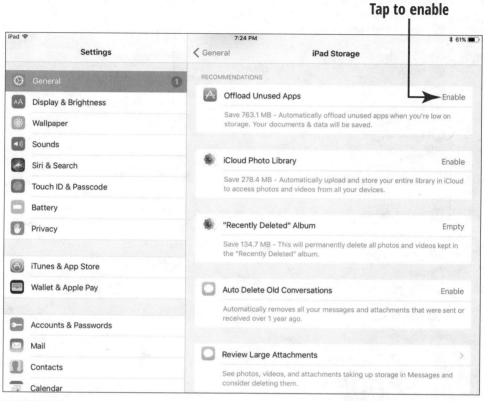

FIGURE 6-9

- To offload an individual app, scroll down to find the app, tap it, and then tap the Offload App option, seen in Figure 6-10; tap Offload App again to confirm. The offloaded apps icon is grayed out on your iPad's Home screen, indicating that the app is not loaded but its data still is.

3. You can restore an app by simply tapping its grayed-out icon (when the app is ready to use the icon will no longer by grayed out) or by reinstalling it from the App Store.

Offloading apps is a great idea if the app itself is of a significant size, but otherwise may not be very handy unless you're just super-strapped for space. Often, most of your iPad's memory is taken up by the data used in apps, not necessarily by the apps themselves.

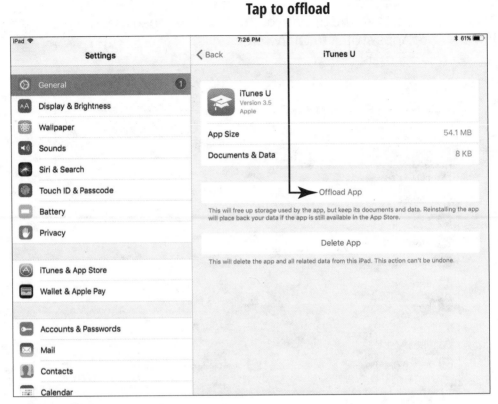

Tap to offload

FIGURE 6-10

Update Apps

App developers update their apps all the time, so you may want to check for those updates. The App Store icon on the Home screen displays the number of available updates in a red circle.

To check for updates:

1. Tap the App Store icon on the Home screen.

2. Tap the Updates button to access the Updates screen and then tap the Update button for any item you want to update. Note that if you have Family Sharing turned on, you can tap a folder titled Family Purchases to display apps that are shared across your family's devices. To update all, tap the Update All button.

TIP

You can download multiple apps at one time. If you choose more than one app to update instead of downloading apps sequentially, several items will download simultaneously.

3. You may be asked to confirm that you want to update or to enter your Apple ID; after you do, tap OK to proceed. You may also be asked to confirm that you are over a certain age or agree to terms and conditions; if so, scroll down the terms dialog and, at the bottom, tap Agree. The download progress is displayed.

TIP

If you have an iCloud account that you have activated on several devices and update an app on your iPad, any other Apple iOS devices are also updated automatically and vice versa.

iOS 11 performs what Apple calls "intelligently scheduled updates," meaning that updates to apps and the iOS happen at times when your iPad isn't using much power; for example, when you're connecting to the Internet via Wi-Fi. And speaking of updating, iOS 11 studies your habits and can update apps that require updated content, such as Facebook or Apple's Stocks app, around the time you usually check them so that you have instant access to current information.

Customize Individual App Settings

Some apps allow you to customize their settings via the Settings app. These customizable settings are typically to let you tell an app how you'd like to interact with it, as opposed to it telling you what to do all the time.

1. To see a list of apps that you can customize settings for, tap the Settings app on your Home screen.

2. Swipe down the screen until you see the names of apps you've installed.

3. Tap the name of an app to see the features that you can customize, as illustrated in Figure 6-11.

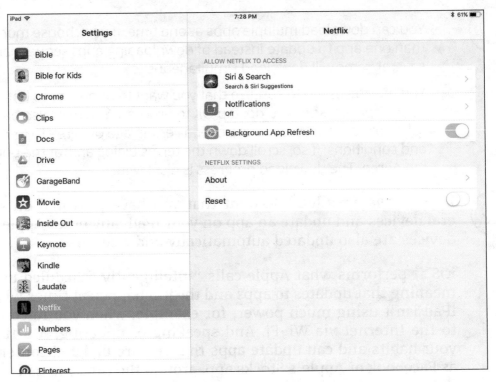

FIGURE 6-11

Chapter **7**

Managing Contacts

ontacts is the iPad equivalent of the dog-eared address book that used to sit by your phone. The Contacts app is simple to set up and use, and it has some powerful features beyond simply storing names, addresses, and phone numbers.

For example, you can pinpoint a contact's address in iPad's Maps app. You can use your contacts to address email and Facebook messages and Twitter tweets quickly. If you store a contact record that includes a website, you can use a link in Contacts to view that website instantly. In addition, of course, you can easily search for a contact by a variety of criteria, including how people are related to you, such as family or mutual friends, or by groups you create.

In this chapter, you discover the various features of Contacts, including how to save yourself time spent entering contact information by syncing contacts with such services as iCloud.

Add a Contact

To add a contact to Contacts:

1. Tap the Contacts icon on the Home screen. An alphabetical list of contacts appears, like the one shown in Figure 7-1.

FIGURE 7-1

2. Tap the Add button, the button with the small plus sign (+) on it in the upper-right corner of the Contacts list. A blank New Contact page opens (see Figure 7-2). Tap in any field, and the onscreen keyboard displays.

3. Enter any contact information you want.

Only one of the First, Last, or Company fields is required.

TECHNICAL
STUFF

4. To scroll down the contact's page and see more fields, flick up on the page with your finger.

FIGURE 7-2

5. If you want to add information (such as a mailing or street address), you can tap the relevant Add field, which opens additional entry fields.

6. To add an information field, such as Nickname or Job Title, tap Add Field toward the bottom of the page. In the Add Field dialog that appears (see Figure 7-3), choose a field to add.

TIP

You may have to flick the page up with your finger to view all the fields.

TIP

If your contact has a name that's difficult for you to pronounce, consider adding the Phonetic First Name or Phonetic Last Name field, or both, to that person's record (refer to Step 6).

7. Tap the Done button in the upper-right corner when you finish making entries. The new contact appears in your address book. Tap it to see details (see Figure 7-4).

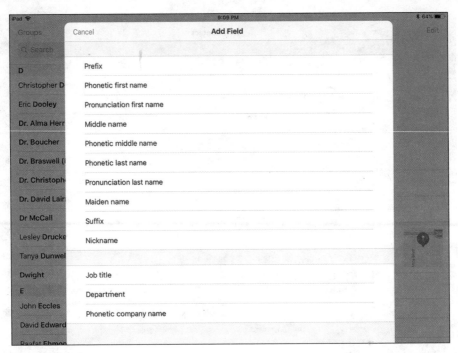

FIGURE 7-3

FIGURE 7-4

TIP

You can choose a distinct ringtone or text tone for a new contact. Just tap the Ringtone or Text Tone field in the New Contact form to see a list of options. When that person calls either on the phone or via FaceTime or texts you via SMS, MMS, or iMessage, you will recognize him or her from the tone that plays.

Sync Contacts with iCloud

You can use your iCloud account to sync contacts from your iPad to iCloud to back them up. These also become available to your email account, if you set one up.

TIP

You can also use iTunes to sync contacts among all your Apple devices and even a Windows PC. See Chapter 4 for more about making iTunes settings.

To sync contacts with iCloud:

1. On the Home screen, tap Settings, tap the name of your Apple ID account (at the top of the screen), and then tap iCloud.

2. In the iCloud settings shown in Figure 7-5, make sure that the On/Off switch for Contacts is set to On (green) in order to sync contacts.

3. To choose which email account to sync with, tap Accounts & Passwords in the Settings list on the left and in the Accounts section, tap the email account you want to use (it will usually be listed as iCloud).

4. In the following screen (see Figure 7-6), toggle the Contacts switch to On to merge contacts from that account via iCloud.

TIP

You can use the iTunes Wi-Fi Sync feature in iPad Settings under General to sync with iTunes wirelessly from a computer connected to the same Wi-Fi network.

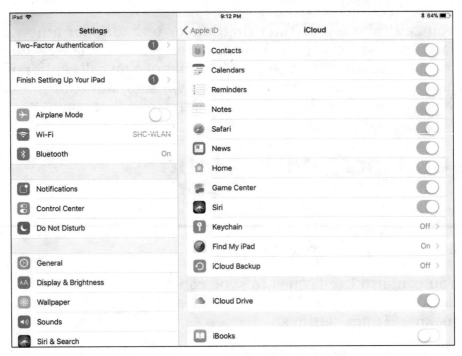

FIGURE 7-5

FIGURE 7-6

Assign a Photo to a Contact

To assign a photo to a contact:

1. With Contacts open, tap a contact to whose record you want to add a photo.

2. Tap the Edit button.

3. On the Info page that appears (see Figure 7-7), tap Add Photo.

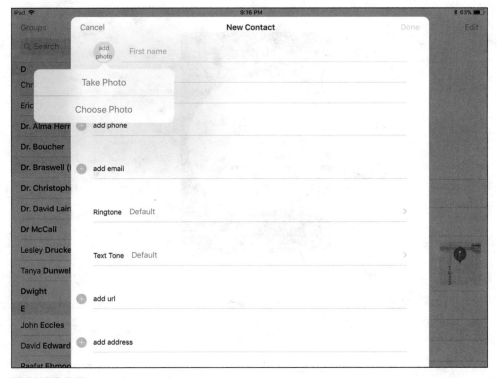

FIGURE 7-7

4. In the popover that appears, tap Choose Photo to choose an existing photo.

You could also choose Take Photo to take that contact's photo on the spot.

5. In the Photos dialog that appears, choose a source for your photo (such as Favorites, Camera Roll, or other album).

6. In the photo album that appears, tap a photo to select it. The Move and Scale dialog, shown in Figure 7-8, appears.

Center the photo the way you want it by dragging it with your finger.

FIGURE 7-8

7. Tap the Choose button to use the photo for this contact.

8. Tap Done to save changes to the contact. The photo appears on the contact's Info page (see Figure 7-9).

While in the Photos dialog, in Step 6, you can modify the photo before saving it to the contact information. You can unpinch your fingers on the iPad screen to expand the photo and move it around the space to focus on a particular section. Then tap the Choose button to use the modified version.

FIGURE 7-9

Add Social Media Information

iPad users can add social media information to their Contacts so that they can quickly tweet (send a short message to) others using Twitter, comment to a contact on Facebook, and more. Social media platforms available in Contacts are

» Twitter

» Facebook

» Flickr

» LinkedIn

» Myspace

» Sina Weibo

To add social media information to contacts:

1. Open the Contacts app.

2. Tap the Edit button in the upper-right corner of the screen.

3. Scroll down and tap Add Social Profile.

   You may add multiple social profiles if you like.

4. Twitter is the default service that pops up, but you can easily change it to a different service by tapping "Twitter" and selecting from the list of services, shown in Figure 7-10. Tap Done after you've selected the service you'd like to use.

5. Enter the information for the social profile as needed.

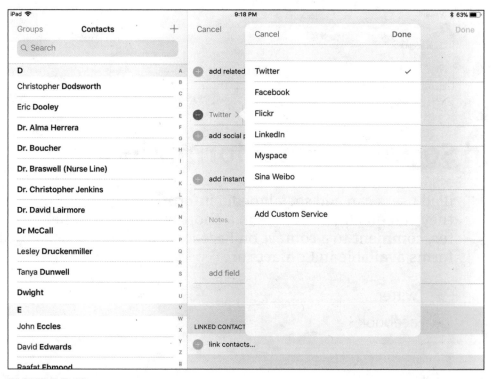

FIGURE 7-10

6. Tap Done, and the information is saved. The social profile account is now displayed when you select the contact, and you can send tweets, Facebook messages, or what-have-you by simply tapping the username, tapping the service you want to use to contact the person, and then tapping the appropriate command (such as Facebook posting).

Designate Related People

You can quickly designate relationships in a contact record if those people are saved to Contacts. One great use for this feature is using Siri to simply say "FaceTime Manager" to FaceTime someone who is designated in your contact information as your manager.

There's a setting for Linked Contacts in the Contacts app when you're editing a contact's record. Using this setting isn't like adding a relation; rather, if you have records for the same person that have been imported into Contacts from different sources, such as Google or Twitter, you can link them to show only a single contact.

To designated contacts as related to you:

1. Tap a contact and then tap Edit.

2. Scroll down the record and tap Add Related Name. The field labeled Mother (see Figure 7-11) now appears.

3. Tap the blue Information button (looks like a circle with an "i") in Related Name field, and your Contacts list appears. Tap the related person's name, and it appears in the field (see Figure 7-12).

4. Tap Add Related Name and continue to add additional names as needed.

5. Tap Done to complete the edits.

After you add relations to a contact record, when you select the person in the Contacts main screen, all the related people for that contact are listed there.

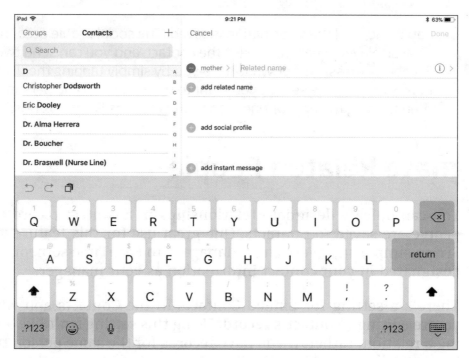

FIGURE 7-11

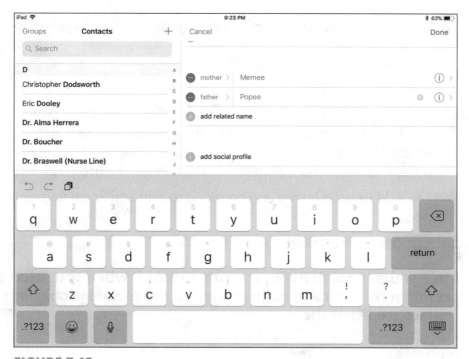

FIGURE 7-12

Set Individual Ringtones and Text Tones

If you want to hear a unique tone when you receive a Message or FaceTime call from a particular contact, you can set up this feature in Contacts. For example, if you want to be sure that you know instantly whether your spouse, sick friend, or boss is FaceTiming, you can set a unique tone for that person.

TIP

If you set a custom tone for someone, that tone will be used when that person texts or contacts you by FaceTime.

To set up custom tones, follow these steps:

1. Tap to add a new contact or select a contact in the list of contacts and tap Edit.

2. Tap the Ringtone field in a new contact or tap Edit and then the Ringtone field in an existing contact, and a list of tones appears (see Figure 7-13).

FIGURE 7-13

TIP

You can set a custom text tone to be used when the person sends you a text message. Tap Text Tone instead of Ringtone in Step 2 and then follow the remaining steps.

3. Scroll up and down to see the full list. Tap a tone, and it previews. When you hear one you like, tap Done.

TIP

If your Apple devices are synced via iCloud, setting a unique ringtone for an iPad contact also sets it for use with FaceTime and Messages on your iPhone and Mac. See Chapter 3 for more about iCloud.

Search for a Contact

If you're like most iPad users, your Contacts list will expand exponentially over time. iOS 11 makes it simple to search what can grow to be a seemingly never-ending list of contacts:

1. With Contacts open, tap in the Search field at the very top of your Contacts list on the left (see Figure 7-14). The onscreen keyboard opens.

2. Type the first letters of either the first or last name or company. All matching results appear, as shown in Figure 7-15. For example, typing "App" may display Johnny Appleseed and Apple, Inc. in the results, both of which have "App" as the first three letters of the first or last part of the name or address.

TIP

You can use the alphabetical listing along the right side of All Contacts and tap a letter to locate a contact. Also, you can tap and drag to scroll down the list of contacts on the All Contacts page.

3. Tap a contact in the results to display that person's Information page.

TIP

You can search by phone number simply by entering the phone number in the Search field until the list narrows to the person you're looking for. This may be a good way to search for all contacts in your town or company, for example.

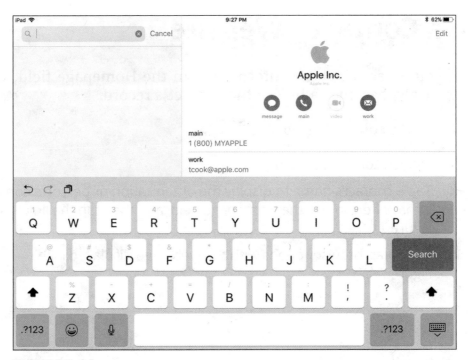

FIGURE 7-14

FIGURE 7-15

Go to a Contact's Website

If you entered website information in the Homepage field, it auto-matically becomes a link in the contact's record.

To view a contact's website:

1. Open a contact's record.

2. Tap a contact's name to display the organization or person's contact information, locate the Homepage field, and then tap the link (see Figure 7-16).

3. The Safari browser opens with the web page displayed (see Figure 7-17).

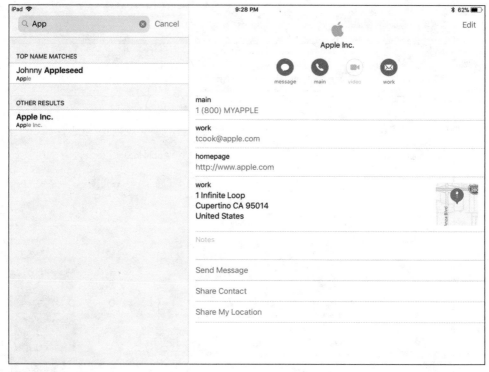

FIGURE 7-16

FIGURE 7-17

TIP

You can go directly back to Contacts after you follow a link to a website. Simply tap Contacts in the upper-left corner of the screen, and you're whisked back to the Info page for the contact you last visited.

Address Email Using Contacts

If you entered an email address for a contact, the address automatically becomes a link in the contact's record.

To address an email from a contact:

1. Open Contacts.

2. Tap a contact's name to display the person's contact information and then tap the email address link (see Figure 7-18).

FIGURE 7-18

3. The New Message dialog appears, as shown in Figure 7-19. Initially, the title bar of this dialog reads New Message, but as you type a subject, New Message changes to the specific title.

4. Tap in a field and use the onscreen keyboard to enter a subject and message.

5. Tap the Send button. The message goes on its way.

FIGURE 7-19

Share a Contact

After you've entered contact information, you can share it with others via an email, text message, and other methods.

1. With Contacts open, tap a contact name to display its information.

2. On the Information page, scroll down and tap Share Contact. In the dialog that appears, shown in Figure 7-20, tap the method you'd like to use to share the contact.

FIGURE 7-20

TIP

To share with an AirDrop-enabled device that is nearby, use the AirDrop button in the screen, shown in Figure 7-20. Just select a nearby device, and your contact is transmitted to that person's device (such as a smartphone, a Mac with macOS with the AirDrop folder open in Finder, or a tablet).

3. Use the onscreen keyboard to enter a recipient's information if emailing or sharing via text message.

TIP

If the person is saved in Contacts, you can just type his or her name here.

4. Tap the Send button if sharing with email or text message. The message goes to your recipient with the contact information attached as a .vcf file. (This vCard format is commonly used to transmit contact information.)

TIP

When somebody receives a vCard containing contact information, he or she needs only to click the attached file to open it. At this point, depending on the email or contact management program, the recipient can perform various actions to save the content. Other iPad and iPod touch users can easily import .vcf records as new contacts in their own Contacts apps.

View a Contact's Location in Maps

If you've entered a person's address in Contacts, you have a shortcut for viewing that person's location in the Maps application:

1. Open Contacts.

2. Tap the contact you want to view to display that contact's information.

3. Tap Edit, then tap Add Address, and enter the address information.

4. Tap Done and then tap the Address field. Maps opens and displays a map of the address (see Figure 7-21).

TIP

This task works with more than your friends' addresses. You can save information for your favorite restaurant or movie theater or any other location and use Contacts to jump to the associated website in the Safari browser or to the address in Maps. For more about using Safari, see Chapter 9. For more about the Maps application, see the bonus chapter at www.dummies.com.

FIGURE 7-21

Delete a Contact

When it's time to remove a name or two from your Contacts, it's easy to do:

1. With Contacts open, tap the contact you want to delete.

2. On the Information page (refer to Figure 7-4), tap the Edit button.

3. On the Info page that displays, drag your finger upward to scroll down and then tap the Delete Contact button at the bottom (see Figure 7-22).

FIGURE 7-22

4. The confirming dialog, shown in Figure 7-23, appears; tap the Delete Contact button to confirm the deletion.

TIP

During this process, if you change your mind before you tap Delete, tap the Cancel button in Step 4. Be careful: After you tap Delete, there's no going back! Your contact is deleted from your iPad and also any other device that syncs to your iPad via iCloud, Google, or other means.

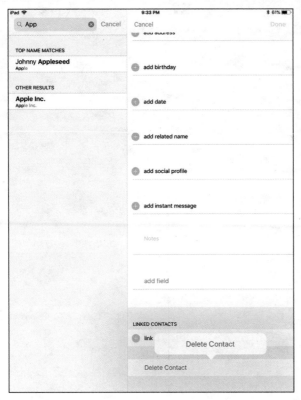

FIGURE 7-23

Chapter **8**

Getting Social with Your iPad

aceTime is an excellent video-calling app that lets you call people who have FaceTime on their devices using either a phone number or an email address. You and your friend, colleague, or family member can see each other as you talk, which makes for a much more personal calling experience.

iMessage is a feature available through the preinstalled Messages app for instant messaging (IM). IM involves sending a text message to somebody's iPad, iPod touch, Mac running macOS 10.8 or later, or iPhone (using the person's phone number or email address to carry on an instant conversation). You can even send audio and video via Messages.

Social media apps keep you in close digital contact with friends and family and have become as important a digital staple as email, if not more so for some folks. Facebook and Twitter are two of the most popular social media apps.

Facebook is a platform for sharing posts about your life, with or without photos and video, and allows you to be as detailed as you please in your posts. Twitter, on the other hand, is meant to share information in quick bursts, allowing users only 140 characters in which to alert you to their latest comings and goings.

In this chapter, I introduce you to FaceTime and the Messages app and review their simple controls. You also take a look at finding, installing, and customizing Facebook and Twitter. In no time, you'll be socializing with all and sundry.

Understand Who Can Use FaceTime

Here's a quick rundown of the device and information you need for using FaceTime's various features:

>> You can use FaceTime to call people over a Wi-Fi connection who have an iPhone 4 or later, an iPad 2 or a third-generation iPad or later, all iPad mini and iPad Pro models, a fourth-generation iPod touch or later, or a Mac (running macOS 10.6.6 or later). If you want to connect over a 3G/4G cellular connection, you're limited to iPhone 4s or later and iPad third generation or later (as long as the iPad supports cellular data).

>> You can use a phone number to connect with anybody with either an iOS device or a Mac and an iCloud account.

>> The person you're contacting must have allowed FaceTime to be used in Settings.

Get an Overview of FaceTime

FaceTime works with the iPad's built-in cameras so that you can call other folks who have a device that supports FaceTime. You can use

FaceTime to chat while sharing video images with another person. This preinstalled app is useful for seniors who want to keep up with distant family members and friends and see (as well as hear) the latest-and-greatest news.

You can make and receive calls with FaceTime using a phone number or an email account and make calls to those with an iCloud account. When connected, you can show the person on the other end what's going on around you. Just remember that you can't adjust audio volume from within the app or record a video call. Nevertheless, on the positive side, even though its features are limited, this app is straightforward to use.

You can use your Apple ID and iCloud account to access FaceTime, so it works pretty much right away. See Chapter 3 for more about getting an Apple ID.

If you're having trouble using FaceTime, make sure that the FaceTime feature is turned on. That's quick to do: Tap Settings on the Home screen, tap FaceTime, and then tap the FaceTime On/Off switch to turn it On (green), if it isn't already. On this Settings screen, you can also select the phone number and/or email addresses that others can use to make FaceTime calls to you, as well as which one of those is displayed as your caller ID.

To view information for recent calls, open the FaceTime app and then tap the Information button on a recent call, and iPad displays that person's information. You can tap the contact to call the person back.

Make a FaceTime Call with Wi-Fi or 3G/4G (LTE)

If you know that the person you're calling has FaceTime available on his device, adding that person to your iPad Contacts is a good idea so you can initiate FaceTime calls from within Contacts if you like or from the Contacts list you can access through the FaceTime app.

When you call somebody using an email address, the person must be signed in to his Apple iCloud account and have verified that the address can be used for FaceTime calls.

To make a FaceTime call:

1. Tap the FaceTime icon to launch the app.

2. Tap to choose a Video or Audio call in the upper left of the screen. Video includes your voice and image; Audio includes only your voice.

3. If your contact doesn't appear in the Recents list (under a field like Enter Name on the left), tap the Enter Name, Email, or Number field and begin to enter a contact's name; a list of matching contacts appears, or you can tap the plus sign (+) to open your complete Contacts list, scroll to locate a contact who has associated a device with FaceTime, tap that contact, and then tap the appropriate method to initiate a call (see Figure 8-1).

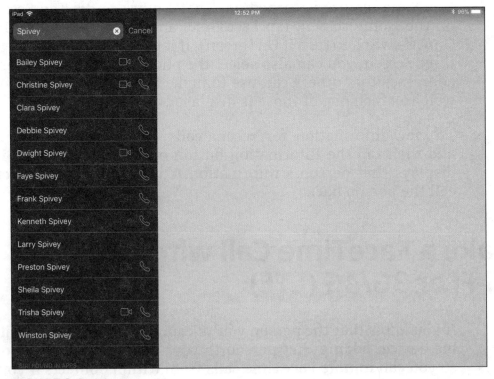

FIGURE 8-1

You see a Camera button if that contact's device supports FaceTime video and a Phone button if the contact's device supports FaceTime audio. (If you haven't saved this person in your contacts and you know the phone number to call or email, you can just enter that information in the Enter Name, Email, or Number field.)

4. When the person accepts the call, you see a large screen that displays the recipient's image and a small screen referred to as a Picture in Picture (PiP) containing your image superimposed (see Figure 8-2).

FIGURE 8-2

If you use FaceTime over a 3G or 4G(LTE) connection, you may incur costly data usage fees. To avoid extra cost, in Settings under Cellular, set the iPad Cellular Calls switch for FaceTime to Off.

Accept and End a FaceTime Call

If you're on the receiving end of a FaceTime call, accepting the call is about as easy as it gets.

If you'd rather not be available for calls, you can go to Settings and turn on the Do Not Disturb feature. This feature stops any incoming calls or notifications other than for the people you've designated as exceptions to Do Not Disturb. After you turn on Do Not Disturb, you can use the feature's settings to schedule when it's active, allow calls from certain people, or allow a second call from the same person in a three-minute interval to go through.

To accept and end a FaceTime call, follow these steps:

1. When the call comes in, tap the Accept button to take the call (see Figure 8-3).

   To reject the call, tap the Decline button.

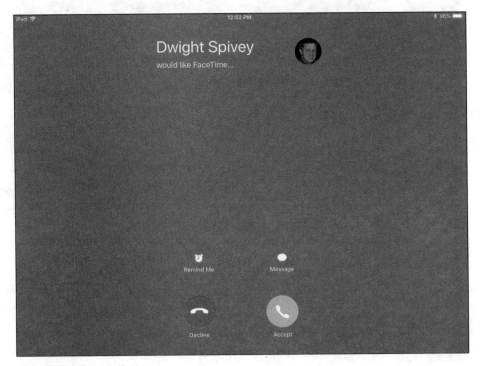

FIGURE 8-3

2. Chat away with your friend, swapping video images. To end the call, tap the End button (the red button in Figure 8-4).

FIGURE 8-4

Switch Views

When you're on a FaceTime call, you might want to use iPad's built-in, rear–facing camera to show the person you're talking to what's going on around you.

1. Tap the Switch Camera button (to the left of the End Call button in Figure 8-5) to switch from the front-facing camera that's displaying your image to the back-facing camera that captures whatever you're looking at.

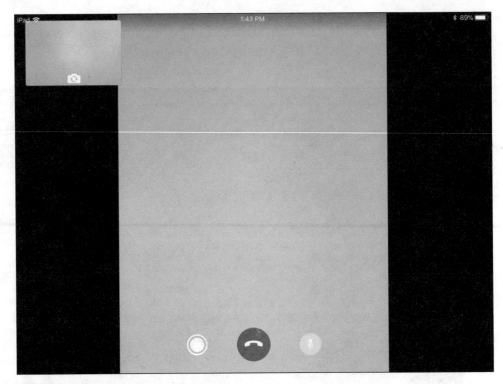

FIGURE 8-5

2. Tap the Switch Camera button again to switch back to the front camera displaying your image.

TIP

To mute sound during a call, tap the Mute button, which looks like a microphone with a line through it (refer to Figure 8-5). Tap the button again to unmute your iPad.

Set Up an iMessage Account

iMessage is a feature available through the preinstalled Messages app that allows you to send and receive instant messages (IMs) to others using an Apple iOS device or suitably configured Macs. iMessage is a way of sending instant messages through a Wi-Fi network, but you can send messages through your cellular connection without having iMessage activated, assuming your iPad supports cellular data.

TECHNICAL STUFF

Instant messaging differs from email or tweeting in an important way. Whereas you might email somebody and wait for days or weeks before that person responds, or you might post a tweet that could sit there awhile before anybody views it, with instant messaging, communication happens almost immediately. You send an IM, and it appears on somebody's Apple device right away.

Assuming that the person wants to participate in a live conversation, the chat begins immediately, allowing a back-and-forth dialogue in real time.

To set up an iMessage account:

1. To set up Messages, tap Settings on the Home screen.

2. Tap Messages. The settings shown in Figure 8-6 appear.

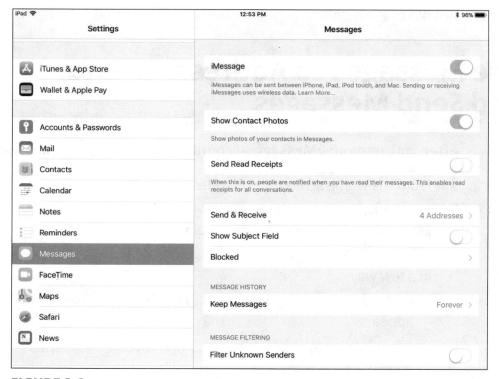

FIGURE 8-6

3. If iMessage isn't set to On (refer to Figure 8-6), tap the On/Off switch to turn it On (green).

TIP Be sure that the phone number and/or email account associated with your iPad under the Send & Receive setting is correct. (It should be set up automatically based on your iCloud settings.) If it isn't, tap the Send & Receive field, add an email or phone, and then tap Messages to return to the previous screen.

4. To allow a notice to be sent to the sender when you've read a message, tap the On/Off switch for Send Read Receipts. You can also choose to show a subject field in your messages.

5. Press the Home button to leave Settings.

TIP To enable or disable email accounts used by Messages, tap Send & Receive and then tap an email address to enable (check mark appears to the left) or disable it (no check mark appears to the left).

Use Messages to Address, Create, and Send Messages

After you set your iMessage account, you're ready to use Messages.

1. From the Home screen, tap the Messages button.

2. Tap the New Message button in the top-right corner of the Messages list (on the left of the screen) to begin a conversation.

3. In the form that appears (see Figure 8-7), you can address a message in a few ways:

- Begin to type a name in the To field, and a list of matching contacts appears.

- Tap the Dictation key on the onscreen keyboard and speak the address.

- Tap the plus (+) button on the right side of the address field, and the Contacts list is displayed.

FIGURE 8-7

4. Tap a contact on the list you chose from in Step 3. If the contact has both an email address and a phone number stored, the Info dialog appears, allowing you to tap one or the other, which addresses the message.

5. To create a message, simply tap in the message field (near the bottom of the screen if the onscreen keyboard is collapsed), shown in Figure 8-8, and type your message.

6. To send the message, tap the Send button (the round blue button with the white arrow in Figure 8-8). When your recipient (or recipients) responds, you'll see the conversation displayed on the screen. Tap in the message field again to respond to the last comment.

TIP

You can address a message to more than one person by simply choosing more recipients in Step 2 of the preceding list.

FIGURE 8-8

Read Messages

When you receive a message, it's as easy to read as email — easier, to be honest!

1. Tap Messages on the Home screen.

2. When the app opens, you see a list of text conversations you've engaged in.

3. Tap a conversation to see the message string, including all attachments, as shown in Figure 8-9.

4. To view all attachments of a message, tap Details (the encircled *i* in the upper-right corner) and scroll down.

FIGURE 8-9

Clear a Conversation

When you're done chatting, you might want to delete a conversation to remove the clutter before you start a new chat.

1. With Messages open and your conversations displayed, swipe to the left on the message you want to delete.

2. Tap the Delete button next to the conversation you want to get rid of (see Figure 8-10).

Tap the Hide Alerts button to keep from being alerted to new messages in the conversation. Swipe again and tap the Show Alerts button to reactivate alerts for the conversation.

TIP

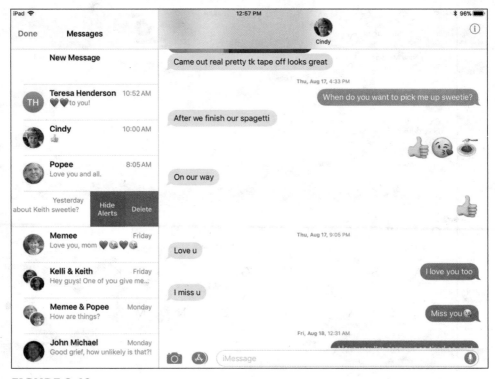

FIGURE 8-10

Send Emojis in Place of Text

Emojis are small pictures that can help convey a feeling or idea — for example, smiley faces and sad faces to show emotions, thumbs–up to convey approval, and the like.

To send an emoji in place of text:

1. From within a conversation, tap the Emoji key on the onscreen keyboard. If you can't see the keyboard, tap in the Message field to display it.

2. When the emojis appear (see Figure 8-11), swipe left and right to find the right emoji for the moment and tap to select it. You can add as many as you like to the conversation.

FIGURE 8-11

Utilizing the App Drawer

The App Drawer allows you to add items that spice up your messages with information from other apps that are installed on your iPad, as well as drawings and other images from the web.

To use the App Drawer:

1. Tap the App Drawer icon (looks like an A) to the left of the iMessage field in your conversation. The App Drawer will display at the bottom of the screen.

2. Tap an item in the App Drawer to see what it offers your messaging.

The App Drawer is populated by

» **The App Store:** Tap the App Store all the way to the left of the App Drawer to find tons of stickers, games, and apps for your messages.

» **Digital Touch:** Allows you to send special effects in Messages. These can range from sending your heartbeat to sketching a quick picture to sending a kiss.

» **Other apps you have installed may also appear if they have the ability to add functions and information to your messages.** For example, send the latest scores using ESPN or let your friend know what the weather's like nearby using icons from the AccuWeather app. Another example could be using Fandango's app to send movie information, as illustrated in Figure 8-12.

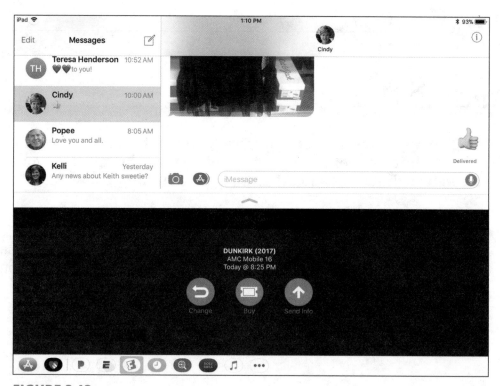

FIGURE 8-12

Digital Touch is one of the most personal ways to send special effects to others, so take a closer look at it:

1. To send a Digital Touch in a message, open a conversation and tap the Digital Touch button (black oval containing a red heart), shown in Figure 8-13.

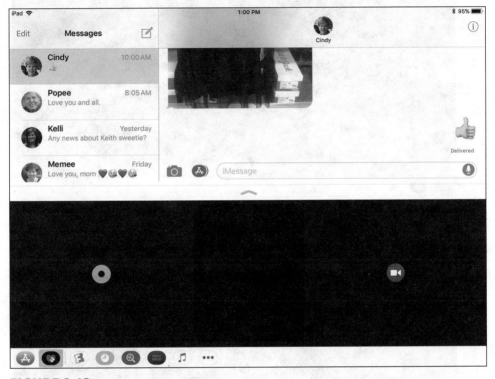

FIGURE 8-13

2. In the Digital Touch window, tap the gray expansion arrow (seen in Figure 8-13 in the very middle of the screen immediately under the message field) to open the full window. Tap the Information button in the lower right (a gray circle with a white letter *i*), and you see a list of the gestures and what they do (see Figure 8-14).

3. Perform a gesture in the Digital Touch window, and it will go to your recipient, as I've done in Figure 8-15.

FIGURE 8-14

FIGURE 8-15

Send and Receive Audio

When you're creating a message, you can also create an audio message:

1. With Messages open, tap the New Message button.

2. Enter an addressee's name in the To field.

3. Tap and hold the Audio button (the microphone symbol to the right of the screen in the message field).

4. Speak your message or record a sound or music near you as you continue to hold down the Audio button.

5. Release the Audio button when you're finished recording.

6. Tap the Send button (an upward-pointing arrow at the top of the recording circle). The message appears as an audio track in the recipient's Messages inbox (see Figure 8-16). To play the track, the recipient just taps the Play button.

FIGURE 8-16

Send a Photo or Video

When you're creating a message, you can also send a picture or create a short video message:

1. With Messages open, tap the New Message button.

2. Tap the Camera button. In the tool palette that appears (see Figure 8-17), tap the Photo button to take a picture and then return to the message.

FIGURE 8-17

3. If you prefer to capture a video, with the palette in Figure 8-17 displayed:

   a. Tap Camera.

   b. When Camera opens, swipe to Video and tap the red Record button.

c. Tap the red Stop button when you've recorded what you want to record.

d. Tap Done in the upper-right corner if the video is up to your standards and then tap the Send button. Your video is attached to your message.

Send a Map of Your Location

When responding to a message, you can also send a map showing your current location.

1. Tap a message and then tap the Details button in the upper-right corner.

2. Tap Send My Current Location (see Figure 8-18), and a map will be inserted as a message attachment.

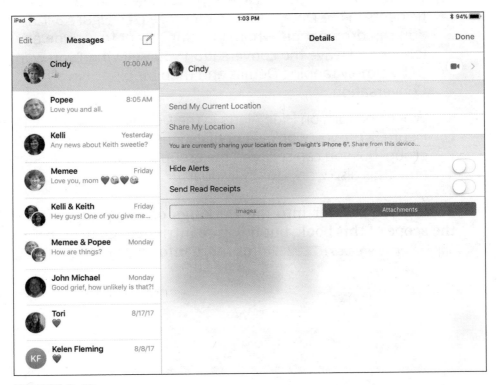

FIGURE 8-18

TIP

You can also share your location in the middle of a conversation rather than send a map attachment with your message. In the screen shown in Figure 8-18, tap Share My Location and then tap Share for One Hour, Share Until End of Day, or Share Indefinitely. A map showing your location appears above your conversation until you stop sharing.

Understand Group Messaging

If you want to start a conversation with a group of people, you can use group messaging. Group messaging is great for keeping several people in the conversational loop.

With iOS 8 came a lot of group messaging functionality, including the following features:

» When you participate in a group message, you see all participants in the Details for the message (see Figure 8-19). You can drop people whom you don't want to include any longer and leave the conversation yourself when you want to by simply tapping Details and then tapping Leave This Conversation.

» When you turn on Hide Alerts in the Details in a message (see Figure 8-19), you won't get notifications of messages from this group, but you can still read the group's messages at a later time (this also works for individuals).

Taking you further into the workings of group messages is beyond the scope of this book, but if you're intrigued, go to `https://support.apple.com/en-us/HT202724` for more information.

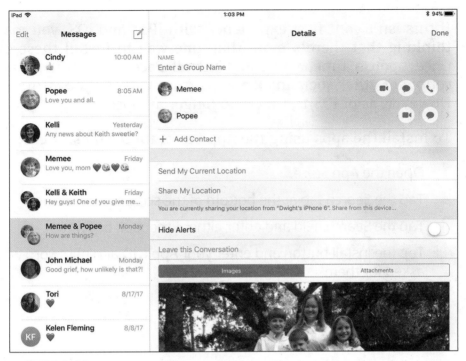

FIGURE 8-19

Activate the Hide Alerts Feature

If you don't want to get notifications of new messages from an individual or group for a while, you can use the Hide Alerts feature:

1. With a message open, tap Details.

2. Tap the Hide Alerts switch to turn the feature on (refer to Figure 8-19).

3. Later, return to Details and tap the Hide Alerts switch again to turn the feature off.

Finding and Installing Facebook and Twitter

To begin using Facebook and Twitter, you first need to find and then install them on your iPad.

If this isn't your first experience with iPad and iOS, you may be thinking that there's more than one way to install these apps. Once upon a time, you could install Facebook, Twitter, and a couple of other social media apps from within the Settings app. However, as of iOS 11, that's no longer an option.

To install the apps using the App Store, follow these steps:

1. Open the App Store.

2. Tap the Search tab at the bottom of the screen.

3. Tap the Search field and enter either Facebook or Twitter.

4. Tap the Install button and enter your Apple ID and password when asked for them.

If you've had the app installed before but have since deleted it, you will instead see a cloud with a downward-pointing arrow (see Figure 8-20); tap that to begin the download.

FIGURE 8-20

The app will download and install on one of your Home screens.

Creating a Facebook Account

You can create a Facebook account from directly within the app, or if you have an account already, you can simply use that account information to log in.

To create an account in the Facebook app, follow these steps:

1. Launch the newly downloaded Facebook app.

2. Tap the Sign Up for Facebook option near the bottom of the screen, as seen in Figure 8-21 (you almost need binoculars to see it).

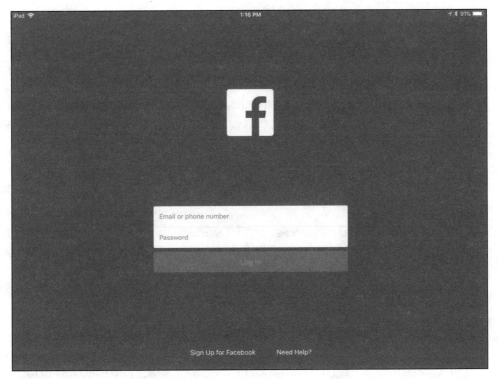

FIGURE 8-21

3. Tap Get Started and walk through the steps to complete the registration of your account.

4. When finished, you'll be logged into your account in the Facebook app.

TIP

You may also create a Facebook account by visiting its website at www.facebook.com.

Customize Facebook Settings for Your iPad

Facebook has a few settings that you'll want to configure when entering your account information into the Settings app:

1. Open the Settings app.

2. Tap Facebook.

3. Toggle the switches, seen in Figure 8-22, On (green) or Off for the following options:

- **Background App Refresh:** Allows Facebook to refresh its content in the background or, put another way, when you aren't actually using it.

- **Cellular Data (if your iPad supports it):** Allows Facebook to refresh itself and lets you post updates when you aren't connected to a Wi-Fi network.

- **Upload HD:** If you record HD video on your iPad, allows you to upload that high-quality video to Facebook. Keep in mind that HD video files are very large files and will therefore consume vast quantities of your cellular data allotment, as well as take much longer to upload.

4. Tap the remaining items in the Allow Facebook to Access section (Photos, Siri & Search, and Notifications) to customize how Facebook can interact with these iOS 11 features. For example, tap Photos and allow or deny Facebook access to the Photos app, as illustrated in Figure 8-23.

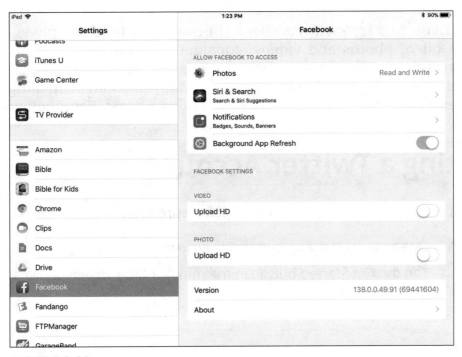

FIGURE 8-22

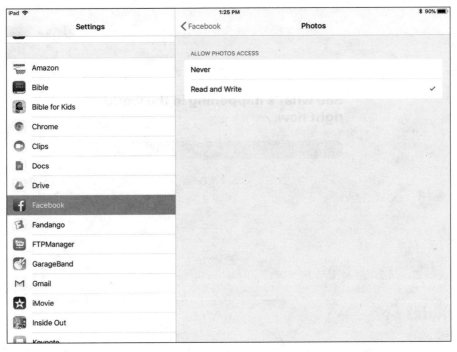

FIGURE 8-23

WARNING

If you're a frequent Facebook user and you tend to upload quite a bit of photos and videos, consider toggling the Cellular Data switch to Off. If you have an account with a cellular provider that provides a limited amount of data, you could be in danger of exceeding your data allotment if you're a heavy Facebook user.

Creating a Twitter Account

To create an account in the Twitter app, follow these steps:

1. Open the Twitter app by tapping its icon.

2. Tap the Get Started button in the middle of the screen, as illustrated in Figure 8-24.

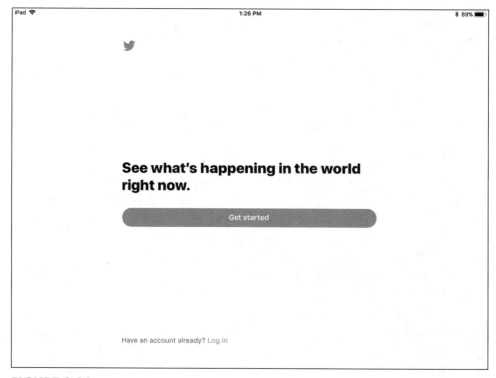

FIGURE 8-24

If you already have a Twitter account, tap the tiny blue Log In button at the very bottom of the screen to log in.

3. The app asks you a series of friendly questions to help you create your account.

4. When you're done, the app logs you into your new account.

Just like Facebook, you can create an account on the Twitter website at www.twitter.com.

Customize Twitter Settings for Your iPad

Like Facebook, Twitter also has a handful of options that you need to consider when installing it:

1. Open the Settings app.

2. Tap Twitter.

3. Tap Siri & Search and toggle the Search & Siri Suggestions switch On (green) or Off. This option, if enabled, allows Siri to learn how you use the Twitter app and offer suggestions to you based on that information.

4. Toggle the Background App Refresh switch, seen in Figure 8-25, On (green) or Off to allow Twitter to refresh its content in the background (when you're not using the app).

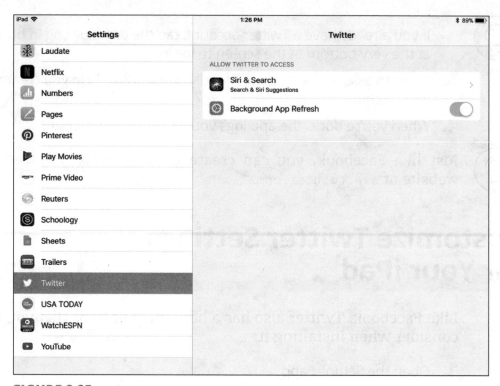

FIGURE 8-25

Chapter **9**

Browsing with Safari

Getting on the Internet with your iPad is easy, by using its Wi-Fi or 3G/4G (LTE) capabilities. After you're online, the built-in browser (software that helps you navigate the Internet's contents), Safari, is your ticket to a wide world of information, entertainment, education, and more. Safari will look familiar to you if you've used it on a PC or Mac computer, though the way you move around by using the iPad touchscreen may be new to you. If you've never used Safari, this chapter takes you by the hand and shows you all the basics of making Safari work for you.

In this chapter, you see how to go online with your iPad. You see how to navigate among web pages and use iCloud tabs to share your browsing experience between devices. Along the way, you see how to place a bookmark for a favorite site or place a web clip on your

Home screen. You can also view your browsing history, save online images to your Photo Library, post photos to sites from within Safari, or email or tweet a link to a friend. You also explore Safari's Reader and Reading List features and learn how to keep yourself safer while online by using private browsing. Finally, you review the simple steps involved in printing what you find online.

Connect to the Internet

How you connect to the Internet depends on which connections are available:

» You can connect to the Internet via a Wi-Fi network. You can set up this type of network in your own home using your computer and some equipment from your Internet provider. You can also connect over public Wi-Fi networks, referred to as *hotspots*.

You'll probably be surprised to discover how many hotspots your town or city has. Look for Internet cafés, coffee shops, hotels, libraries, and transportation centers (such as airports or bus stations). Many of these businesses display signs alerting you to their free Wi-Fi.

» You can use the paid data network provided by AT&T, Sprint, T-Mobile, Verizon, or most any other cellular provider, to connect by using 3G or 4G (LTE) from just about anywhere you can get coverage through a cellular network. Of course, you have to have an iPad model that supports cellular connections to hop on the Internet this way.

To enable 3G/4G (LTE) data, tap Settings and then tap Cellular. Toggle the switch (just tap it) to turn on the Cellular Data setting.

WARNING

Browsing the Internet using a 3G/4G (LTE) connection can eat up your data plan allotment quickly if your plan doesn't include unlimited data access. If you think you'll be using the Internet a good deal with your iPad away from a Wi-Fi connection, double-check your data allotment with your cellular provider.

To connect to a Wi-Fi network, you have to complete a few steps:

1. Tap Settings on the Home screen and then tap Wi-Fi.

2. Be sure that Wi-Fi is set to On (green) and choose a network to connect to by tapping it.

Network names should appear automatically when you're in range of them. When you're in range of a public hotspot, if access to several nearby networks is available, you may see a message asking you to tap a network name to select it. After you select one (or if only one network is available), you may see a message asking for your password. Ask the owner of the hotspot (for example, a hotel desk clerk or business owner) for this password or enter your own network password if you're connecting to your home network.

Free public Wi-Fi networks usually don't require passwords, or the password is posted prominently for all to see (if you can't find the password, don't be shy to ask someone).

3. Tap the Join button when prompted. Once done, you're connected! Your iPad will now recognize the network and connect without repeatedly entering the password.

After you connect to public Wi-Fi, someone else can track your online activities because these are unsecured networks. Avoid accessing financial accounts, or sending emails with sensitive information in them, when connected to a public hotspot.

Explore Safari

Safari will become your new best friend when it comes to surfing the World Wide Web, so it's a good idea to learn what it offers as a web-surfing tool.

Here's how to get around in Safari:

1. After you're connected to a network, tap Safari on the Dock at the bottom of the Home screen. Safari opens, probably displaying the Apple iPad Home page the first time you go online (see Figure 9-1).

Previous button
Next button   Address/Search field   Show/Hide Tabs button
Bookmarks button   Share button

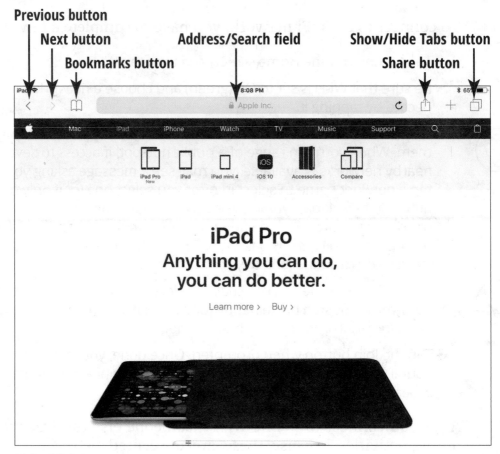

FIGURE 9-1

2. Put two fingers together on the screen and spread them apart to expand the view (also known as zooming in). Double-tap the screen with a single finger to restore the default view size.

TIP
Using your fingers on the screen to enlarge or reduce the size of a web page allows you to view what's displayed at various sizes, giving you more flexibility than the double-tap method.

3. Put your finger on the screen and flick upward to scroll down on the page.

4. To return to the top of the web page, put your finger on the screen and drag downward or tap the Status bar at the very top of the screen twice.

TIP

When you zoom in, you have more control by using two fingers to drag from left to right or from top to bottom on the screen. When you zoom out, one finger works fine for making these gestures.

Navigate among Web Pages

Web pages are chock full of information and gateways to other web resources. To navigate the landscape of web pages in Safari:

1. Tap in the Address field just under the Status bar. The onscreen keyboard appears (see Figure 9-2).

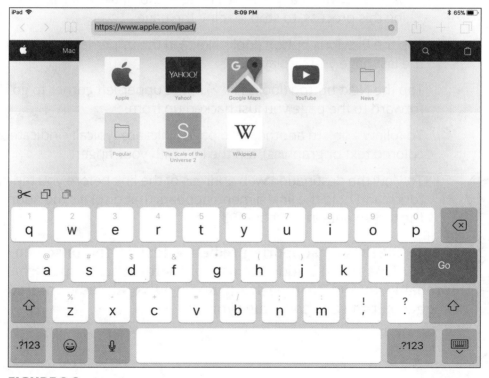

FIGURE 9-2

2. Enter a web address; for example, you can go to www.dummies.com.

By default, AutoFill is turned on in iPad, causing entries you make in fields, such as the Address field and Password fields, to automatically display possible matching entries.

You can turn off AutoFill by using iPad Settings for Safari.

3. Tap the Go key on the keyboard (refer to Figure 9-2). The website appears.

- If a page doesn't display properly, tap the Reload button at the right end of the Address field.

- If Safari is loading a web page and you change your mind about viewing the page, you can stop loading the page. Tap Cancel (looks like an X), which appears at the right end of the Address field during this process, to stop loading the page.

4. Tap the Previous button (looks like <) in the upper-left corner to go to the last page you displayed.

5. Tap the Next button (looks like >) in the upper-left corner to go forward to the page you just backed up from.

6. To follow a link to another web page (links are typically indicated by colored text or graphics), tap the link with your finger.

To view the destination web address of the link before you tap it, just touch and hold the link; a menu appears that displays the address at the top, as shown in Figure 9-3.

Apple QuickType supports predictive text in the onscreen keyboard. This feature adds the capability for iPad to spot what you probably intend to type from text you've already entered and suggests it to save you time typing.

FIGURE 9-3

Use Tabbed Browsing

Tabbed browsing is a feature that allows you to have several websites open at one time so that you can move easily among those sites.

1. With Safari open and a web page already displaying, tap the Show/Hide Tabs button in the upper-right corner (refer to Figure 9-1). The new Tab view appears.

2. To add a new page (meaning that you're opening a new website), tap the New Page button (shaped like a plus [+] symbol) in the upper right of the screen (see Figure 9-4). A page with your favorite sites and an address bar appears.

You can get to the same new page by simply tapping in the address bar from any site.

TIP

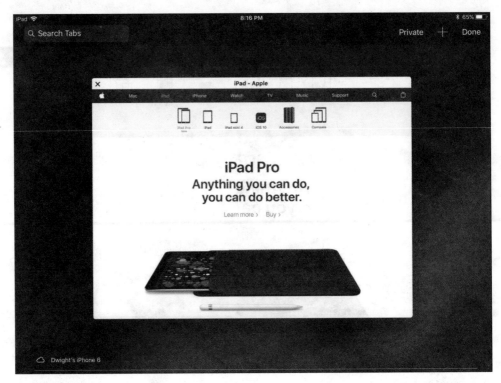

FIGURE 9-4

3. Tap in the Address field and use the onscreen keyboard to enter the web address for the website you want to open. Tap the Go key. The website opens on the page.

Repeat Steps 1 to 3 to open as many new web pages as you'd like.

4. You can now switch among open sites by tapping outside the keyboard to close it and tapping the Show/Hide Tabs button and scrolling among recent sites. Find the one you want and then tap it.

You can easily rearrange sites in the tabs window. Just touch-and-hold the tab you want to move and then drag it to the right or left in the list until it's in the spot you'd like it to be (the other sites in the window politely move to make room). To drop it in the new location, simply remove your finger from the screen.

5. To delete a tab, tap the Show/Hide Tabs button, scroll to locate the tab, and then tap the Close button in the upper-left corner of the tab (looks like an X; it may be difficult to see on some sites, but trust me, it's there).

View Browsing History

As you move around the web, your browser keeps a record of your browsing history. This record can be handy when you want to visit a site that you viewed previously but whose address you've now forgotten.

To view your browsing history:

1. With Safari open, tap the Bookmarks button.

TIP

After you master the use of the Bookmarks button options, you might prefer a shortcut to view your History list. Tap and hold the Previous button at the bottom left on any screen, and your browsing history for the current session appears. You can also tap and hold the Next button to look at sites you backtracked from.

2. On the menu shown in Figure 9-5, tap the History tab (looks like a clock).

FIGURE 9-5

3. In the History list that appears (see Figure 9-6), tap a site to navigate to it. Tap Done to leave History and return to browsing.

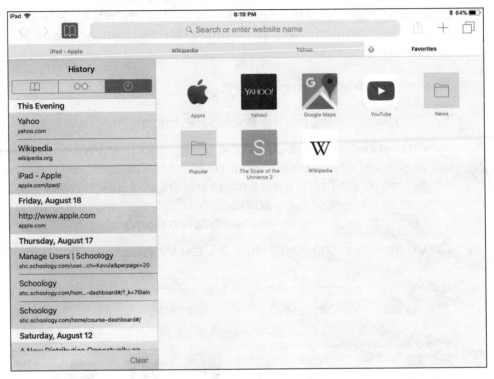

FIGURE 9-6

TIP

To clear the history, tap the Clear button in the bottom of the History list (refer to Figure 9-6) and on the screen that appears, tap an option: The Last Hour, Today, Today and Yesterday, or All Time. This button is useful when you don't want your spouse or grandchildren to see where you've been browsing for anniversary, birthday, or holiday presents!

Search the Web

If you don't know the address of the site that you want to visit (or you want to research a topic or find other information online), get acquainted with Safari's Search feature on iPad. By default, Safari uses the Google search engine.

To search the web:

1. With Safari open, tap in the Address field (refer to Figure 9-1). The onscreen keyboard appears.

To change your default search engine from Google to Yahoo!, Bing, or DuckDuckGo, from the Home screen, tap Settings, tap Safari, and then tap Search Engine. Tap Yahoo!, Bing, or DuckDuckGo, and your default search engine changes.

2. Enter a search term. With recent versions of Safari, the search term can be a topic or a web address because of what's called the Unified smart search field. You can tap one of the suggested sites or complete your entry and tap the Go key (see Figure 9-7) on your keyboard.

3. In the search results that are displayed, tap a link to visit that site.

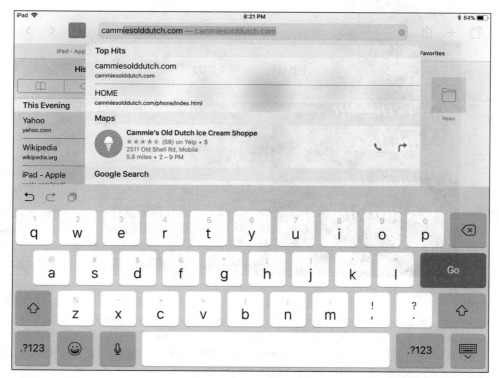

FIGURE 9-7

Add and Use Bookmarks

Bookmarks are a way to save favorite sites so that you can easily visit them again.

To add and use bookmarks:

TIP

1. With a site open that you want to bookmark, tap the Share button.

   If you want to sync your bookmarks on your iPad browser, go to Settings on iPad and make sure that iCloud is set to sync with Safari.

2. On the menu that appears (see Figure 9-8), tap Add Bookmark.

FIGURE 9-8

3. In the Add Bookmark dialog, shown in Figure 9-9, edit the name of the bookmark if you want. Tap the name of the site and use the onscreen keyboard to edit its name.

FIGURE 9-9

4. Tap the Save button in the upper-right corner. The item is saved to your Favorites by default.

5. To go to the bookmark, tap the Bookmarks button.

6. On the Bookmarks menu that appears (see Figure 9-10), if you saved a site to a folder tap to open the folder, and then tap the bookmarked site that you want to visit.

TIP

When you tap the Bookmarks button, you can tap Edit in the lower right of the Bookmarks menu and then use the New Folder option (in the lower left) to create folders to organize your bookmarks or folders. When you next add a bookmark, you can then choose, from the dialog that appears, any folder to which you want to add the new bookmark.

FIGURE 9-10

Save Links and Web Pages to Safari Reading List

The Safari Reading List provides a way to save content that you want to read at a later time so that you can easily call up that content again. You essentially save the content rather than a web page address, which allows you to read the content even when you're offline. You can scroll from one item to the next easily.

To save content to the Reading List, follow these steps:

1. Displaying a site that you want to add to your Reading List, tap the Share button.

2. On the menu that appears (refer to Figure 9-8), tap the Add to Reading List button. The site is added to your Reading List.

3. To view your Reading List, tap the Bookmarks button and then tap the Reading List tab (the middle tab with the eyeglasses icon near the top of the Bookmarks menu).

TIP

If you want to see both the Reading List material you've read and the material you haven't read, tap the Show Unread button in the bottom-left corner of the Reading List. To see all reading material, tap the Show All button.

4. On the Reading List that appears (see Figure 9-11), tap the content that you want to revisit and resume reading.

FIGURE 9-11

TIP

To delete an item, with the Reading List displaying, swipe right to left on an item; a Delete button appears. Tap this button to delete the item from the Reading List. To save an item for offline (when you're not connected to the Internet) reading, tap the Save Offline button when you swipe.

Enjoy Reading More with Safari Reader

The Safari Reader feature gives you an e-reader type of experience right within your browser, removing other stories and links as well as those distracting advertisements.

When you're on a site where you're reading content (such as an article), Safari displays a Reader button on the left side of the Address field for sites that support this feature (see Figure 9-12).

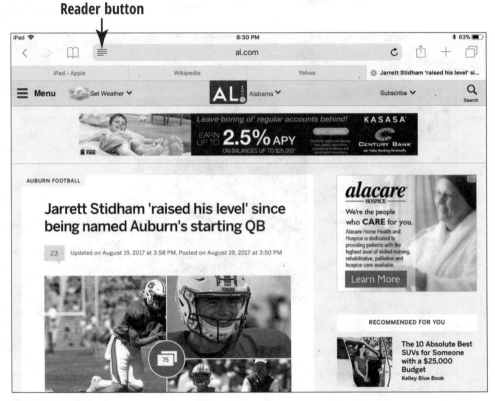

FIGURE 9-12

1. Tap the Reader button. The content appears in a reader format (see Figure 9-13).

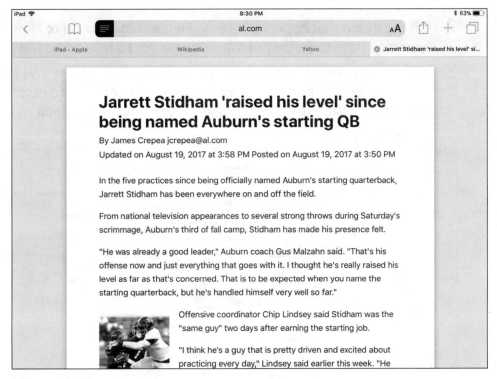

FIGURE 9-13

2. Scroll down the page. The entire content is contained in this one long page.

3. When you finish reading the material, just tap the Reader button again to leave that view.

Tap the AA button at the top right of the Address field to adjust the background color, font, and font size for the article.

TIP

Add Web Clips to the Home Screen

The Web Clips feature allows you to save a website as an icon on your Home screen so that you can go to the site at any time with one tap:

1. With Safari open and displaying the site you want to add, tap the Share button.

2. On the menu that appears (refer to Figure 9-8), tap Add to Home Screen (you may have to swipe the menu from right to left to find the button).

3. In the Add to Home dialog that appears (see Figure 9-14), you can edit the name of the site to be more descriptive, if you like. To do so, tap the name of the site and use the onscreen keyboard to edit its name.

FIGURE 9-14

4. Tap the Add button in the upper right. The site is added to your Home screen.

TIP

You can have from 11 to 15 Home screens on your iPad (depending on the model) to accommodate all the web clips you create and apps you download. (There is a limit to how many items will fit on these screens; however, you can place up to 135 apps in folders on Home screens and up to 24 folders per Home screen.)

Save an Image to Your Photo Library

Sometimes you stumble across an image on a website you'd like to save. Follow these steps to do so:

1. Display a web page that contains an image you want to copy.

2. Tap and hold the image. The menu shown in Figure 9-15 appears.

   Some websites are set up to prevent you from copying images on them, or they display a pop-up stating that the contents on the site are copyrighted and shouldn't be copied.

3. Tap the Save Image option (see Figure 9-15). The image is saved to your Camera Roll.

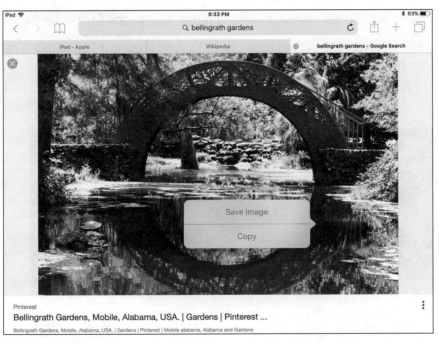

FIGURE 9-15

Be careful about copying images from the Internet and using them for business or promotional activities. Most images are copyrighted, and you may violate the copyright even if you simply use an image in (say) a brochure for your association or a flyer for your community group. Note that some search engines' advanced search settings offer the option of browsing only for images that aren't copyrighted.

Send a Link

If you find a great site that you want to share, you can easily send a link in a variety of ways (via Messages, Mail, Twitter, Facebook, or even saving a link to Reminders or Notes).

1. With Safari open and the site that you want to share displaying, tap the Share button.

2. On the menu that appears (refer to Figure 9-8), tap the method you want to use for sharing the link (I use Messages for this example).

3. On the message form that appears (see Figure 9-16), enter a recipient in the To field.

4. Tap the Send button; the message is sent.

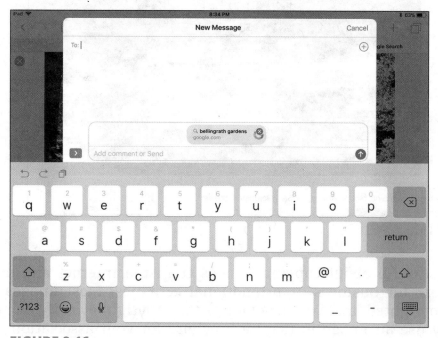

FIGURE 9-16

Make Privacy Settings

Apple has provided some privacy settings for Safari that you should consider using.

Private Browsing automatically stops Safari from using AutoFill to save information used to complete certain entries as you type, and erases some browsing history information. This feature can keep your online activities more private. To enable Private Browsing:

1. Tap the Show/Hide Tabs button (refer to Figure 9-1).

2. Tap Private in the upper-right corner; you're now in Private Browsing Mode, as illustrated in Figure 9-17.

3. Tap the Private button in the upper-right corner again to disable Private Browsing.

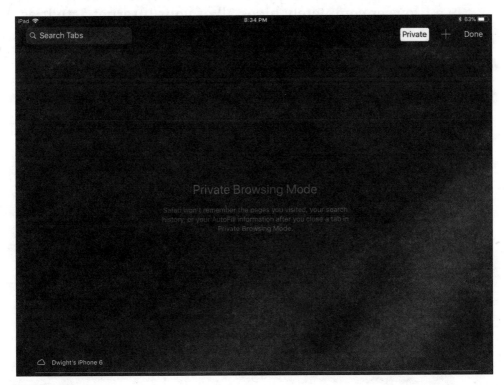

FIGURE 9-17

Cookies are small files that document your browsing history so that you can be recognized by a site the next time you go to or move within that site. Cross-site tracking is a technique used by some sites to collect your data via cookies, whether you've directly visited that site or not. Safari in iOS 11 provides a new feature called Prevent Cross-Site Tracking to stop just this sort of activity. Go to Settings from the Home screen and in Safari toggle the Prevent Cross-Site Tracking switch to On (green). A cousin setting is the Block All Cookies option, and it can be found directly under the Prevent Cross-Site Tracking option.

WARNING

Blocking all cookies may cause some websites not to function properly. If you find you're unable to use a website in the way it's intended, try disabling the Block All Cookies option (if it's enabled).

Toggle the Ask Websites Not To Track Me switch in Safari settings to turn on the Do Not Track feature (see Figure 9-18). This setting stops some sites from tracking your online activities, but no privacy setting in a browser completely hides all of your Internet activities.

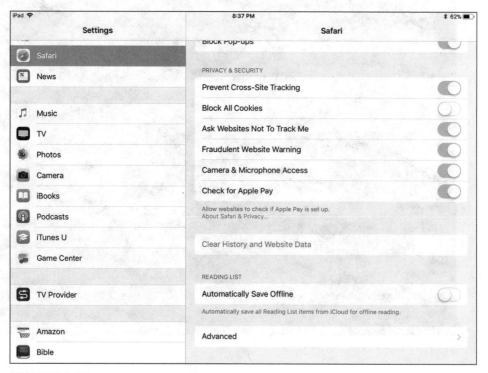

FIGURE 9-18

TIP

You can also tap the Clear History and Website Data option (refer to Figure 9-18) to manually clear your browsing history, saved cookies, and other data.

Print a Web Page

If you have a wireless printer that supports Apple's AirPrint technology, you can print web content using a wireless connection:

1. With Safari open and the site that you want to print displaying, tap the Share button.

TIP

If you don't have an AirPrint-compatible wireless printer or don't want to use an app to help you print wirelessly, just email a link to the web page to yourself, open the link on your computer, and print from there.

2. On the menu that appears (refer to Figure 9-8), scroll to the right in the bottom row of buttons and then tap Print.

3. In the Printer Options dialog that appears (see Figure 9-19), tap Select Printer. In the list of printers that appears, tap the name of your wireless printer.

4. Tap either the plus or minus button in the Copy field to adjust the number of copies to print.

If your printer supports two-sided printing, you'll also see a Double-Sided On/Off switch.

5. Tap Print to print the displayed page.

TIP

The Mac applications Printopia (www.decisivetactics.com/products/printopia) and HandyPrint (www.netputing.com/applications/handyprint-v5) make any shared or network printer on your home network visible to your iPad. Printopia has more features, but will cost you, whereas HandyPrint is free.

FIGURE 9-19

Understand iCloud Tabs

The iCloud Tabs feature allows you to access all browsing history among your different devices from any device. If you begin to research a project on your iPad before you leave home, you can then pick up where you left off as you sit in a waiting room with your iPad.

To use iCloud tabs:

1. Tap Settings and then tap your Apple ID (at the top of the screen); swipe down and check to make sure that the iPad is using the same iCloud account as your other devices.

2. Open Safari on another device and tap the Show/Hide Tabs button. Scroll down to see a list of every device using your iCloud account.

   All items in your iPad's browsing history are displayed on the other devices.

Chapter **10**

Working with Email in Mail

S taying in touch with others by using email is a great way to use your iPad. You can access an existing account using the handy Mail app supplied with your iPad or sign in to your email account using the Safari browser. In this chapter, you take a look at using Mail, which involves adding an existing email account by way of Settings. Then you can use Mail to write, format, retrieve, and forward messages from that account.

Mail offers the capability to mark the messages you've read, delete messages, and organize your messages in a small set of folders, as well as use a handy search feature. You can create a VIP list so that you're notified when that special person sends you an email.

In this chapter, you read all about Mail and its various features.

Add an Email Account

You can add one or more email accounts, including the email account associated with your iCloud account, using iPad Settings. If you have an iCloud, Microsoft Exchange (often used for business accounts), Gmail, Yahoo!, AOL, or Outlook.com (this includes Microsoft accounts from Live, Hotmail, and so on) account, iPad pretty much automates the setup.

To set up iPad to retrieve messages from your email account at one of these popular providers:

1. Tap the Settings icon on the Home screen.

2. In Settings, tap Accounts & Passwords, and the screen shown in Figure 10-1 appears.

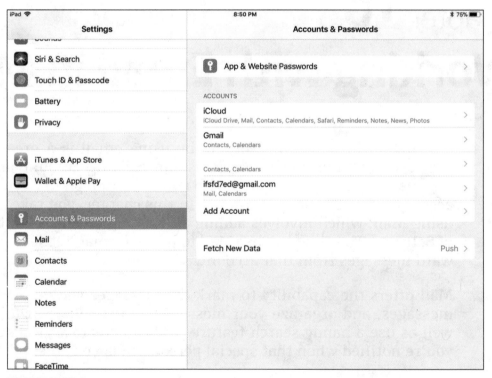

FIGURE 10-1

3. Tap Add Accounts, found under the Accounts section. The options shown in Figure 10-2 appear.

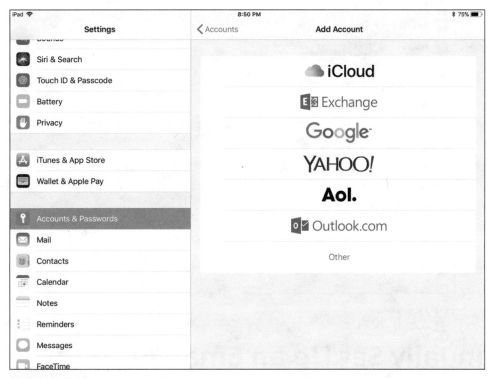

FIGURE 10-2

4. Tap iCloud, Google, Yahoo!, AOL, Exchange, or Outlook.com. Enter your account information in the form that appears and tap Sign In or, for AOL and Outlook accounts, tap Next.

5. After iPad takes a moment to verify your account information, on the next screen (shown in Figure 10-3), you can tap any On/Off switch to have services from that account synced with iPad.

6. When you're done, tap Save. The account is saved, and you can now open it using Mail.

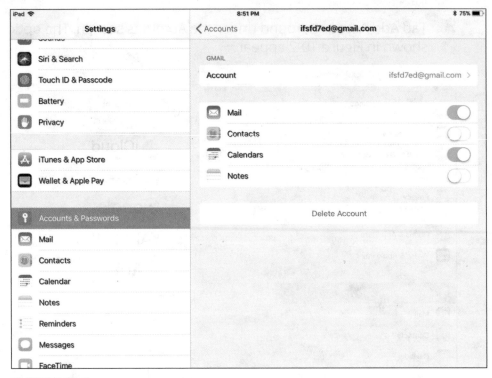

FIGURE 10-3

Manually Set Up an Email Account

You can also set up most popular email accounts, such as those available through Earthlink or a cable provider's service, by obtaining the host name from the provider. To set up an existing account with a provider other than iCloud, Gmail (Google), Yahoo!, AOL, Exchange, or Outlook.com, you enter the account settings yourself:

1. Tap the Settings icon on the Home screen.

2. In Settings, tap Accounts & Passwords and then tap the Add Account button (refer to Figure 10-1).

3. On the screen that appears (refer to Figure 10-2), tap Other.

4. On the screen shown in Figure 10-4, tap Add Mail Account.

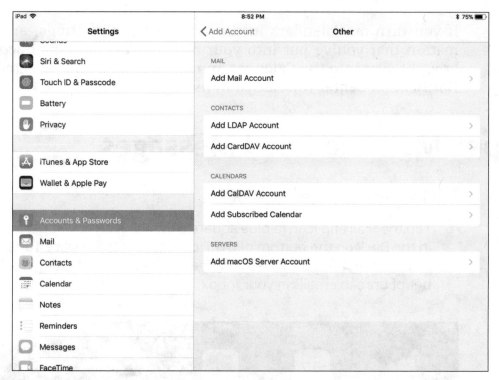

FIGURE 10-4

5. In the form that appears, enter your name and an account email address, password, and description and then tap Next. iPad takes a moment to verify your account and then returns you to the Accounts & Passwords page, with your new account displayed.

TIP

iPad will probably add the outgoing mail server (SMTP) information for you. If it doesn't, you may have to enter it yourself. If you have a less mainstream email service, you may have to enter the mail server protocol (POP3 or IMAP — ask your provider for this information) and your password.

6. To make sure that the account is set to receive email, tap the account name. In the dialog that appears, toggle the On/Off switch for the Mail field to On (green) and then tap the Accounts button to return to Mail settings. You can now access the account through iPad's Mail app.

If you turn on Calendars in the email account settings, any information that you've put into your calendar in that email account is brought over into the Calendar app on your iPad and reflected in the Notification Center (discussed in more detail in Chapter 17).

Open Mail and Read Messages

To open mail and read messages:

1. Tap the Mail app icon (a blue square containing an envelope) located in the Dock on the bottom of the Home screen (see Figure 10-5). A red circle on the icon, called a badge, may appear indicating the number of unread emails in your Inbox.

FIGURE 10-5

2. In the Mail app (see Figure 10-6), tap the Inbox whose contents you want to display.

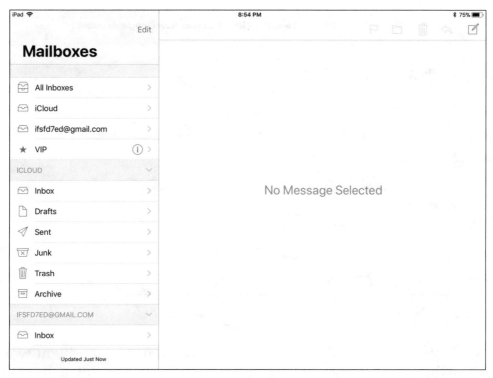

FIGURE 10-6

3. Tap a message to read it. It opens on the right side (see Figure 10-7).

4. If you need to scroll to see the entire message, just place your finger on the screen and flick upward to scroll down.

Email messages that you haven't read are marked with a blue circle in your Inbox. After you read a message, the blue circle disappears. You can mark a read message as unread to help remind you to read it again later. With the Inbox displayed, swipe to the right (starting your swipe just a little in from the edge of the screen) on a message and then tap Unread. If you swipe quickly to the right, you don't need to tap; it will just mark as unread automatically.

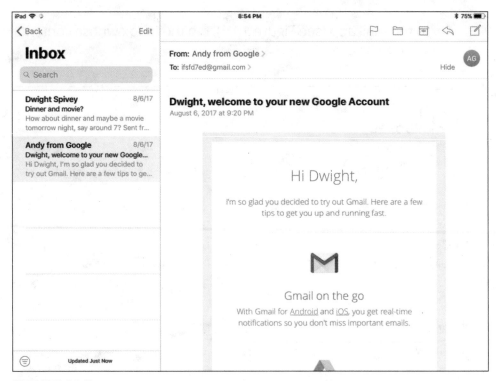

FIGURE 10-7

TIP

If you have an iPad that supports cellular data and you want to avoid having messages retrieved while you're not using Wi-Fi, you can stop retrieval of data, including email, by tapping Settings, Cellular, and then the On/Off switch on the Cellular Data option. Now you'll get data on your device only if you're logged in to a Wi-Fi network.

Reply To or Forward Email

To reply to or forward email:

1. With an email message open, tap the Reply/Forward button, which looks like a left-facing arrow (refer to Figure 10-7). Then tap Reply, Reply All (available if there are multiple recipients), or Forward in the menu that appears (see Figure 10-8).

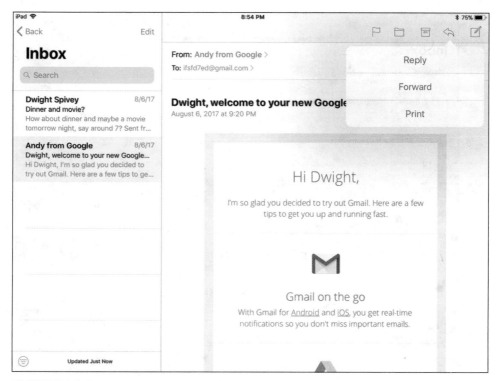

FIGURE 10-8

2. In the new email message that appears (see Figure 10-9), tap in the To field and enter another addressee if you like (you have to do this if you're forwarding); next, tap in the message body and enter a message (see Figure 10-10).

If you want to move an email address from the To field to the Cc or Bcc field, tap and hold the address and drag it to the other field.

TIP

3. Tap the Send button in the upper-right corner, and the email goes on its way.

If you tap Forward to send the message to somebody else and the original message had an attachment, you're offered the option of including or omitting the attachment.

TIP

FIGURE 10-9

FIGURE 10-10

Create and Send a New Message

To create and send a new message:

1. With Mail open, tap the New Message button in the upper-right corner (this looks like a page with a pencil on it). A blank email appears (see Figure 10-11).

FIGURE 10-11

2. Enter a recipient's address in the To field. If you have addresses in Contacts, tap the plus sign (+) in the Address field to choose an addressee from the Contacts list that appears.

3. If you want to send a copy of the message to other people, tap the Cc/Bcc field. When the Cc and Bcc fields open, enter addresses in either or both. Use the Bcc field to specify recipients of blind carbon copies, which means that no other recipients are aware that that person received this reply.

4. Enter the subject of the message in the Subject field.

5. Tap in the message body and type your message.

6. If you want to check a fact or copy and paste some part of another message into your draft message, swipe down near the top of the email to display your Inbox and other folders. Locate the message, and when you're ready to return to your draft, tap the Subject of the email, which is displayed near the bottom of the screen.

7. When you've finished creating your message, tap Send.

Format Email

You can apply some basic formatting to email text. You can use bold, underline, and italic formats, and indent text using the Quote Level feature.

To format an email:

1. Press and hold the text in a message you're creating and choose Select or Select All to select a single word or all the words in the email (see Figure 10-12).

TIP

When you make a selection, handles appear that you can drag to add adjacent words to your selection. If the menu disappears after you select the text, just tap one of the selection handles, and it will reappear.

2. To see more tools (such as adding attachments or inserting drawings), tap the arrow on the toolbar that appears; to apply bold, italic, or underline formatting, tap the BIU button.

3. In the toolbar that appears (see Figure 10-13), tap Bold, Italic, or Underline to apply formatting.

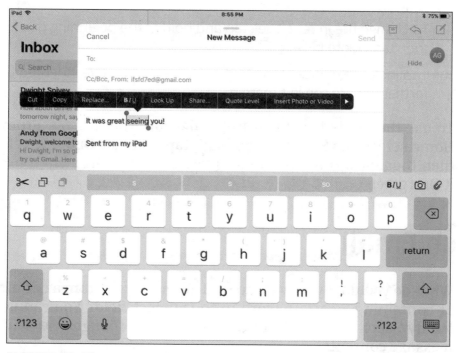

FIGURE 10-12

FIGURE 10-13

4. To change the indent level, tap and hold at the beginning of a line and then tap Quote Level.

5. Tap Increase to indent the text or Decrease to move indented text farther toward the left margin.

To use the Quote Level feature, make sure that it's on. From the Home screen tap Settings, tap Mail, tap Increase Quote Level, and then toggle (tap) the Increase Quote Level On/Off switch to turn it On (green).

Search Email

What do you do if you want to find all messages from a certain person or containing a certain word in the Subject field? You can use Mail's handy Search feature to find these emails (though you can't search message contents).

To search email:

1. With Mail open, tap an account to display its Inbox.

2. In the Inbox, tap in the Search field, and the onscreen keyboard appears.

You can also use the Spotlight Search feature covered in Chapter 2 to search for terms in the To, From, or Subject lines of mail messages.

3. Enter a search term or name, as shown in Figure 10-14. Matching emails are listed in the results (refer to Figure 10-14).

4. Tap the All Mailboxes tab to view messages that contain the search term in one of those fields in any mailbox or tap the Current Mailbox tab to see only matches within the current mailbox (refer to Figure 10-14). (These options may vary slightly, depending on which email service you use.)

To start a new search or go back to the full Inbox, either tap the Delete icon (the circled X) on the far-right end of the Search field to delete the term or tap the Cancel button.

FIGURE 10-14

Mark Email as Unread or Flag for Follow-Up

You can use a simple swipe to access tools that either mark an email as unread after you've read it (placing a blue dot before the message) or flag an email (which places an orange circle before it). If the email is both marked as unread and is flagged, a blue dot in an orange circle will appear in front of the message. These methods help you remember to reread an email that you've already read or to follow up on a message at a later time.

To mark email as unread or to flag it for follow–up:

1. With Mail open and an Inbox displayed, swipe to the left on an email in the Inbox list to display three options: More, Flag, and Trash/Archive. Whether Trash or Archive appears is dependent on the settings for each account.

2. Tap More. On the menu shown in Figure 10-15, you're given several options, including Mark. Tapping Mark accesses both the Mark As Read/Unread and Flag commands. Tapping either command applies it and returns you to your Inbox.

TIP

You can also get to this command by swiping to the right on a message displayed in your Inbox.

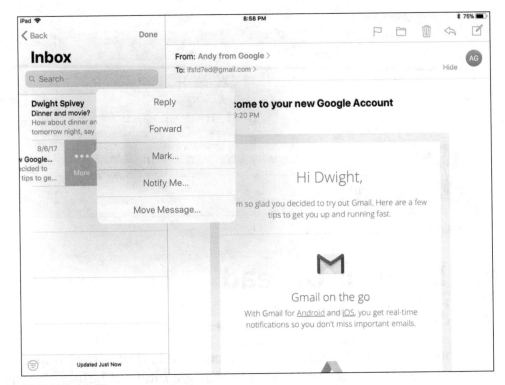

FIGURE 10-15

There's another way to get to the Flag command. Swipe to the left on another email and then tap Flag. An orange circle appears before the email.

TIP

On the menu shown in Figure 10-15, you can also select Notify Me. This option causes Mail to notify you whenever somebody replies to this email thread.

Create an Event from Email Contents

A neat feature in Mail is the ability to create a Calendar event from within an email:

1. To test this out, create an email to yourself mentioning a reservation on a specific airline on a specific date and time; you can also mention another type of reservation, such as for dinner, or mention a phone number.

2. Send the message to yourself and then open Mail.

3. In your Inbox, open the email. (The pertinent information is displayed in underlined blue text.)

4. Tap the underlined text, and in the menu shown in Figure 10-16, tap Create Event. A New Event form from Calendar appears. Enter additional information about the event and then tap Done.

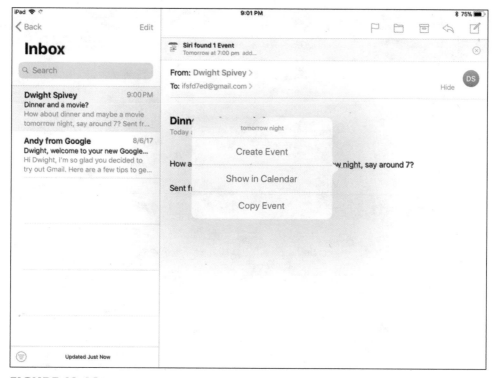

FIGURE 10-16

Delete Email

When you no longer want an email cluttering your Inbox, you can delete it.

1. With the Inbox displayed, tap the Edit button. Circular check boxes are displayed to the left of each message (see Figure 10-17).

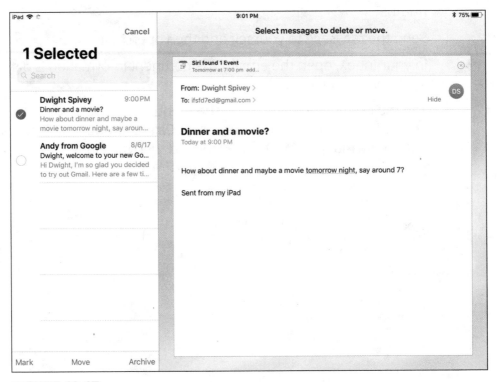

FIGURE 10-17

2. Tap the circle next to the message that you want to delete. A message marked for deletion shows a check mark in the circular check button (refer to Figure 10-17).

You can tap multiple items if you have several emails to delete.

3. Tap the Trash or Archive button at the bottom-left corner of the Inbox dialog. The message is moved to the Trash or Archive folder.

You can also delete an open email by tapping the Trash or Archive icon on the toolbar that runs across the bottom of the screen, or swiping left on a message displayed in an Inbox and tapping the Trash or Archive button that appears.

Organize Email

You can move messages into any of several predefined folders in Mail (these will vary depending on your email provider and the folders you've created on your provider's server).

To move your messages to folders:

1. After displaying the folder containing the message that you want to move (for example, Inbox), tap the Edit button. Circular check boxes are displayed to the left of each message (refer to Figure 10-17).

2. Tap the circle next to the message you want to move.

3. Tap the Move button.

4. In the Mailboxes list that appears (see Figure 10-18), tap the folder where you want to store the message. The message is moved.

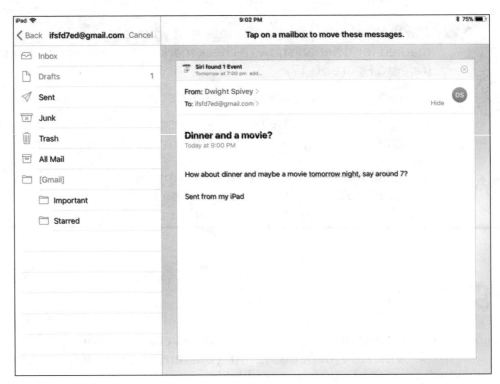

FIGURE 10-18

Create a VIP List

A VIP list is a way to create a list of senders you deem to be more important than others. When any of these senders sends you an email, you'll be notified of it through the Notifications feature of iPad.

1. In the list of all Mailboxes, tap the Info button (circle with lower-case *i*) in the VIP option (see Figure 10-19).

2. Tap Add VIP (see Figure 10-20), and your Contacts list appears. Tap a contact to add that person to the VIP list.

3. Tap a contact to make that person a VIP.

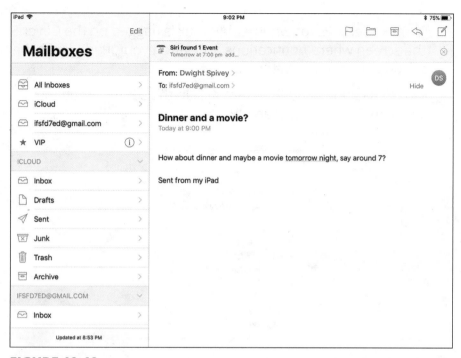

FIGURE 10-19

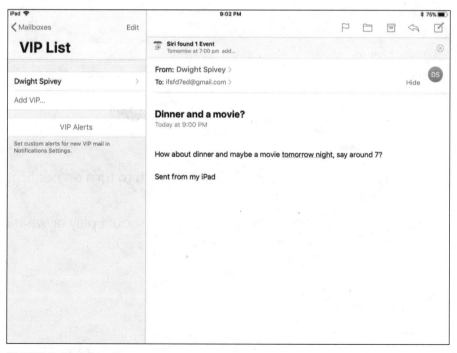

FIGURE 10-20

4. To make settings for whether VIP mail is flagged on the Cover Sheet (the screen where notifications appear on your iPad), press the Home button and then tap Settings.

5. Tap Notifications and then tap Mail. In the settings that appear, shown in Figure 10-21, tap VIP.

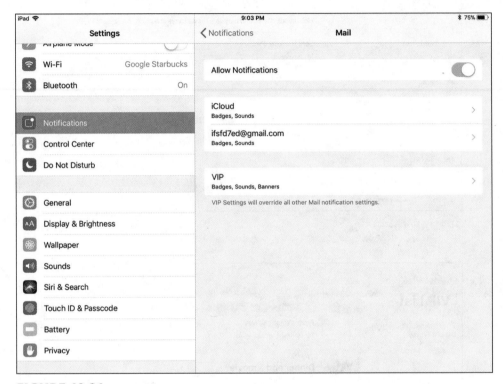

FIGURE 10-21

6. Tap the Show on Lock Screen On/Off switch to turn on notifications for VIP mail.

7. Tap an alert style and choose what sound should play or what badge icon should appear (see Figure 10-22).

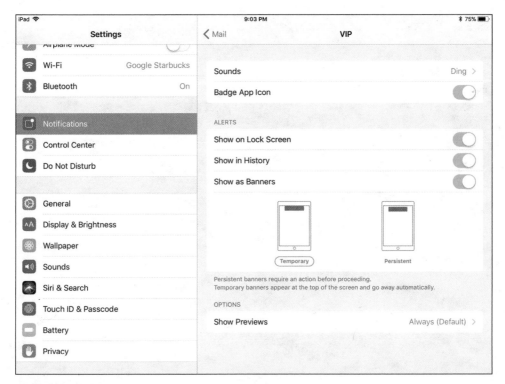

FIGURE 10-22

8. Press the Home button to close Settings. New mail from your VIPs should now appear on the Cover Sheet/Lock Screen when you swipe down from the top of the screen and, depending on the settings you chose, may cause a sound to play or a badge icon to appear on your Lock screen, and a blue star icon to appear to the left of these messages in the Inbox in Mail.

3 Enjoying Media

Chapter **11**

Shopping the iTunes Store

The iTunes Store app that comes preinstalled in iPad lets you easily shop for music, movies, and TV shows. As Chapter 12 explains, you can also get electronic and audiobooks via the iBooks app.

In this chapter, you discover how to find content in the iTunes Store. You can download the content directly to your iPad or to another device and then sync it to your iPad. With the Family Sharing feature, which I cover in this chapter, as many as six people in a family can share purchases using the same credit card. Finally, I cover a few options for buying content from other online stores and using Apple Pay to make real-world purchases using a stored payment method.

TIP

I cover opening an iTunes account and downloading iTunes software to your computer in Chapter 3. If you need to, read Chapter 3 to see how to handle these two tasks before digging into this chapter.

Explore the iTunes Store

Visiting the iTunes Store from your iPad is easy with the built-in iTunes Store app.

TIP

If you're in search of other kinds of content, the Podcasts app and iTunes U app allow you to find and then download podcasts and online courses to your phone.

To check out the iTunes Store, follow these steps:

1. If you aren't already signed in to iTunes, tap Settings and go to iTunes & App Store. Tap Sign In, enter your Apple ID and Password in their respective fields, as shown in Figure 11-1, and then tap Sign In.

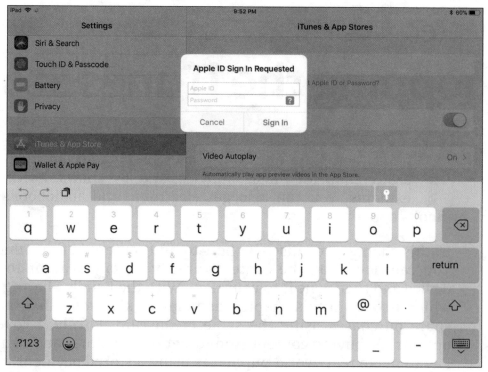

FIGURE 11-1

2. Go to your Home screen and tap the iTunes Store icon.

3. Tap the Music button (if it isn't already selected) in the row of buttons at the bottom of the screen. Swipe up and down the screen, and you'll find several categories of selections, such as New Music, Hot Tracks, and Recent Releases (these category names change from time to time).

4. Flick your finger up to scroll through the featured selections or tap the See All button to see more selections in any category, as shown in Figure 11-2.

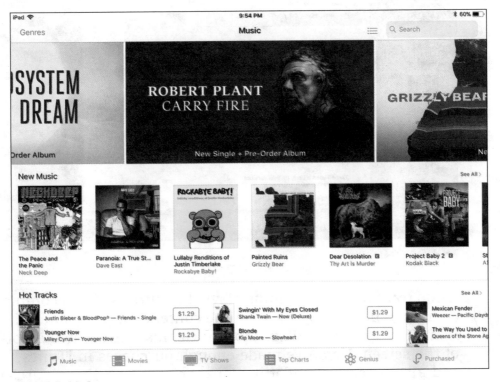

FIGURE 11-2

The navigation techniques in these steps work essentially the same in any of the content categories (the buttons at the bottom of the screen), which include Music, Movies, and TV Shows.

5. Tap the Top Charts tab at the bottom of the screen and then tap the Music tab at the top of the screen. This displays lists of bestselling songs, albums, and music videos in the iTunes Store.

6. Tap any listed item to see more detail about it, as shown in Figure 11-3, and hear a brief preview when you tap the number to the left of a song.

FIGURE 11-3

TIP

If you want to use the Genius playlist feature, which recommends additional purchases based on the contents of your library in the iTunes app on your iPad, tap the Genius button at the bottom of the screen. If you've made enough purchases in iTunes, song and album recommendations appear based on those purchases as well as the content in your iTunes Match library (a fee-based service), if you have one.

Find a Selection

You can look for a selection in the iTunes Store in several ways. You can use the Search feature, search by genre or category, or view artists' pages. Here's how these work:

» Tap the Search field in the upper-right corner of the screen, and the Search field shown in Figure 11-4 appears. Tap in the field and enter a search term using the onscreen keyboard. Tap the Search button on the keyboard or, if a suggestion in the list of search results appeals to you, just tap that suggestion.

FIGURE 11-4

» Tap an item at the bottom of the screen (such as Music) and then tap the Genres button in the upper left of the screen.

A list of genres like the one shown in Figure 11-5 appears.

» On a description page that appears when you tap a selection, you can find more offerings by the people involved with that particular work. For example, for a music selection, tap to display details about it and then tap the Reviews tab at the middle of the page to see all reviews of the album (see Figure 11-6). For a movie (tap Movies at the bottom of the iTunes Store Home page), tap to open details and then tap Reviews, or tap the Related tab to see more movies starring any of the lead actors.

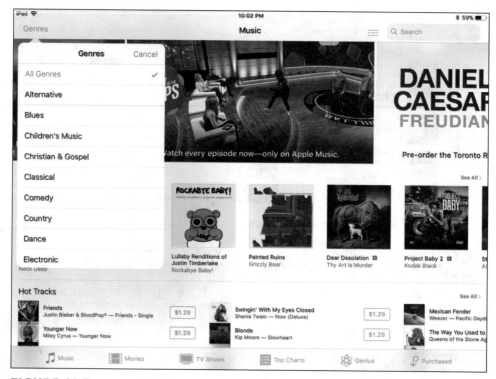

FIGURE 11-5

TIP

If you find a selection that you like, tap the Share button in the top right of its description page to share your discovery with a friend via AirDrop, Mail, Message, Twitter, or Facebook. A message form appears with a link that your friend can tap to view information about the selection. You must have set up an associated account (such as Twitter) before you can use this feature. Tap Settings from the Home screen to set up an account.

FIGURE 11-6

Preview Music, a Video, or an Audiobook

Because you've already set up an iTunes account (if you haven't done so yet, refer to Chapter 3), when you choose to buy an item, it's automatically charged either to the credit or debit card you have on file, to your PayPal account, or against any allowance you have outstanding from an iTunes gift card. You might want to preview an item before you buy it. If you like it, buying and downloading are easy and quick.

TIP

If you don't want to allow purchases from within apps (for examples, Music or TV) but rather want to allow purchases only through the iTunes Store, you can go to the Settings app, tap General, tap Restrictions, then tap Enable Restrictions, and enter a passcode. After you've set a passcode, you can tap individual apps to turn on restrictions for them, as well as for such actions as installing apps, deleting apps, or using Siri.

To preview items in the iTunes Store, follow these steps:

1. Open the iTunes Store app and use any method outlined in earlier tasks to locate a selection that you might want to buy.

2. Tap the item to see detailed information about it, as shown in Figure 11-7.

FIGURE 11-7

3. For a TV show, tap an episode to get further information (refer to Figure 11-7). If you're looking at a music selection, tap the track number or name of a selection to play a preview. For a movie or audiobook selection, tap the Trailers Play button (movies) shown in Figure 11-8.

TIP

Note the Redeem button on some iTunes screens. Tap this button to redeem any iTunes gift certificates that you might get from your generous friends or from yourself.

FIGURE 11-8

Buy a Selection

To buy a selection:

1. When you find an item that you want to buy, tap the button that shows either the price (if it's a selection available for purchase; see Figure 11-9) or the button with the word Get on it (if it's a selection available for free). The button label changes to Buy X, where X is the type of content, such as a song or album, that you're buying. If the item is free, the label changes to Get Song (or whatever item you're purchasing).

TIP

If you want to buy music, you can open the description page for an album and tap the album price, or buy individual songs rather than the entire album. Tap the price for a song and then proceed to purchase it.

FIGURE 11-9

2. Tap the Buy X button. The iTunes Password dialog appears (refer to Figure 11-1).

3. Enter your password and tap OK. The item begins downloading, and the cost, if any, is automatically charged against your account. When the download finishes, tap OK in the Purchase Complete message, and you can then view the content using the Music or Video app, depending on the type of content.

TIP

You can allow content to be downloaded over your 3G/4G(LTE) cellular network if you aren't near a Wi-Fi hotspot and you have an iPad model that supports cellular data. If you aren't near a Wi-Fi hotspot, downloading over your cellular network might be your only option. Tap Settings, tap iTunes & App Store, scroll down, and set the Use Cellular Data setting switch to On (green).

WARNING

You could incur hefty data charges with your provider if you run over your allotted data.

Rent Movies

In the case of movies, you can either rent or buy content. If you rent, which is less expensive but only a one-time deal, you have 30 days from the time you rent the item to begin watching it. After you have begun to watch it, you have 24 hours from that time left to watch it on the same device, as many times as you like.

TIP

Some movies are offered in high–definition versions. These HD movies look pretty good on that crisp, colorful iPad screen. If your selection is available in SD, it won't have quite as high quality (still very good, mind you), but it will take up less bandwidth to download or stream it to your iPad. SD is also a bit cheaper than an HD movie to rent or purchase.

To rent movies:

1. With the iTunes Store open, tap the Movies button.

2. Locate the movie you want to rent and tap it, as shown in Figure 11-10.

3. In the detailed description of the movie that appears, tap the Rent button (if it's available for rental); see Figure 11-11.

4. The Purchase window appears; tap the Purchase button to confirm the transaction. The movie begins to download to your iPad immediately, and your account is charged the rental fee.

5. After the download is complete, you can use the TV app to watch it. (See Chapter 15 to read about how this app works.)

TIP

You can also download content to your computer and sync it to your iPad. Refer to Chapter 3 for more about this process.

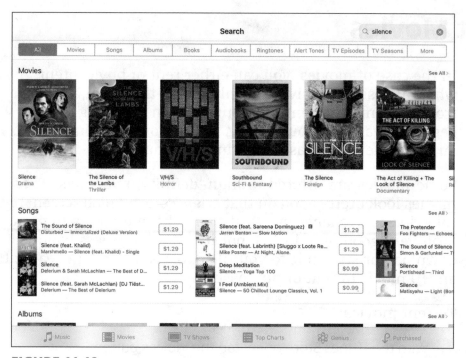

FIGURE 11-10

FIGURE 11-11

Shop Anywhere Else

One feature that's missing from the iPad is support for Adobe Flash, a format of video playback that many online video-on-demand services and interactive games use (although development for Flash has stopped and services are moving away from it). However, most (if not all) online stores that sell content such as movies and music have added iPad-friendly videos to their collections, so you have alternatives to iTunes for your choice of movies and TV shows. You can also shop for music from sources other than iTunes, such as Amazon.com.

You can open accounts at one of these stores by using your computer or your iPad's Safari browser and then following the store's instructions for purchasing and downloading content.

TIP For non–iPad-friendly formats, you can download the content on your computer and stream it to your iPad using Air Video (for $5.99) on the iPad and Air Video Server (for free) using your Mac or Windows computer. For more information, go to www.inmethod. com/air-video/index.html.

Enable Auto-Downloads of Purchases from Other Devices

With iCloud, you can make a purchase or download free content on any of your Apple devices, and iCloud automatically shares those purchases with all your Apple devices.

TIP To use iCloud, first set up an iCloud account. See Chapter 3 for detailed coverage of iCloud, including setting up your account.

To enable this auto-download feature on iPad:

1. Tap Settings on the Home screen.
2. Tap iTunes & App Store.

3. In the options that appear, scroll down and then set the switch to On for any category of purchases you want to auto-download to your iPad from other Apple devices: Music, Apps, or Books & Audiobooks (see Figure 11-12).

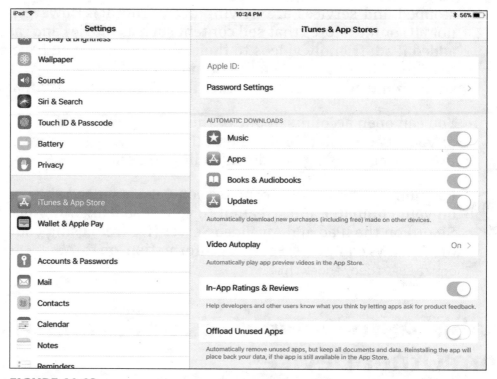

FIGURE 11-12

TIP

At this point, Apple doesn't offer an option of auto-downloading video content using these settings, probably because video is such a memory and bandwidth hog.

Set Up Family Sharing

Family Sharing is a feature that allows as many as six people in your family to share whatever anybody in the group has purchased from the iTunes, iBooks, and App Stores even though you don't share Apple IDs. Your family must all use the same credit card to purchase items (tied to whichever Apple ID is managing the family), but you can approve purchases by children under 13 years of age. (This age can vary depending on your country or region.) You can also share calendars, photos, and a family calendar. (See Chapter 16 for information about Family Sharing and Calendar and Chapter 14 for information on sharing photos in a family album.)

To turn on Family Sharing:

1. Tap Settings and then tap the Apple ID at the top of the screen.

2. Tap Set Up Family Sharing.

3. Tap Get Started. On the next screen, you can add a photo for your family. Tap Continue.

4. On the Share Purchases screen, tap Share Purchases from a different account to use another Apple account.

5. Tap Continue and check the payment method that you want to use. Tap Continue.

6. On the next screen, tap Add Family Member. Enter the person's name (assuming that this person is listed in your contacts) or email address. An invitation is sent to the person's email. When the invitation is accepted, the person is added to your family (see Figure 11-13).

TECHNICAL STUFF

The payment method for this family is displayed under Shared Payment Method in this screen. All those involved in a family have to use a single payment method for family purchases.

There's also a link called Create a Child Account. When you click this link and enter information to create the ID, the child's account is automatically added to your Family and retains the child status until he or she turns 13. If a child accesses iTunes to buy something, he or she gets a prompt to ask permission. You get an Ask to Buy notification on your phone as well as via email. You can then accept or decline the purchase, giving you control over family spending in the iTunes Store.

FIGURE 11-13

Chapter **12**

Reading Books

A traditional e-reader is a device that's used primarily to read the electronic version of books, magazines, and newspapers. Apple has touted the iPad as a great e-reader, and although it isn't a traditional e-reader device like the Kindle Paperwhite, you don't want to miss this cool functionality.

Apple's free app that turns your iPad into an e-reader is iBooks, which also enables you to buy and download books from Apple's iBooks Store (offering more than 2.5 million books and growing). You can also use one of several other free e-reader apps — for example Kindle or Nook. Then you can download books to your iPad from a variety of online sources, such as Amazon and Google, so that you can read to your heart's content.

In this chapter, you discover the options available for reading material and how to buy books. You also learn how to navigate a book or periodical and adjust the brightness and type, as well as how to search books and organize your iBooks libraries.

Discover E-Reading

An *e-reader* is any electronic device that enables you to download and read books, magazines, PDF files, or newspapers. Many e-readers use E Ink technology to create a paper-like reading experience. These devices are typically portable and dedicated only to reading the electronic version of published materials.

The iPad is a bit different from an e-reader. It isn't only for reading books, and you have to use iBooks or download another e-reader app to enable it as an e-reader (though the apps are usually free).

When you buy a book online (or get one of many free publications), it downloads to your iPad in a few seconds (or minutes, depending on your Internet connection speed and the size of the files being downloaded) using a Wi-Fi or 3G/4G/LTE connection if your iPad model supports cellular data. The iPad offers several navigation tools to move around an electronic book, which you explore in this chapter.

Find Books with iBooks

You'll need to find some good books to read before you begin learning the ins and outs of iBooks. Here's how to find materials in iBooks.

1. To shop using iBooks, tap the iBooks application icon to open it. (It's on your first Home screen.)

2. In the iBooks library that opens (see Figure 12-1), you see a bookshelf; yours probably has only one free book already downloaded to it. (If you don't see the bookshelf, tap the My Books button in the lower-left corner to go there.) Tap the Featured button at the bottom of the screen, and you're taken to the iBooks Store with featured titles displayed.

3. In the iBooks Store, shown in Figure 12-2, featured titles are shown. You can do any of the following to find a book:

   - Tap the Search field in the upper-right corner of the screen and type a search word or phrase, using the onscreen keyboard.

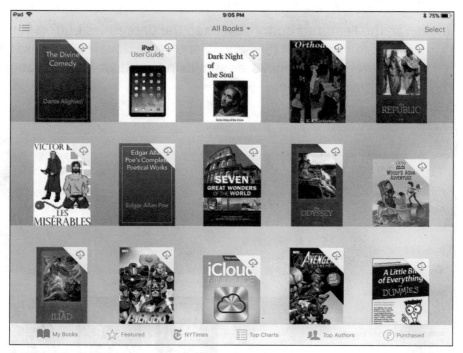

FIGURE 12-1

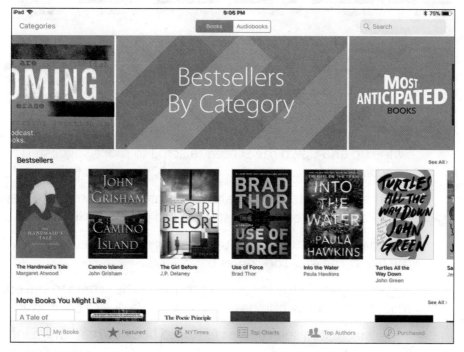

FIGURE 12-2

- Tap the Featured button, then tap the Categories button in the upper-left corner of the screen, and scroll down to see links to popular categories of books, as shown in Figure 12-3. Tap a category to view those selections.

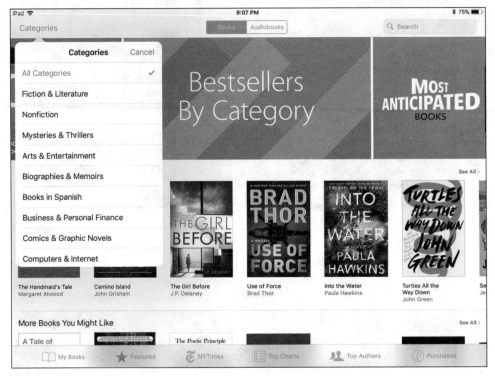

FIGURE 12-3

- Swipe up and down the screen to scroll to more suggested titles on a page.

- Tap the Top Charts button at the bottom of the screen to view both Paid and Free books listed on top bestseller lists.

- Tap the NYTimes button at the bottom of the screen to see a list of the latest *The New York Times* bestsellers.

- Tap Purchased in the lower-right corner of the screen to see only titles that you've already purchased on any Apple device connected via iCloud.

- Tap a suggested selection or featured book to read more information about it.

Many books let you download free samples before you buy. You get to read several pages of the book to see whether it appeals to you, and it doesn't cost you a dime! Look for the Sample button (usually directly under the price of the book) when you view book details.

Explore Other E-Book Sources

Beyond using iBooks, the iPad is capable of using other e-reader apps to read book content from other bookstores. You first have to download another e-reader application, such as Kindle from Amazon or the Barnes & Noble Nook reader from the App Store (see Chapter 6 for how to download apps). You can also download a non-vendor-specific app such as Bluefire Reader, which handles ePub and PDF formats, as well as the format that most public libraries use (protected PDF). Then use the app's features to search for, purchase, and download content.

The Kindle e-reader application is shown in Figure 12-4. After downloading the free app from the App Store, you just open the app and enter the email address and password associated with your Amazon account. Any content you've already bought from the Amazon.com Kindle Store from your computer or Kindle Fire tablet is archived online and can be placed on your Kindle Home page on the iPad for you to read anytime you like. Tap the Device tab to see titles stored on iPad rather than in Amazon's Cloud library. To enhance your reading experience, use such features as changing the background to a sepia tone or changing font. To delete a book from this reader, press and hold the title with your finger, and the Remove from Device button appears; simply tap the button to remove the book from your iPad.

E-books are everywhere! You can get content from a variety of other sources, such as Project Gutenberg, Google Play, and some publishers like Baen. Download the content using your computer, if you like, then just add the items to Books in iTunes, and sync them to your iPad. You can also open items from a web link or email, and they're copied to iBooks for you. You can also make settings to iCloud so that books are pushed across your Apple devices or you can place them in an online storage service (such as Dropbox or Google Drive) and access them from there.

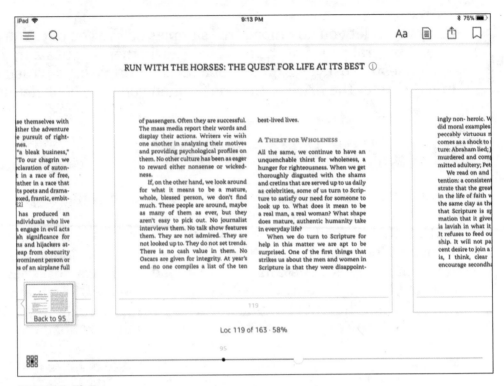

FIGURE 12-4

TECHNICAL STUFF

E-books come in different formats, and iBooks won't work with formats other than ePub or PDF (for example, it can't use such formats as the Kindle's Mobi and AZW).

Buy Books

If you've set up an account with iTunes, you can buy books at the iBooks Store using the iBooks app. (See Chapter 3 for more about iTunes.)

1. Open iBooks, tap Featured, and begin looking for a book.

2. When you find a book in the iBooks Store, either in Featured titles or by searching, you can buy it by tapping it and then tapping the Price button or the Get button (if it's free), as shown in Figure 12-5.

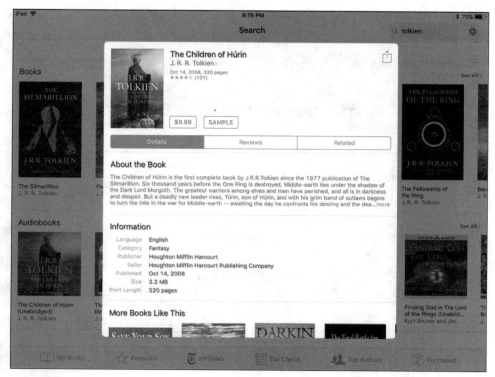

FIGURE 12-5

3. A confirmation dialog sheet will appear at the bottom of the screen, as shown in Figure 12-6. Tap either the Purchase or Get button, depending on the cost of the book.

TIP If you have signed in, your purchase is accepted immediately.

4. Tap Enter Password, enter your password in the Password field, and tap Done.

5. The book appears on your bookshelf, and the cost is charged to whichever credit card you specified when you opened your iTunes account. Tap the Read button that appears and read your tome.

TIP Books that you've downloaded to your computer can be accessed from any Apple device through iCloud. Content can also be synced with your iPad by using the Lightning-to-USB cable and your iTunes account, or by using the wireless iTunes Wi-Fi Sync setting on the General Settings menu. See Chapter 3 for more about syncing.

FIGURE 12-6

Navigate a Book

Getting around in iBooks is half the fun! To navigate a book:

1. Open iBooks and, if your Library (the bookshelf) isn't already displayed, tap the My Books button.

2. Tap a book to open it. The book opens to its title page or the last spot you read on any compatible device, as shown in Figure 12-7.

3. Take any of these actions to navigate the book:

   • **To go to the book's Table of Contents:** Tap the Table of Contents button at the top of the page and then tap the name of a chapter to go to it (see Figure 12-8).

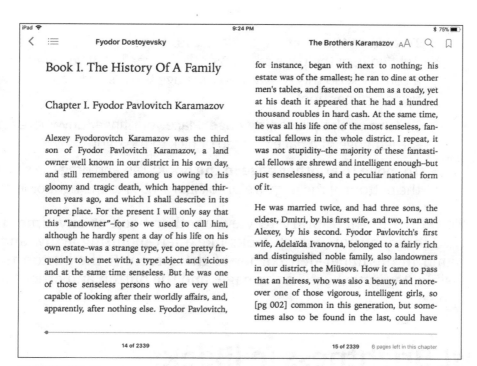

FIGURE 12-7

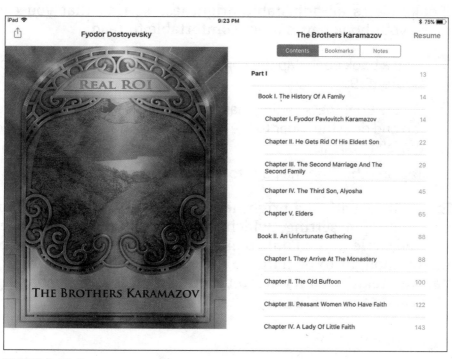

FIGURE 12-8

- **To turn to the next page:** Place your finger anywhere along the right edge of the page and tap or flick to the left. If you want to see a cool trick, do this slowly, and the page turns slowly, as if you were using a paper book.

- **To turn to the preceding page:** Place your finger anywhere on the left edge of a page and tap or flick to the right.

- **To move to another page in the book:** Tap and drag the slider at the bottom of the page (refer to Figure 12-7) to the right or left.

To return to the Library to view another book at any time, tap the Library button, which looks like a left-pointing arrow and is found in the upper-left corner of the screen. If the button isn't visible, tap anywhere on the page, and the button and other tools appear.

Adjust Brightness in iBooks

iBooks offers an adjustable brightness setting that you can use to make your book pages more comfortable to read.

1. With a book open, tap the Fonts button (looks like AA), shown in Figure 12-9.

2. On the Brightness setting that appears at the top (refer to Figure 12-9), tap and drag the slider to the right to make the screen brighter or to the left to dim it.

3. Tap anywhere on the page to close the Fonts dialog.

Experiment with the brightness level that works for you or try out the Sepia setting, which you find by tapping the sepia-colored circle in the Fonts dialog. Bright-white screens are commonly thought to be hard on the eyes, so setting the brightness halfway relative to its default setting or less is probably a good idea (and saves on battery life).

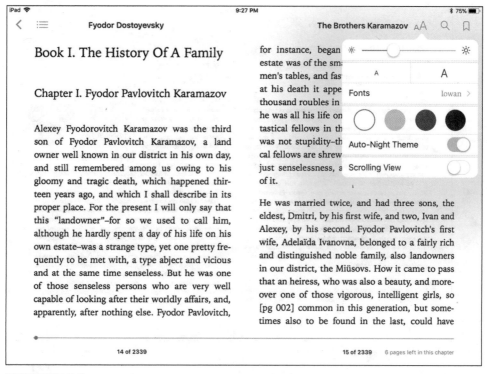

FIGURE 12-9

Change the Font Size and Type

If the type on your screen is a bit small for you to make out, you can change to a larger font size or choose a different font for readability:

1. With a book open, tap the Fonts button, shown in Figure 12-10.

2. In the Fonts dialog that appears, tap the button with a smaller A, on the left, to use smaller text (refer to Figure 12-10), or the button with the larger A, on the right, to use larger text.

3. Tap the Fonts button. The list of fonts shown in Figure 12-11 appears.

4. Tap a font name to select it. The font changes on the book page.

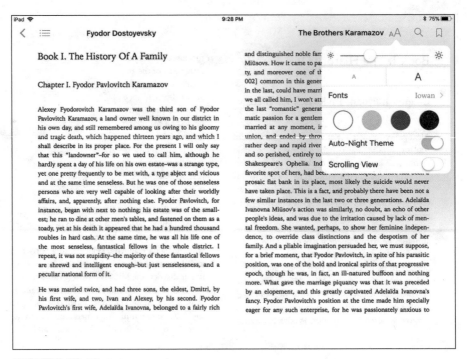

FIGURE 12-10

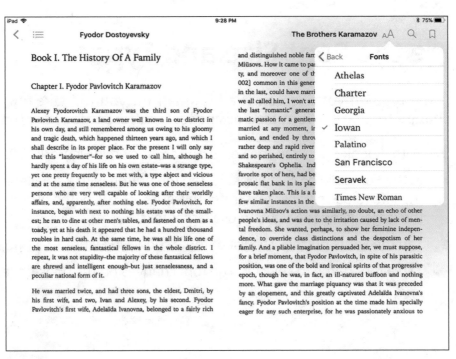

FIGURE 12-11

5. If you want a sepia tint on the pages, which can be easier on the eye, tap the Back button in the upper left of the Fonts list to redisplay the Fonts dialog and then tap one of the screen color options (the colored circles) to activate it.

6. Tap outside the Fonts dialog to return to your book.

TIP Some fonts appear a bit larger on your screen than others because of their design. If you want the largest font, use Iowan.

Search in Your Book

You may want to find certain sentences or references in your book. iBooks has a built-in Search feature that makes it simple.

To search in your book:

1. With a book displayed, tap the Search button shown in Figure 12-12. The onscreen keyboard appears.

2. Enter a search term and then tap the Search key on the keyboard. iBooks searches for any matching entries.

3. Use your finger to scroll down the entries (see Figure 12-13).

4. Flick your finger to scroll down the search results and then use either the Search Web or Search Wikipedia button at the bottom of the Search dialog if you want to search for information about the search term online. Tap a result, and you're taken to the page containing that result with a highlight applied to it.

TIP You can also search for other instances of a particular word while in the book pages by pressing your finger on the word for just a moment and then releasing; a toolbar will appear. Tap the right-facing arrow and then tap Search.

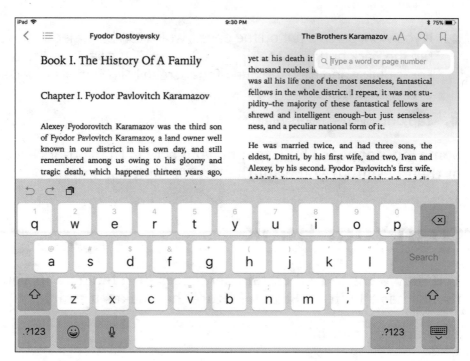

FIGURE 12-12

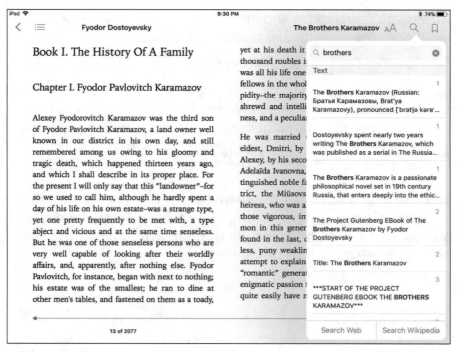

FIGURE 12-13

Use Bookmarks and Highlights

Bookmarks and highlights in your e-books operate like favorite sites that you save in your web browser: They enable you to revisit a favorite passage or refresh your memory about a character or plot point.

To add bookmarks and highlights:

1. To bookmark a page, display that page and tap the Bookmark button in the top-right corner (see Figure 12-14).

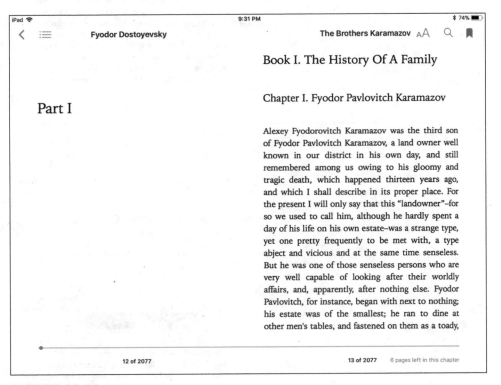

FIGURE 12-14

2. To highlight a word or phrase, press and release a word, and the toolbar shown in Figure 12-15 appears.

3. Tap the Highlight button. A colored highlight is placed on the word, and the toolbar shown in Figure 12-16 appears.

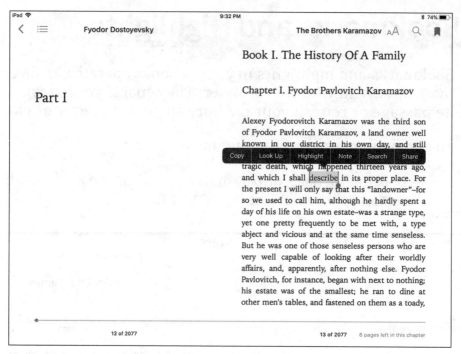

FIGURE 12-15

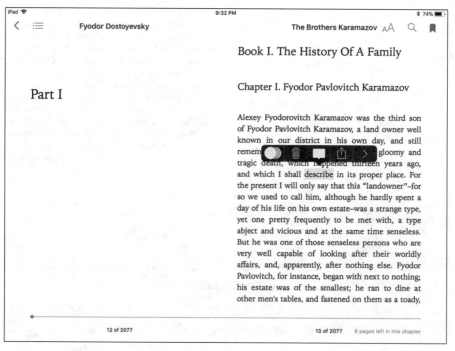

FIGURE 12-16

4. Tap one of these four buttons (from left to right):

- **Colors:** Displays a menu of colors that you can tap to change the highlight color as well as an underline option.

- **Remove Highlight** (looks like a trashcan): Removes the highlight.

- **Note:** Lets you add a note to the item.

- **Share:** Allows you to share the highlighted text with others via AirDrop, Messages, Mail, Notes, Twitter, or Facebook, or to copy the text.

5. You can also tap the arrow button at the right side of the toolbar to access Copy, Look Up, Highlight, Note, Search, and Share tools. Tap outside the highlighted text to close the toolbar.

6. To go to a list of bookmarks and notes (including highlighted text), tap the Table of Contents button in the upper left of the screen.

7. In the Table of Contents, tap the Bookmarks tab shown in Figure 12-17; all bookmarks are displayed. If you want to see highlighted text and associated notes, you display the Notes tab.

8. Tap a bookmark in the bookmark list to go to that location in the book.

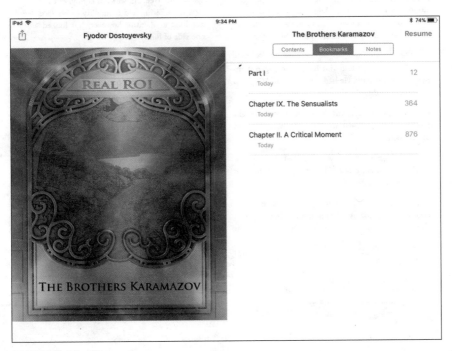

FIGURE 12-17

TIP

iPad automatically bookmarks where you left off reading in a book so that you don't have to mark your place manually. If you use any other device registered to your iTunes or iCloud account, you also pick up where you left off reading.

Check Words in the Dictionary

As you read a book, you may come across unfamiliar words. Don't skip over them — take the opportunity to learn a new word!

To check words in the dictionary:

1. With a book open, press and release your finger on a word, and the toolbar shown in Figure 12-18 appears.

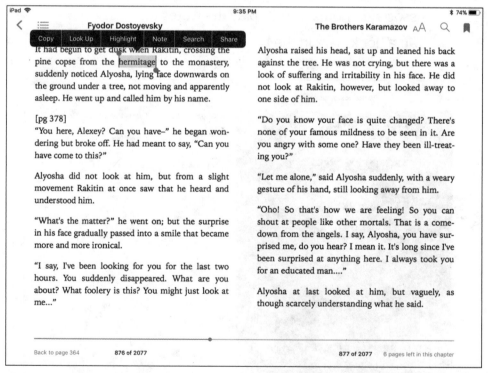

FIGURE 12-18

2. Tap the Look Up button. A dialog appears, as shown in Figure 12-19, which offers several options for looking up the term.

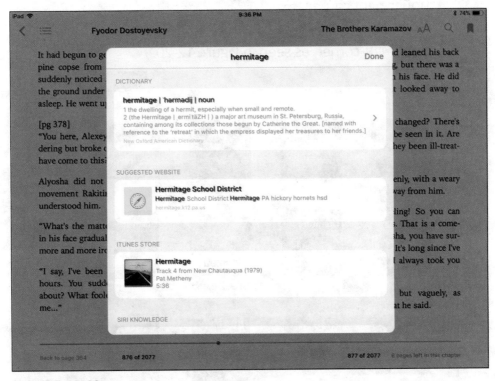

FIGURE 12-19

To see the definition, tap the Dictionary option and scroll down to view more.

When you finish reviewing the definition, tap Done in the upper-right corner, and the definition disappears.

Organize Books in Collections

iBooks lets you create and name collections of books to help you organize them by your own logic, such as Tear Jerkers, Work-Related, and Great Recipes. You can place a book in only one collection, however.

To organize books in collections:

1. To create a collection from the Library bookshelf, tap Select in the upper-right corner.

2. On the screen that appears, tap a book and then tap Move in the upper-left corner, as seen in Figure 12-20.

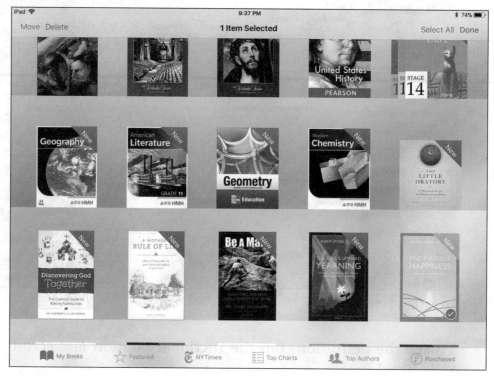

FIGURE 12-20

3. In the Collections screen shown in Figure 12-21, tap New Collection. On the blank line that appears, type a name.

4. Tap Done on the keyboard, which returns you to the Collections screen.

5. Tap the collection you want to add your book; this takes you to the bookshelf for the collection you just created, and your book is contained there.

FIGURE 12-21

6. To add another book to the collection, follow these steps:

   a. Tap the Collections drop-down menu (the title that appears is the name of the collection you're currently viewing) in the upper center of the screen and choose All Books.

   b. Tap Select in the upper-right corner, tap the book (or books) you want to move to the collection, and then tap the Move button that appears in the top of the screen.

   c. In the dialog that appears, tap the collection to which you'd like to move the book, and the book now appears on the bookshelf in that collection (see Figure 12-22).

7. To delete a book from a collection with the collection displayed, tap Select, tap the book, tap Delete, and then tap Delete again to confirm.

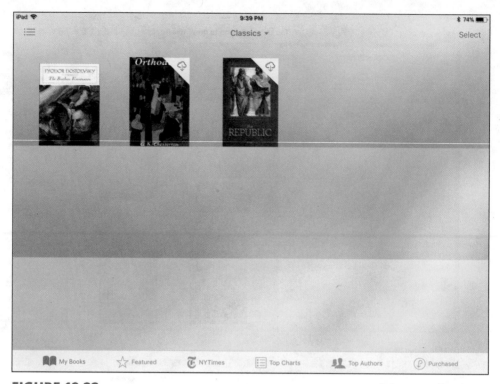

FIGURE 12-22

TIP

To delete a collection with the Collections dialog displayed, select the collection that you want to delete and then tap Edit. Tap the Delete button (looks like a minus sign) to the left of the collection and then tap Delete to get rid of it. A message appears, asking you to tap Delete Collection and Content (to remove the contents of the collection from your iPad) or Delete Collection Only.

TECHNICAL
STUFF

If you choose Delete Collection Only, all titles within a deleted collection are returned to their original collections in your library; the default collection is All Books.

Chapter **13**

Enjoying Music and Podcasts

Pad includes an iPod-like app called Music that allows you to take advantage of its amazing little sound system to play your favorite music.

In this chapter, you get acquainted with the Music app and its features that allow you to sort and find music and control playback. You also get an overview of AirPlay for accessing and playing your music over a home network or over any connected device (this also works with videos and photos). Finally, I introduce you to Podcasts for your listening pleasure.

View the Library Contents

The Library in Music contains the music or other audio files that you've placed on your iPad, either by purchasing them through the iTunes Store or copying them from your computer. The following steps show you how to work with those files on your iPad:

1. Tap the Music app, located in the Dock on the Home screen, and the Music window opens, as shown Figure 13-1.

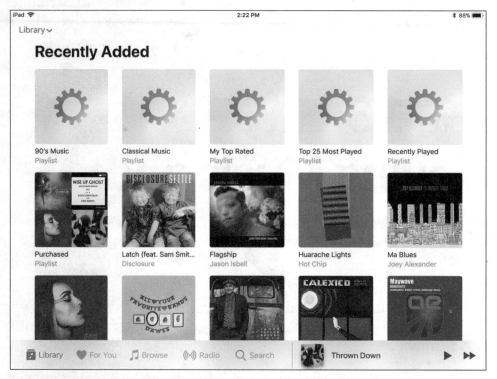

FIGURE 13-1

2. Swipe down the screen to scroll through the Recently Added section of the Music app's Library.

3. Tap the Library button in the upper-left corner and tap a category (see Figure 13-2) to view music by Playlists, Artists, Albums, Songs, or Downloaded Music. Tap Library in the upper-left corner again to return to the screen you were on.

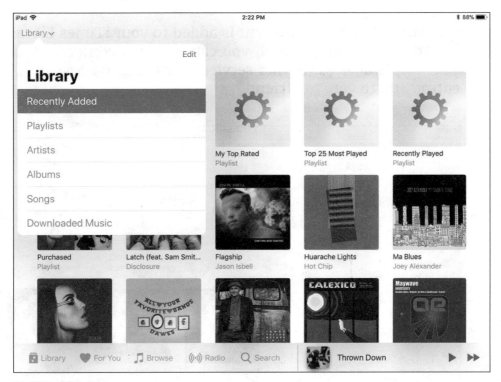

FIGURE 13-2

TIP

iTunes has several free items that you can download and use to play around with the features in Music. You can also sync content (such as iTunes Smart Playlists stored on your computer or other Apple devices) to your iPad, and play it using the Music app. (See Chapter 3 for more about syncing and Chapter 11 for more about getting content from iTunes.)

4. Tap Edit in the upper-right corner of the Library list to edit the list of categories, as seen in Figure 13-3. Tap the check box to the left of categories that you'd like to sort your Music Library by; uncheck those you don't want to use.

5. Tap Done when you're finished.

TIP

Apple offers a service called iTunes Match (visit `https://support.apple.com/en-us/HT204146` for more information). You pay $24.99 per year for the capability to match the music you've bought from other providers (and stored in the iTunes Library on your computer) to what's in the iTunes Library. If there's a match (and there usually is), that content is added to your iTunes Library on iCloud. Then, using iCloud, you can sync the content among all your Apple devices. Is this service worth $24.99 a year? That's entirely up to you, my friend.

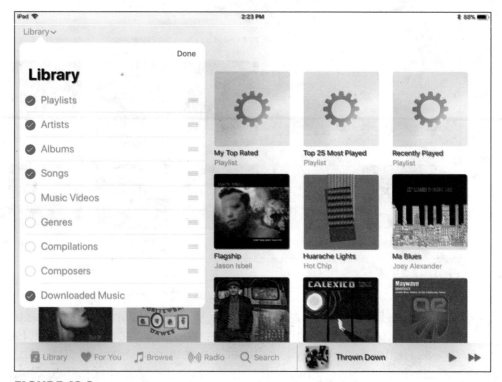

FIGURE 13-3

Create Playlists

You can create your own playlists to put tracks from various sources into collections of your choosing:

1. Tap the Playlists category in the Library list.

2. Tap the New button in the upper-right corner. In the dialog that appears (see Figure 13-4), tap Playlist Name and enter a title for the playlist.

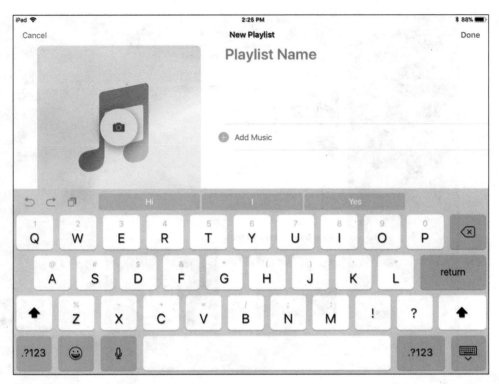

FIGURE 13-4

3. Tap Add Music and then tap a category, such as Songs or Artists, to display songs.

4. In the list of selections that appears (see Figure 13-5), drill down through the options if necessary (the options you see depend on the first selection you made), and tap the plus sign next to each item you want to include.

5. Tap the Done button and then tap Done on the next screen to return to the Playlists screen.

6. Your playlist appears in the list, and you can now play it by tapping the list name and then tapping a track to play it.

TIP

To search for a song in your music libraries, use the Spotlight Search feature. From your first Home screen, you can swipe down from the screen outside the Dock and enter the name of the song. A list of search results appears.

FIGURE 13-5

Search for Music

You can search for an item in your Music Library by using the Search feature:

1. With Music open, tap the Search button at the bottom of the screen (see Figure 13-6). The Search screen appears showing Recent Searches and Trending Searches, along with a Search field at the top of the screen.

2. Enter a search term in the Search field. Results are displayed, narrowing as you type, as shown in Figure 13-7.

3. Tap an item to play it.

TIP

You can enter an artist's name, a lyricist's or a composer's name, or a word from the item's title in the Search field to find what you're looking for.

FIGURE 13-6

FIGURE 13-7

Play Music

After you know how to find your music, you can have some real fun by playing it!

TIP

You can use Siri to play music hands-free. Just press and hold the Home button, and when Siri appears, say something like "Play 'L.A. Woman'" or "Play 'Fields of Gold.'"

To play music on your iPad, follow these steps:

1. Locate the music that you want by using the methods described in previous tasks in this chapter.

2. Tap the item you want to play. If you're displaying the Songs category, you don't have to tap an album to open a song; you need only tap a song to play it. If you're using any other categories, you have to tap items, such as albums (or multiple songs from one artist), to find the song you want to hear.

TIP

Home Sharing is a feature of iTunes that you can use to share music among up to five devices that have Home Sharing turned on. After Home Sharing is set up via iTunes, any of your devices can stream music and videos to other devices, and you can even click and drag content between devices using iTunes. For more about Home Sharing, visit this site: www.apple.com/support/homesharing.

3. Tap the item you want to play from the list that appears; it begins to play (see Figure 13-8).

4. Tap the currently playing song title in the lower right of the screen to open it, displaying playback controls. Use the Previous and Next buttons at the bottom of the screen shown in Figure 13-9 to navigate the audio file that's playing:

- The Previous button takes you back to the beginning of the item that's playing if you tap it or rewinds the song if you press and hold it.

- The Next button takes you to the next item if you tap it or fast-forwards the song if you press and hold it.

Use the Volume slider on the bottom of the screen (or the Volume buttons on the side of your iPad) to increase or decrease the volume.

FIGURE 13-8

FIGURE 13-9

5. Tap the Pause button to pause playback. Tap the button again to resume playing.

TIP

You can also use music controls for music that's playing from the lock screen.

6. Tap and drag the red line (it appears gray until you touch it) near the middle of the screen (underneath the album art) that indicates the current playback location. Drag the line to the left or right to "scrub" to another location in the song.

7. If you don't like what's playing, here's how to make another selection: Tap the downward-pointing arrow at the top of the playback controls to view other selections in the album that's playing.

TIP

Family Sharing allows up to six members of your family to share purchased content even if they don't share the same iTunes account. You can set up Family Sharing under iCloud in Settings. See Chapter 11 for more about Family Sharing.

Shuffle Music

If you want to play a random selection of the music in an album on your iPad, you can use the Shuffle feature.

1. Tap the name of the currently playing song at the bottom of the screen.

2. Swipe up on the screen until you see Up Next.

3. Tap the Shuffle button located just above Up Next, which looks like two lines crossing to form an X (see Figure 13-10). Your content plays in random order.

4. Tap the Repeat button (refer to Figure 13-10) to play the songs over again continuously.

TIP

If you're playing music and have set the Volume slider as high as it goes and you're still having trouble hearing, consider using earbuds/headphones with your iPad. These cut out extraneous noises and improve the sound quality of what you're listening to.

FIGURE 13-10

Use 3.5mm stereo earbuds or headphones; insert them in the headphone jack of your iPad. If you have an iPad with a Lightning connector, you can also use earbuds that use a Lightning connector, or you can use a Lightning-to-3.5mm adaptor with standard 3.5mm earbuds/headphones.

You might also look into purchasing Bluetooth earbuds, which allow you to listen wirelessly. For a top-of-the-line wireless experience, try out Apple's AirPods (go to www.apple.com/airpods for more info); they're getting rave reviews, and for good reason.

Use AirPlay

The AirPlay streaming technology is built into the iPad, iPod touch, Macs, PCs running iTunes, and iPhone. Streaming technology allows you to send media files from one device that supports AirPlay to be played on another. You can send (for example) a movie that you've purchased on your iPad or a slideshow of your photos to be played on your Apple TV, then control the TV playback from your iPad. You can also send music to be played over compatible speakers. Check out the Apple Remote app, which you can use to control your Apple TV.

You can use the AirPlay button in the Control Center, which you display by swiping up from the bottom edge of your iPad screen, to take advantage of AirPlay in a few ways:

» Purchase Apple TV and stream video, photos, and music to the TV.

» Purchase AirPort Express and attach it to your speakers to play music.

» If you buy AirPort Express, you can stream audio directly to your speakers.

TIP

If you're interested in using AirPlay, visit an Apple Store and find out which hardware combination will work best for you.

» Get AirPlay-compatible speakers. With these, you don't need AirPort Express at all because you can AirPlay to the speakers directly. Apple's new HomePod (www.apple.com/homepod) is yet another of their new musically-oriented products garnering rave reviews and may be exactly what you're looking for in a home audio system that does much more than simply play music.

To use AirPlay with another AirPlay-enabled device on your network or in close proximity, swipe up from the bottom of your screen and tap the AirPlay button in the Control Center; then select the AirPlay device to stream the content to or choose your iPad to move the playback back to it.

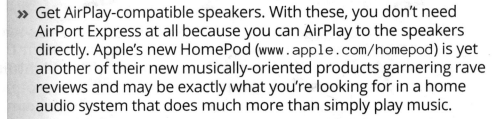

If you get a bit antsy watching a long movie, one of the beauties of AirPlay is that you can still use your iPad to check email, browse photos or the Internet, or check your calendar while the media file is playing on the other device.

Play Music with Radio

You can access Radio by tapping the Radio button at the bottom of the Music screen, as seen in Figure 13-11.

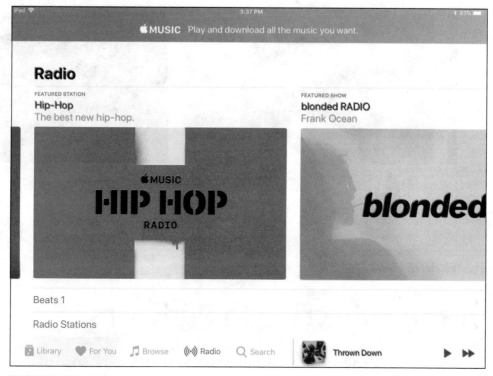

FIGURE 13-11

Swipe from left to right, and you'll find lots of music categories to listen to or tap Radio Stations to see the entire gamut of Radio's offerings (see Figure 13-12).

TECHNICAL STUFF

At one time the Radio feature was free in the Music app, but now it's tied into Apple's Music service, which is subscription-based. So, if you want to listen to stations in Radio, you'll have to become a member of Apple Music, or you can listen to Apple's flagship radio station, Beats 1, for free. To learn more about Apple Music (which is a great service), visit www.apple.com/music.

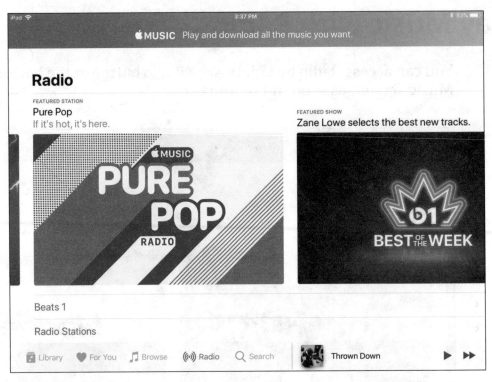

FIGURE 13-12

Find and Subscribe to Podcasts

First, what the heck is a podcast? A podcast is sort of like a radio show that you can listen to at any time. You'll find podcasts covering just about any subject imaginable, including

» News of the day

» Sports

» Gardening

» Cooking

» Education

» Comedy

» Religion

The Podcasts app is the vehicle by which you'll find and listen to podcasts on your iPad.

To search Apple's library of podcasts and subscribe to them (which is free, by the way):

1. Tap the Podcasts icon on the home screen to open it.

2. There are three ways to discover podcasts:

   - Tap Browse at the bottom of the screen and then tap Featured. There you'll find podcasts that are featured by the good folks at Apple, as shown in Figure 13-13.

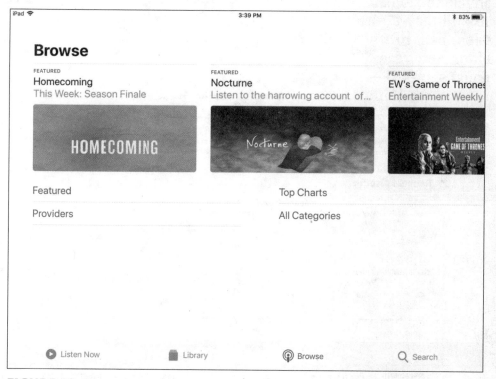

FIGURE 13-13

   - Tap Browse at the bottom of the screen and tap Top Charts; you'll be greeted with lists of the most popular podcasts. Tap the All Categories button in the upper-right corner to sift through the podcasts based on the category (such as Arts, Health, or Music).

- Tap Search and then tap the Search field at the top of the screen. When the keyboard appears, type the name or subject of a podcast to see a list of results.

3. When you find a podcast that intrigues you, tap its name to see its information page, which will be similar to the one in Figure 13-14.

4. Tap the Subscribe button (refer to Figure 13-14). The podcast appears in the Library section of the app, and the newest episode will be downloaded to your iPad.

FIGURE 13-14

5. Tap Library in the toolbar at the bottom of the screen and then tap the name of the podcast you subscribed to and view its information screen.

6. Tap the More button (looks like a circle containing three dots) and then tap the Settings icon (looks like a gear) to see the settings for the podcast. From here (see Figure 13-15), you can customize how the podcast downloads and organizes episodes.

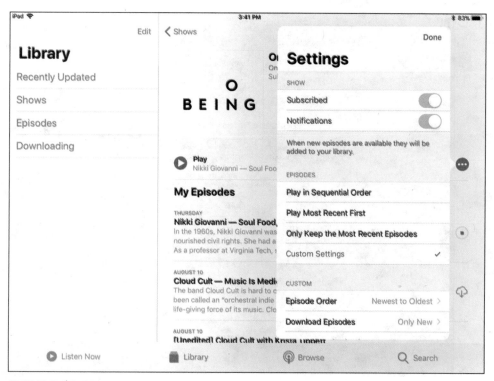

FIGURE 13-15

Play Podcasts

Playing podcasts is a breeze and works very much like playing audio files in the Music app.

1. Open the Podcasts app and tap Library at the bottom of the screen.

2. Tap the name of the podcast you'd like to listen to.

3. Tap the episode you want to play. The episode begins playing; you can see the currently playing episode near the bottom of the screen, just above the toolbar.

4. Tap the currently playing episode in the lower right of the screen to open the playback controls, shown in Figure 13-16.

5. Drag the line in the middle of the screen to scrub to a different part of the episode or tap the Rewind or Fast Forward buttons to the left and right of the Pause/Play button, respectively.

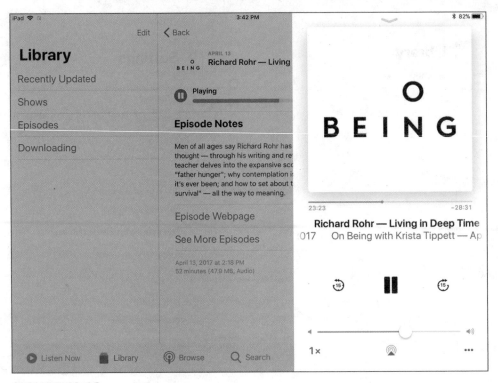

FIGURE 13-16

6. Adjust the playback speed by tapping the 1x icon in the lower left of the Play controls. Each tap increases or decreases playback speed.

7. Adjust the volume by dragging the Volume slider near the bottom of the screen or using the Volume buttons on the side of your iPad.

Tap the Listen Now button in the toolbar at the bottom of the app's screen to see a list of the newest episodes that have been automatically downloaded to your iPad.

TIP

Chapter **14**

Taking and Sharing Photos

With its gorgeous screen, the iPad is a natural for taking and viewing photos. It supports most common photo formats, such as JPEG, TIFF, and PNG. You can shoot your photos by using the built-in cameras in iPad with built-in square or panorama modes. With recent iPad models, you can edit your images using smart adjustment filters. You can also sync photos from your computer, save images that you find online to your iPad, or receive them by email, MMS, or iMessage.

The Photo Sharing feature lets you share groups of photos with people using iCloud on an iOS device or on a Mac or Windows computer with iCloud access. Your iCloud Photo Library makes all this storage and sharing easy.

When you have taken or downloaded photos to play with, the Photos app lets you organize photos and view photos in albums, one by one, or in a slideshow. You can also view photos by the years in which they were taken, with images divided into collections by the location or time you took them. You can also AirDrop (iPad, 4th generation, and newer), email, message, or tweet a photo to a friend, print it, share it via AirPlay, or post it to Facebook.

Finally, you can create time-lapse videos with the Camera app, allowing you to record a sequence in time, such as a flower opening as the sun warms it or your grandchild stirring from sleep. You can read about all these features in this chapter.

Take Pictures with the iPad Cameras

The cameras in the iPad are just begging to be used, no matter which model you have!

To go to the camera with the lock screen displayed, swipe up from the bottom of the screen and tap the Camera app icon in the Control Center to go directly to the Camera app. You can also swipe from right to left in Cover Sheet to access Camera.

1. Tap the Camera app icon on the Home screen to open the app.

2. If the image type on the lower-right side of the screen (see Figure 14-1) is set to Video, tap and slide up to choose Photo (the still camera).

iPad's front- and rear-facing cameras allow you to capture photos and video (see Chapter 15 for more about the video features) and share them with family and friends. Newer models offer an 8-megapixel iSight camera (up to 12-megapixel with iPad Pro!) with such features as

» Phase Detection Autofocus

» Image stabilization to avoid fuzzy moving targets

» True Tone Flash (with iPad Pro), a sensor that tells iPad when a flash is needed

FIGURE 14-1

The following are options for taking pictures after you've opened the Camera app:

» You can set the Pano (for panorama) and Square options using the image type control below the Capture button (the large white or red circle, depending on the image type selected). These controls let you create square images like those you see on the popular Instagram site. With Pano selected, tap to begin to take a picture and pan across a view and then tap Done to capture a panoramic display.

» If your iPad supports it, tap the Flash button when using the rear camera, then select a flash option:

- On, if your lighting is dim enough to require a flash

- Off, if you don't want iPad to use a flash

- Auto, if you want to let iPad decide for you

» To use the High Dynamic Range or HDR feature, tap the HDR setting and tap to turn it on. This feature uses several images, some underexposed and some overexposed, and combines the best ones into one image, sometimes providing a more finely detailed picture.

HDR pictures can be very large in file size, meaning they'll take up more of your iPad's memory than standard pictures.

» If you want a time delay before the camera snaps the picture, tap the Time Delay button (looks like a timer), then tap 3s or 10s for a 3- or 10-second delay, respectively.

» Move the camera around until you find a pleasing image. You can do a couple of things at this point to help you take your photo:

- Tap the area of the grid where you want the camera to autofocus.

- Place two fingers apart from each other on the screen and then pinch them together (still touching the screen) to display a digital zoom control. Drag the circle in the zoom bar to the left to zoom in or out on the image.

» Tap the Capture button; you've just taken a picture, and it's stored in the Photos app gallery automatically.

You can also use a Volume button (located on the right side of your iPad) to capture a picture or start or stop video camera recording.

» Tap the Switch Camera button above the Capture button to switch between the front camera and rear camera. You can then take selfies (pictures of yourself), so go ahead and tap the Capture button to take another picture.

» To view the last photo taken, tap the thumbnail of the latest image directly beneath the Capture button; the Photos app opens and displays the photo.

» While viewing the image in Photos, tap the Share button (it's the box with an arrow coming out of it, located in the bottom-left corner of the screen) to display a menu that allows you to

AirDrop, email, or instant message the photo, assign it to a contact, use it as iPad wallpaper, tweet it, post it to Facebook, share via iCloud Photo Sharing or Flickr, or print it (see Figure 14-2).

FIGURE 14-2

» You can tap images to select more than one.

» To delete the image, have it displayed and tap the Trash button in the bottom-right corner of the screen. Tap Delete Photo in the confirming menu that appears.

TIP

You can use the iCloud Photo Sharing feature to automatically sync your photos across various devices. Turn on iCloud Photo Sharing by tapping Settings on the Home screen and then tapping Photos.

Save Photos from the Web

The web offers a wealth of images that you can download to your Photo Library.

TIP A number of sites protect their photos from being copied by applying an invisible overlay. This blank overlay image ensures that you don't actually get the image you're tapping. Even if a site doesn't take these precautions, be sure that you don't save images from the web and use them in ways that violate the rights of the person or entity that owns them.

To save an image from the web, follow these steps:

1. Open Safari and navigate to the web page containing the image you want.

TIP For more about how to use Safari to navigate to or search for web content, see Chapter 9.

2. Press and hold the image. A menu appears at the bottom of the screen, as shown in Figure 14-3.

3. Tap Save Image. The image is saved to your Camera Roll album in the Photos app, as shown in Figure 14-4.

TIP If you want to capture your iPad screen as a photo, the process is simple. Press the Sleep/Wake button and Home button simultaneously; the screen flashes white, and the screen capture is complete. A preview of the capture displays in the lower-left corner for a few seconds. Tap the capture if you want to make edits or save it to another app. Alternatively, simply wait about three to four seconds until the capture preview disappears, and the capture is automatically saved in PNG format to your Recently Added album.

TIP To save a picture sent as an email attachment in Mail, tap the attachment icon, and the picture opens. Press the screen until a menu appears and then tap Save.

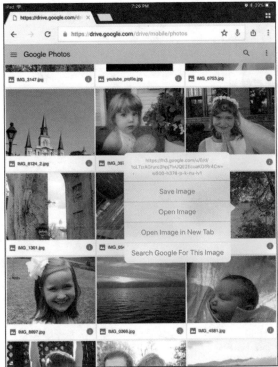

FIGURE 14-3

FIGURE 14-4

View an Album

The Photos app organizes your pictures into albums, using such criteria as the folder or album on your computer from which you synced the photos or photos captured using the iPad camera (saved in the Camera Roll album). You may also have albums for images that you synced from other devices through iTunes or shared via Photos.

To view your albums:

1. Tap the Photos app icon on the Home screen.

2. Tap the Albums button at the bottom of the screen to display your albums, as shown in Figure 14-5.

3. Tap an album. The photos in it are displayed.

FIGURE 14-5

TIP

You can associate photos with faces and events. When you do, additional tabs appear at the bottom of the screen when you display an album containing that type of photo.

View Individual Photos

You can view photos individually by opening them from within an album.

TIP

With the 3D Touch feature, you can preview a photo before you open it. Tap lightly to select the photo. Tap with a medium press to display a preview, then press harder to open the photo.

To view individual photos:

1. Tap the Photos app icon on the Home screen.

2. Tap Albums (refer to Figure 14-5).

3. Tap an album to open it; then, to view a photo, tap it. The picture expands, as shown in Figure 14-6.

FIGURE 14-6

4. Flick your finger to the left or right to scroll through the album to look at the individual photos in it.

5. You can tap the Back button in the upper-left corner (looks like a left-pointing arrow) and then the Albums button to return to the Album view.

You can place a photo on a person's information record in Contacts. For more about how to do this, see Chapter 7.

TIP

Edit Photos

iPad Photos isn't Photoshop, but it does provide some tools for editing photos. To edit photos:

1. Tap the Photos app on the Home screen to open it.

2. Locate and display a photo you want to edit.

3. Tap the Edit button in the upper right of the screen; the Edit Photo screen shown in Figure 14-7 appears.

FIGURE 14-7

4. At this point, you can take three possible actions with these tools:

- **Crop:** To crop the photo to a portion of its original area, tap the Crop button. You can then tap any corner of the image and drag inward or outward to remove areas of the photo. Tap Crop and then Save to apply your changes.

- **Filters:** Apply any of nine filters (such as Vivid, Mono, or Noir) to change the look and feel of your image. These effects adjust the brightness of your image or apply a black-and-white tone to your color photos. Tap the Filters button in the middle of the tools at the bottom of the screen and scroll to view available filters. Tap one and then tap Apply to apply the effect to your image.

- **Adjustments:** Tap Light, Color, or B&W to access a slew of tools that you can use to tweak contrast, color intensity, shadows, and more.

5. If you're pleased with your edits, tap the Done button. A copy of the edited photo is saved.

Each of the editing features has a Cancel button. If you don't like the changes you made, tap this button to stop making changes before you save the image.

Organize Photos

You'll probably want to organize your photos to make it simpler to find what you're looking for:

1. If you want to create your own album, open the Camera Roll album.

2. Tap the Select button in the top-right corner and then tap individual photos to select them. Small check marks appear on the selected photos (see Figure 14-8).

3. Tap the Add To button at the bottom of the screen and then tap New Album.

If you've already created albums, you can choose to add the photo to an existing album at this point.

FIGURE 14-8

4. Enter a name for a new album and then tap Save. If you create a new album, it appears in the Photos main screen with the other albums that are displayed.

You can also choose the Share or Delete buttons when you've selected photos in Step 2 of this task. This allows you to share or delete multiple photos at a time.

TIP

View Photos by Years and Locations

You can view your photos in logical categories, such as by date or a location where they were taken. These so-called smart groupings let you, for example, view all photos taken this year or all the photos from your summer vacation.

To view your photos by years and locations, follow these steps:

1. Tap Photos on the Home screen to open the Photos app.

2. Tap Photos at the bottom of the screen on the left. The display of photos by date appears (see Figure 14-9).

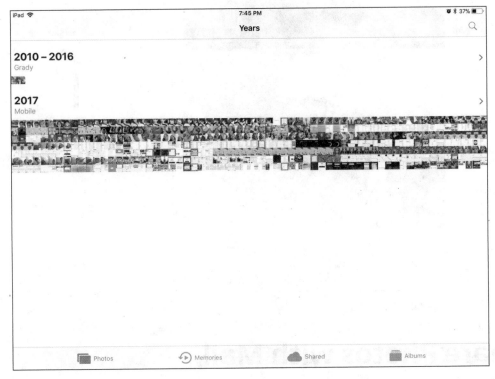

FIGURE 14-9

3. Tap a year or years on the left; you see collections of photos by location and date (see Figure 14-10).

4. Tap a collection, and you can view the individual "moments" in that collection by category, such as Groups & People, Places, Related, and more.

To go back to larger groupings, such as from a moment in a collection to the larger collection to the entire last year, just keep tapping the Back button at the top left of the screen.

FIGURE 14-10

Share Photos with Mail, Twitter, or Facebook

You can easily share photos stored on your iPad by sending them as email attachments, as a text message, by posting them to Facebook, sharing them via iCloud Photo Sharing or Flickr, or as tweets on Twitter.

To share photos:

1. Tap the Photos app icon on the Home screen.

2. Tap the Photos or Albums button and locate the photo you want to share.

3. Tap the photo to select it and then tap the Share button. (It looks like a box with an arrow jumping out of it.) The menu shown in Figure 14-11 appears. Tap to select additional photos, if you want them.

FIGURE 14-11

4. Tap the Mail, Message, Twitter, iCloud Photo Sharing, Facebook, Flickr, or any other option you'd like to use.

5. In the message form that appears, make any modifications that apply in the To, Cc/Bcc, or Subject fields and then type a message for email or enter your Facebook posting or Twitter tweet.

6. Tap the Send or Post button, and the message and photo are sent or posted.

TIP

You can also copy and paste a photo into documents, such as those created in the Pages word-processor app. To do this, tap a photo in Photos and tap Share. Tap the Copy command. In the destination app, press and hold the screen and tap Paste.

Share a Photo Using AirDrop

AirDrop provides a way to share content, such as photos with others who are nearby and who have an AirDrop–enabled device (iPhones, iPads, and more recent Macs that can run macOS 10.10 or later).

Follow the steps in the previous task to locate a photo you want to share.

1. Tap the Share button.

2. If an AirDrop-enabled device is in your immediate vicinity (such as within 30 feet or so), you see the device listed in the Tap to share with AirDrop section directly underneath the selected image (see Figure 14-12). Tap the device name and your photo is sent to the other device.

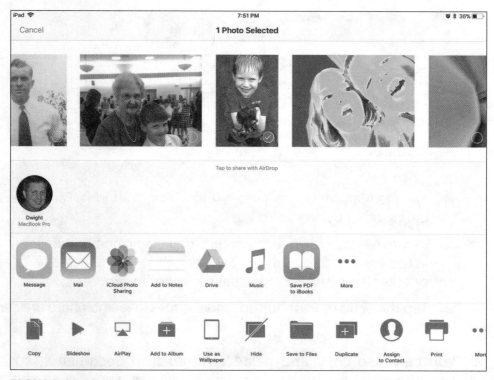

FIGURE 14-12

TIP

Other iOS devices (iPads or iPads) must have AirDrop enabled to use this feature. To enable AirDrop, open the Control Center (swipe up from the bottom of any screen) and tap AirDrop, shown in Figure 14-13. Choose Contacts Only or Everyone to specify whom you can use AirDrop with.

AirDrop button

FIGURE 14-13

Share Photos Using iCloud Photo Sharing

iCloud Photo Sharing allows you to automatically share photos using your iCloud account:

1. Open the Photos app and tap a photo to view it.

2. Tap the Share button in the upper right of a photo.

3. In the Share screen that opens, tap to select the photos you want to share and then tap iCloud Photo Sharing.

4. Enter a comment if you like (see Figure 14-14) and then tap Post. The photos are posted to your iCloud Photo Library.

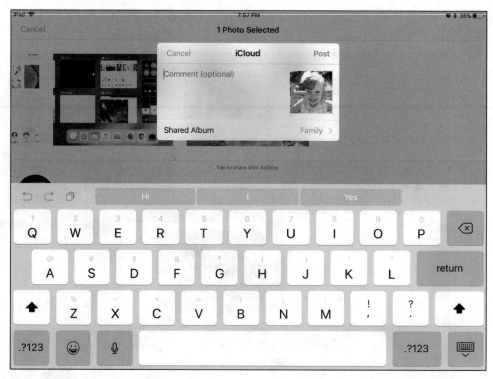

FIGURE 14-14

Work in iCloud Photo Library

iCloud Photo Library automatically backs up all your photos and videos to the cloud:

1. Open the Settings app and then tap Photos.

2. Toggle the iCloud Photo Library switch to On (green) to post all your photos to this library in the cloud.

TIP

If you want to automatically make photos available to your other devices from iCloud, also toggle the My Photo Stream switch to On.

3. Press the Home button on your iPad and then tap the Safari app icon to open it.

4. Go to iCloud.com using your browser, sign in, and click Photos to view all photos and videos stored in the iCloud Library.

Print Photos

If you have a printer that's compatible with Apple's AirPrint technology, you can print photos from your iPad.

1. With Photos open, locate the photo you want to print and tap it to maximize it.

2. Tap the Share button. On the menu that appears (refer to Figure 14-11), scroll in the bottom row of buttons to the far right and then tap Print.

3. In the Printer Options dialog that appears (see Figure 14-15), tap an available printer in the list or Select Printer. iPad presents you with a list of any compatible wireless printers on your local network.

4. Tap the plus or minus symbols in the Copy field to set the number of copies to print.

5. Tap the Print button, and your photo is sent to the printer.

FIGURE 14-15

Run a Slideshow

You can run a slideshow of your images in Photos and even play music and choose transition effects for the show:

1. Tap the Photos app on the Home screen.

2. Open an album containing the photos you want to view.

3. Tap the Slideshow button in the upper-right corner to run the slideshow.

4. Tap the screen and then tap Options in the lower-right corner to see the Slideshow Options dialog, shown in Figure 14-16.

5. If you want to play music along with the slideshow, tap Music and then tap a music selection in the list that appears (see Figure 14-17). Tap Back in the upper-left corner to not make changes and return to the Slideshow Options screen.

FIGURE 14-16

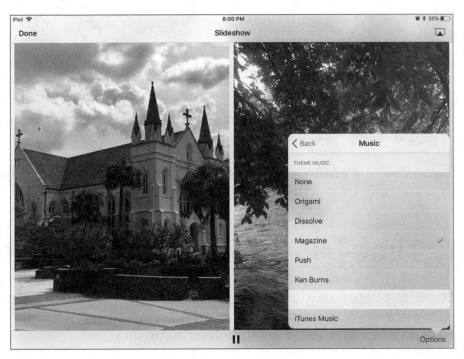

FIGURE 14-17

6. In the Slideshow Options dialog, tap Theme and then tap the transition effect that you want to use for your slideshow. Tap Back in the upper-left corner to not make changes and return to the Slideshow Options screen.

7. Tap the screen while the slideshow is playing and then tap the AirPlay button in the upper-right corner to cast the slideshow to an AirPlay-enabled device nearby, such as an Apple TV.

8. Tap Done and the slideshow plays with the music and theme you selected. Tap the screen and tap Done in the upper-left corner to stop the slideshow at any time.

Delete Photos

You may find that it's time to get rid of some of those old photos of the family reunion or the last community center project. If the photos weren't transferred from your computer, but instead were taken, downloaded, or captured as screenshots on the iPad, you can delete them.

1. Tap the Photos app icon on the Home screen.

2. Tap the Albums tab and then tap an album to open it.

3. Locate and tap on a photo that you want to delete and then tap the Trash icon. In the confirming dialog that appears, tap the Delete Photo button to finish the deletion.

WARNING

If you delete a photo in Photo Sharing, it is deleted on all devices that you shared it with.

Create Time-Lapse Videos from Photos

The Time Lapse feature of Camera allows you to create a time-lapse photo show. iPad captures photos at select intervals, allowing the capture of a dynamic scene (such as a sunset).

To create time-lapse videos from photos:

1. Tap Camera on the Home screen.

2. Swipe the listing of image types on the right side of the screen until Time Lapse is centered under the Capture button (see Figure 14-18).

3. Tap the Capture button. Leave the camera recording as long as you like and then tap the End button. Your new time-lapse images appear in the bottom-left corner. Tap the image and then tap Play.

FIGURE 14-18

Chapter **15**

Creating and Watching Videos

U sing the TV app (formerly known as Videos in earlier iOS versions), you can watch downloaded movies or TV shows, as well as media that you've synced from iCloud on your Mac or PC, and even media that's provided from other content providers, such as cable and streaming video services. The TV app aims to be your one-stop shop for your viewing pleasure.

In addition, iPads sport both a front and rear video camera that you can use to capture your own videos, and by downloading the iMovie app for iPad (a more limited version of the longtime mainstay on Mac computers), you add the capability to edit those videos. Newer iPad Pro models sport cameras that support up to 4K video, which produces rich detail with 8 million pixels per frame. The latest iPad and iPad mini models support HD video up to 1080p.

A few other features of video in newer iPad models include image stabilization to avoid the shakes when recording, more frames shot per second for smoother video, and Cinematic Video Stabilization, which means that your iPad continually autofocuses as you're recording.

In this chapter, I explain all about shooting and watching video content from a variety of sources. For practice, you may want to refer to Chapter 11 first to find out how to purchase or download one of many available TV shows or movies from the iTunes Store.

Capture Your Own Videos with the Built-In Cameras

The camera lens that comes on newer iPads has perks for photographers, including a large aperture and highly accurate sensor, which make for better images all around. In addition, auto image stabilization makes up for any shakiness in the hands holding the iPad, and autofocus has sped up thanks to the fast processors being used. For videographers, you'll appreciate a fast frames-per-second capability as well as a slow-motion feature.

1. To capture a video, tap the Camera app on the Home screen. In iPad, two video cameras are available for capturing video, one from the front and one from the back of the device. (See more about this topic in the next task.)

2. The Camera app opens (see Figure 15-1). Tap and slide the camera-type options below until Video is selected and you see the red Record button. This button is how you switch from the still camera to the video camera.

3. If you want to switch between the front and back cameras, tap the Switch Camera button above the Record button (refer to Figure 15-1).

4. Tap the red Record button to begin recording the video. (The red dot in the middle of this button turns into a red square when the camera is recording.) When you're finished, tap the Record button again. Your new video is now listed under the Record button. Tap the video to play it, share it, or delete it. In the future, you can find and play the video in your Camera Roll or in the Videos album when you open the Photos app.

FIGURE 15-1

TIP

Before you start recording, remember where the camera lens is — while holding the iPad and panning, you can easily put your fingers directly over the lens! Also, you can't pause your recording; when you stop, your video is saved, and when you start recording, you're creating a new video file.

Play Movies or TV Shows with TV

Open the TV app for the first time, and you'll be greeted with a Welcome screen. Tap Continue, and you'll be asked to sign in to your television provider, as shown in Figure 15-2.

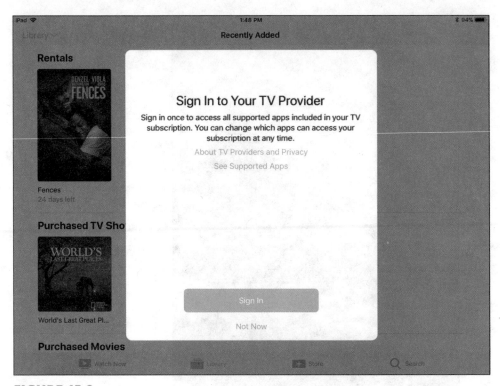

FIGURE 15-2

Signing in will allow you to use the TV app to access content in other apps (like ESPN or Disney), if such services are supported by your TV provider. This way, you need to use only the TV app to access content and sign in, as opposed to having multiple apps to juggle and sign in to.

TIP

Should you decide to skip signing in to your TV provider and worry about it later (or if you've already opened the TV app and cruised right past this part), you can access the same options by going to Settings⇨ TV Provider, tapping the name of your provider (a partial list of which is shown in Figure 15-3), and then entering your account information.

The TV app offers a couple of ways to view movies and TV shows: via third-party providers or items you've purchased or rented from the iTunes Store.

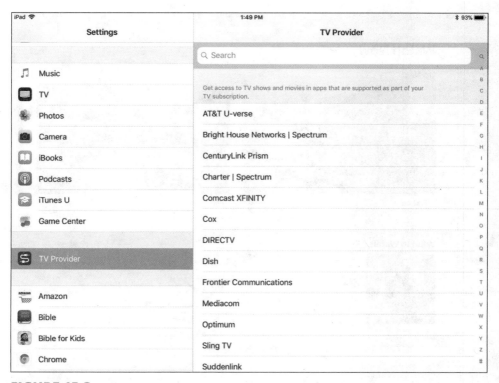

FIGURE 15-3

To access content from third-party providers like NBC, ABC, PBS, and more, tap the Watch Now button in the bottom left of your screen (see Figure 15-4). Swipe to see hit shows and browse by genres like Comedy, Action, and others.

Tap on a show that interests you and then tap an episode to see a description, like I've done in Figure 15-5. Tap Play, and if you have the app that supports the video, it will open automatically. If not, you'll be asked if you'd like to download and install it, as shown in Figure 15-6.

TIP

If your iPad is on the same Wi-Fi network as your computer and both are running iTunes, with the iPad and iTunes set to use the same Home Sharing account, you see the Shared List. With this setup, you can stream videos from iTunes on your computer to your iPad.

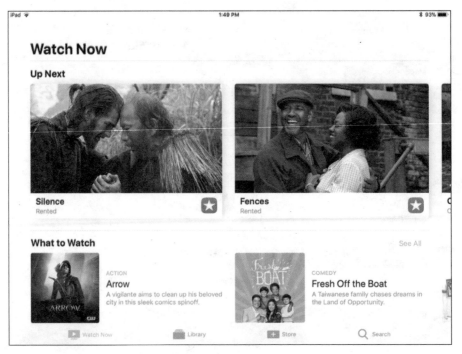

FIGURE 15-4

FIGURE 15-5

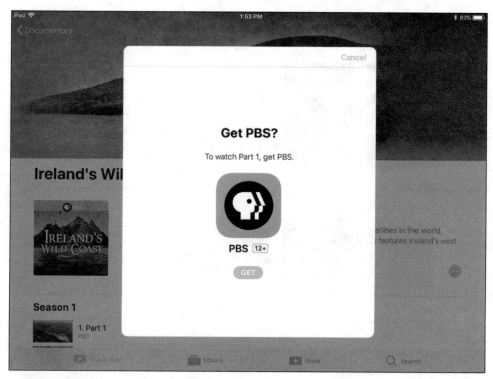

FIGURE 15-6

To access video you've purchased or rented from the iTunes Store, follow these steps:

1. Tap the TV app icon on the Home screen to open the application and then tap Library at the bottom of the screen.

2. On a screen like the one in Figure 15-7, tap a selection from within the categories listed and then tap the video you want to watch. You can also tap the Library button in the upper left to view items in select categories, such as Rentals, TV Shows, or Movies, depending on the content you've downloaded.

   Information about the movie or TV show episodes appears, as shown in Figure 15-8.

3. For TV Shows, tap the episode that you'd like to play; for Movies, the Play button appears right on the description screen. Tap the Play button, and the movie or TV show begins playing (see Figure 15-9). (If you see a small, cloud-shaped icon instead of a Play button, tap it, and the content is downloaded from iCloud.)

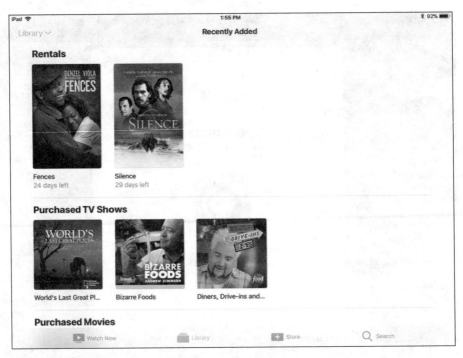

FIGURE 15-7

FIGURE 15-8

The progress of the playback is displayed on the Progress bar showing how many minutes you've viewed and how many remain. If you don't see the bar, tap the screen once to display it briefly, along with a set of playback tools at the bottom of the screen.

FIGURE 15-9

4. With the playback tools displayed, take any of these actions:

- Tap the Pause button to pause playback.

- Tap either Go to Previous Chapter or Go to Next Chapter to move to a different location in the video playback.

TIP

   If a video has chapter support, another button called Scenes appears here for displaying all chapters so that you can move more easily from one to another.

- Tap the circular button on the Volume slider and drag the button left or right to decrease or increase the volume, respectively.

If your controls disappear during playback, just tap the screen, and they'll reappear.

5. To stop the video and return to the information screen, tap the Done button to the left of the Progress bar.

If you've watched a video and stopped it before the end, it opens by default to the last location where you were viewing. To start a video from the beginning, tap and drag the circular button (the *playhead*) on the Progress bar all the way to the left.

Turn On Closed-Captioning

iTunes and iPad offer support for closed-captioning and subtitles. Look for the CC logo on media that you download to use this feature.

Video you record won't have this capability.

If a movie has either closed-captioning or subtitles, you can turn on the feature in iPad.

1. Begin by tapping the Settings icon on the Home screen.

2. Tap General ⇨ Accessibility. On the screen that appears, scroll down and tap Subtitles & Captioning.

3. On the menu that displays (see Figure 15-10), tap the Closed Captions + SDH switch to turn on the feature. Now when you play a movie with closed-captioning, you can tap the Audio and Subtitles button to the left of the playback controls to manage these features.

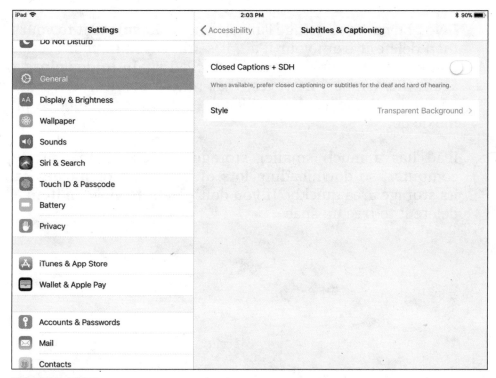

FIGURE 15-10

Delete a Video from the iPad

You can buy videos directly from your iPad, or you can sync via iCloud or iTunes to place content you've bought or created on another device on your iPad.

When you want to get rid of video content on your iPad because it's a memory hog, you can delete it:

1. Open the TV app and go to the TV show or movie you want to delete.

2. Tap the Downloaded button.

3. Tap Remove Download in the options that appear, and the downloaded video will be deleted from your iPad.

If you buy a video using iTunes, sync to download it to your iPad, and then delete it from your iPad, it's still saved in your iTunes Library. You can sync your computer and iPad again to download the video again. Remember, however, that rented movies, when deleted, are gone with the wind. Also, video doesn't sync to iCloud as photos and music do.

TIP

iPad has a much smaller storage capacity than your typical computer, so downloading lots of TV shows or movies can fill its storage area quickly. If you don't want to view an item again, delete it to free up space.

4

Living with Your iPad

Chapter **16**

Keeping On Schedule with Calendar and Clock

Whether you're retired or still working, you have a busy life full of activities (even busier if you're retired, for some unfathomable reason). You may need a way to keep on top of all those activities and appointments. The Calendar app on your iPad is a simple, elegant, electronic daybook that helps you do just that.

In addition to being able to enter events and view them in a list or by the day, week, or month, you can set up Calendar to send alerts to remind you of your obligations and search for events by keywords. You can even set up repeating events, such as birthdays, monthly get-togethers with the girls or guys, or weekly babysitting appointments with your grandchild. To help you coordinate calendars on multiple devices, you can also sync events with other calendar accounts. And by taking advantage of the Family Sharing feature, you can create a Family calendar that everybody in your family can view and add events to.

Another preinstalled app that can help you stay on schedule is Clock. Though simple to use, Clock helps you view the time in multiple locations, set alarms, check yourself with a stopwatch feature, and use a timer.

In this chapter, you master the simple procedures for getting around your calendar, creating a Family calendar, entering and editing events, setting up alerts, syncing, and searching. You also discover the simple ins and outs of using Clock.

View Your Calendar

Calendar offers several ways to view your schedule:

1. Start by tapping the Calendar app icon on the Home screen to open it. Depending on what you last had open and the orientation in which you're holding your iPad, you may see today's calendar, List view, the year, the month, the week, an open event, or the Search screen with search results displayed.

2. Tap the Today button at the bottom of the screen to display Today's view (if it isn't already displayed) and then tap the Search button to see all scheduled events for that day. The Today view with Search open, shown in Figure 16-1, displays your daily appointments for every day in a list, with times listed on the left. Tap an event in the list to get more event details or tap the Cancel button to exit Search.

If you'd like to display events only from a particular calendar, such as the Birthday or US Holidays calendars, tap the Calendars button at the bottom of the screen and select a calendar to view.

3. Tap the Week button to view all events for the current week, as shown in Figure 16-2. In this view, appointments appear against the times listed along the left side of the screen.

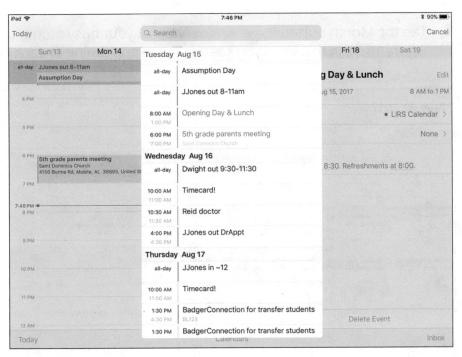

FIGURE 16-1

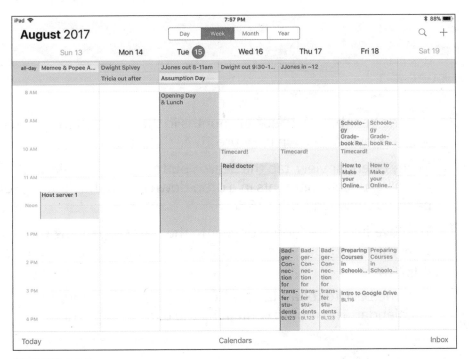

FIGURE 16-2

4. Tap the Month button to get an overview of your busy month (see Figure 16-3). In this view, you see the name and timing of each event.

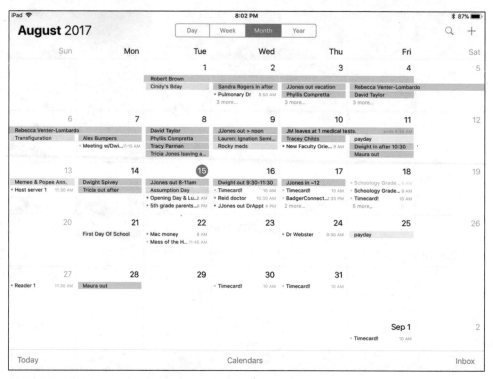

FIGURE 16-3

5. Tap the Year button to see all months in the year so you can quickly move to one, as shown in Figure 16-4.

6. In any calendar view, tap the Search button to see List view, which lists all your commitments in a drop-down list on the right side of the page, as shown in Figure 16-5.

7. To move from one month or year to the next (depending on which view you're in), you can also scroll up or down the screen with your finger.

8. To jump back to today, tap the Today button in the bottom-left corner of Calendar. The month containing the current day is displayed.

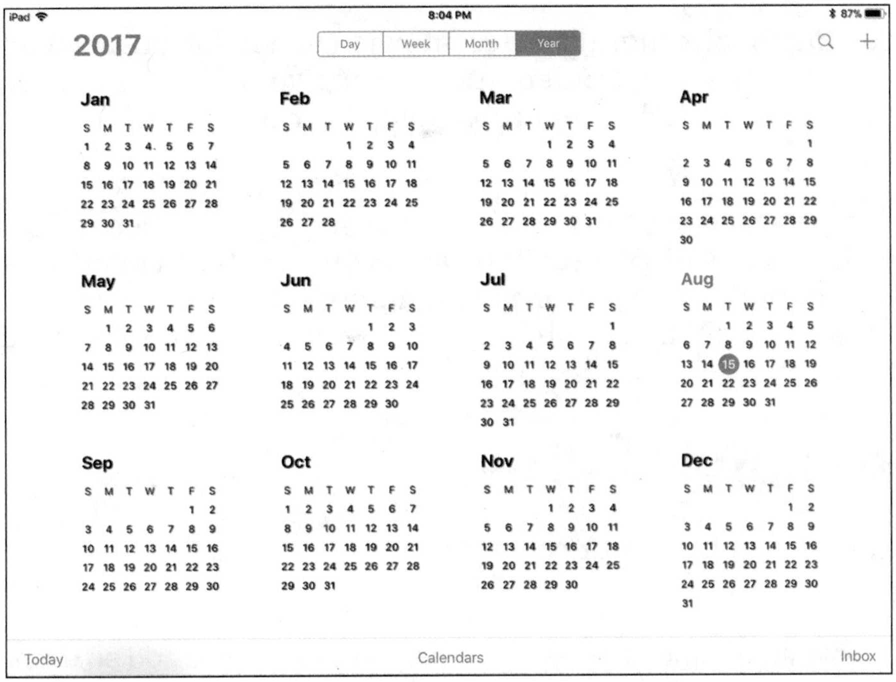

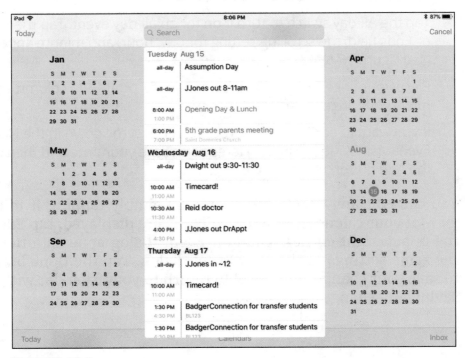

FIGURE 16-4

FIGURE 16-5

TIP

Calendar looks slightly different when you hold your iPad in portrait and landscape orientations. Turn your iPad in both directions to see which orientation you prefer to work in.

TIP

To view any invitation that you accepted, which placed an event on your calendar, tap Inbox in the lower-right corner and a list of invitations is displayed. You can use text within emails (such as a date, flight number, or phone number) to add an event to Calendar. Tap outside the Inbox window to return to the calendar.

Add Calendar Events

To add events to your calendar:

1. With any view displayed, tap the Add button (which looks like a plus symbol) in the upper-right corner of the screen to add an event (refer to Figure 16-4). The New Event dialog appears.

2. Enter a title for the event and, if you want, a location.

3. Tap the All-day switch to turn it on for an all-day event. Tap the Starts or Ends field; the scrolling setting for day, hour, and minute appears (see Figure 16-6).

4. Place your finger on the date, hour, minute, or AM/PM column and move your finger to scroll up or down.

5. If you want to add notes, use your finger to scroll down in the New Event dialog and tap in the Notes field. Type your note and then tap the Add button to save the event.

TIP

You can edit any event at any time by simply tapping it in any view of your calendar. When the details are displayed, tap Edit in the upper-right corner. The Edit Event dialog appears, offering the same settings as the New Event dialog. Tap the Done button to save your changes or Cancel to return to your calendar without saving any changes.

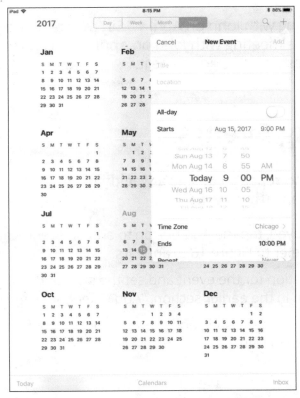

FIGURE 16-6

Add Events with Siri

Play around with this feature and Calendar; it's a lot of fun!

1. Press and hold the Home button or say "Hey Siri."

2. Speak a command, such as "Hey Siri. Create a meeting on October 3 at 2:30 p.m."

3. When Siri asks you whether you're ready to schedule the event, say "Yes." The event is added to Calendar.

TIP

You can schedule an event with Siri in several ways:

» Say "Create event." Siri asks you first for a date and then for a time.

>> Say "I have a meeting with John on April 1." Siri may respond by saying "I don't find a meeting with John on April 1; shall I create it?" You can say "Yes" to have Siri create it.

Create Repeating Events

If you want an event to repeat, such as a weekly or monthly appointment, you can set a repeating event.

1. With any view displayed, tap the Add button to add an event. The New Event dialog (refer to Figure 16-6) appears.

2. Enter a title and location for the event and set the start and end dates and times, as shown in the earlier section, "Add Calendar Events."

3. Scroll down the page, if necessary, and then tap the Repeat field; the Repeat dialog, shown in Figure 16-7, is displayed.

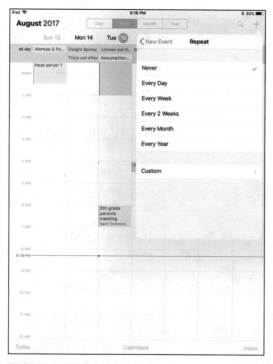

FIGURE 16-7

4. Tap a preset time interval: — Every Day, Week, 2 Weeks, Month, or Year — and you return to the New Event dialog. Tap Custom and make the appropriate settings if you want to set any other interval, such as every two months on the 6th of the month.

5. Tap Done. You return to the Calendar.

View an Event

Tap an event anywhere — on a Day view, Week view, Month view, or List view — to see its details.

Add Alerts

If you want your iPad to alert you when an event is coming up, you can use the Alert feature.

1. Tap the Settings icon on the Home screen and choose Sounds.

2. Scroll down to Calendar Alerts and tap it; then tap any Alert Tone, which causes iPad to play the tone for you. After you've chosen the alert tone you want, tap Sounds to return to Sounds settings. Press the Home button, then tap Calendar, and create an event in your calendar or open an existing one for editing, as covered in earlier tasks in this chapter.

3. In the New Event (refer to Figure 16-6) or Edit Event dialog, tap the Alert field. The Event Alert dialog appears, as shown in Figure 16-8.

4. Tap any preset interval, from 5 Minutes to 2 Days Before or At Time of Event, and you'll return to the New Event or Edit Event dialog.

5. Tap Done in the Edit Event dialog or Add in the New Event dialog to save all settings.

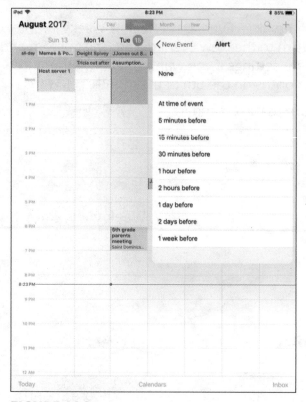

FIGURE 16-8

TIP

If you work for an organization that uses a Microsoft Exchange account, you can set up your iPad to receive and respond to invitations from colleagues in your company. When somebody sends an invitation that you accept, it appears on your calendar. Check with your company network administrator (who will jump at the chance to get her hands on your iPad) or the iPad User Guide to set up this feature if it sounds useful to you.

TIP

iCloud offers individuals functionality similar to Microsoft Exchange.

Search for an Event

1. With Calendar open in any view, tap the Search button in the top-right corner.

2. Tap the Search field to display the onscreen keyboard.

3. Type a word or words to search by and then tap the Search key. While you type, the Results dialog appears, as shown in Figure 16-9.

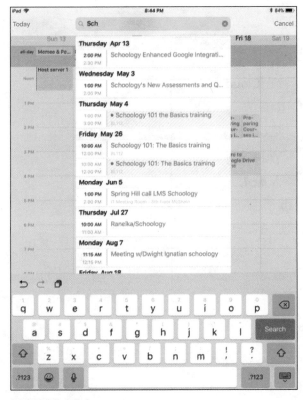

FIGURE 16-9

4. Tap any result to display the event details.

Create a Calendar Account

If you use a calendar available from an online service, such as Yahoo! or Google, you can subscribe to that calendar to read events saved there on your iPad.

1. Tap the Settings icon on the Home screen to get started.

2. Tap the Accounts & Passwords option.

3. Tap Add Account and the Add Account options, shown in Figure 16-10, appear.

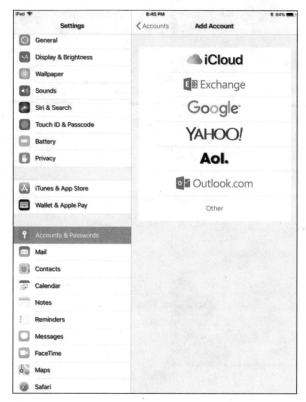

FIGURE 16-10

4. Tap a selection, such as Outlook.com, Gmail, or Yahoo!, depending on the calendar service you'd like to use.

   Turn on Calendars for other accounts that aren't listed by tapping Other.

5. In the next screen that appears (see Figure 16-11), enter your account information for the service (the screen you see will vary, depending on the service you selected in Step 4). If you don't yet have an account for the service, there will be a way on the screen for you to create a new account.

6. Tap Next. iPad verifies your account information.

7. On the following screen (see Figure 16-12), tap the On/Off switch for the Calendars field; your iPad retrieves data from your calendar at the interval you have set to fetch data. Tap Save to save your account settings.

FIGURE 16-11

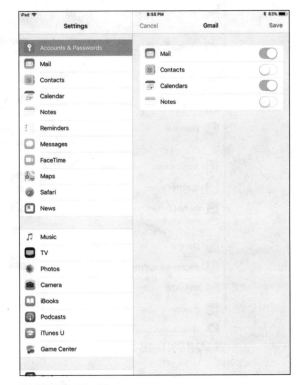

FIGURE 16-12

Use a Family Calendar

If you set up the Family Sharing feature (see Chapter 11 for how to do this), you create a Family calendar that you can use to share family events with up to five other people. After you set up Family Sharing, you have to make sure that the Calendar Sharing feature is on.

1. Tap Settings on the Home screen.

2. Tap the Apple ID and check that Family Sharing is set up (see Figure 16-13). You'll see Family Sharing rather than Set Up Family

Sharing if it has been set up. If you see Set Up Family Sharing, go to Chapter 11 for instructions on setting up Family Sharing.

FIGURE 16-13

3. Tap iCloud. In the iCloud settings, tap the switch for Calendars to turn it on if it isn't already on.

4. Now tap the Home button and then tap Calendars. Tap the Calendars button at the bottom of the screen. Scroll down, and in the Show Calendars dialog that appears, make sure that Family is selected. Tap Done in the upper-right corner of the Show Calendars dialog when finished.

5. Now when you create a new event in the New Event dialog, tap Calendar and choose Family or Show All Calendars. The details of events contain a notation that an event is from the Family calendar.

TIP

If you store birthdays for people in the Contacts app, by default the Calendar app then displays these when the day comes around so that you won't forget to pass on your congratulations! You can turn off this feature by tapping Calendars in the Calendar app and deselecting Birthday Calendar.

Delete an Event

When an upcoming luncheon or meeting is canceled, you should delete the appointment.

1. With Calendar open, tap an event (see Figure 16-14).

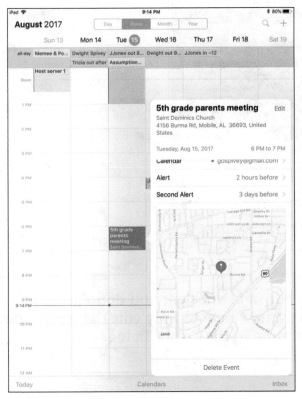

FIGURE 16-14

2. Tap Delete Event at the bottom of the screen.

3. If this is a repeating event, you have the option to delete this instance of the event or this and all future instances of the event (see Figure 16-15). Tap the button for the option you prefer. The event is deleted, and you return to Calendar view.

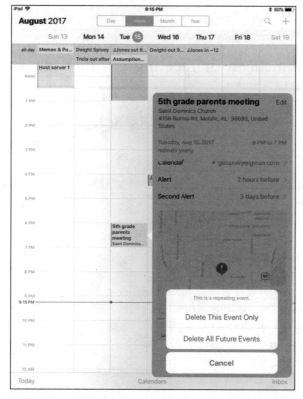

FIGURE 16-15

If an event is moved but not canceled, you don't have to delete the old one and create a new one. Simply edit the existing event to change the day and time in the Event dialog.

TIP

Display Clock

Clock is a preinstalled app that resides on the Home screen along with other preinstalled apps, such as iBooks and Camera.

1. Tap the Clock app to open it. If this is the first time you've opened Clock you'll see the World Clock tab (see Figure 16-16).

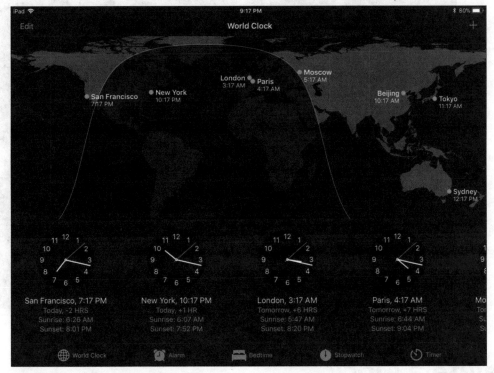

FIGURE 16-16

2. You can add a clock for many (but not all) locations around the world. With Clock displayed, tap the Add button (looks like a plus symbol) in the upper-right corner.

3. Tap a city on the list or tap a letter on the right side to display locations that begin with that letter (see Figure 16-17) and then tap a city. You can also tap in the Search field and begin to type a city name to find and tap a city. The clock appears in the last slot at the bottom.

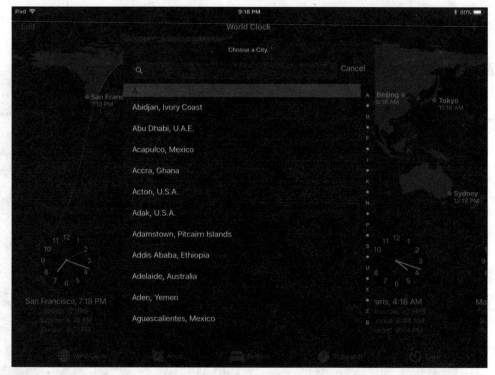

FIGURE 16-17

Delete a Clock

1. To remove a location, tap the Edit button in the top-left corner of the World Clock screen.

2. Tap the minus symbol next to a location to delete it (see Figure 16-18).

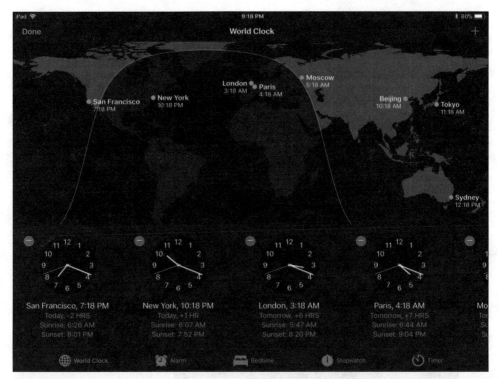

FIGURE 16-18

Set an Alarm

1. With the Clock app displayed, tap the Alarm tab.

2. Tap the Add button (the + in the upper-right corner). In the Add Alarm dialog shown in Figure 16-19, take any of the following actions, tapping Back after you make each setting to return to the Add Alarm dialog:

- Tap Repeat if you want the alarm to repeat at a regular interval, such as every Monday or every Sunday.

- Tap Label if you want to name the alarm, such as "Take Pill" or "Call Glenn."

- Tap Sound to choose the tune the alarm will play.

- Tap the On/Off switch for Snooze if you want to use the Snooze feature.

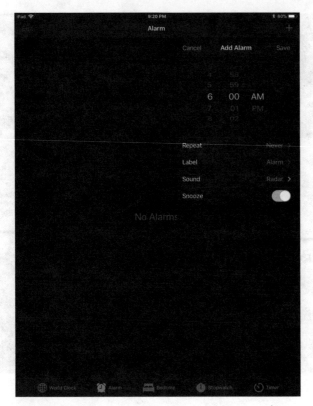

FIGURE 16-19

3. Place your finger on any of the three columns of sliding numbers at the top of the dialog and scroll to set the time you want the alarm to occur; then tap Save. The alarm appears in the Alarm tab.

TIP

To delete an alarm, tap the Alarm tab and tap Edit. All alarms appear. Tap the red circle with a minus in it, and the alarm is deleted. Be careful: When you tap the Delete button, the alarm is unretrievable.

Set Bedtime and Waking Alerts

The Clock can also help you develop better sleeping habits by allowing you to set bedtime and wake alerts and keeping track of your sleep habits.

1. Tap the Bedtime button at the bottom of the Clock app screen.

2. If this is your first time to open the Bedtime feature, tap Get Started and answer the questions you're asked to help configure the Bedtime settings.

3. When you've completed the initial configuration, you will see a screen displaying your bedtime and waking hours (see Figure 16-20).

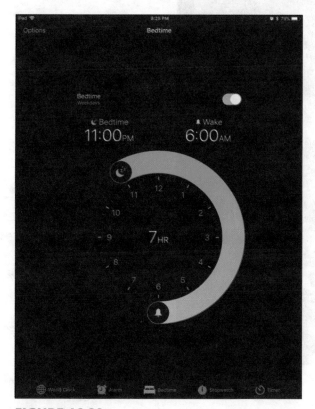

FIGURE 16-20

4. You can manually change the bedtime by pressing the button that looks like a moon and dragging it around the clock face. You can do the same for the wake time by pressing and dragging the button that looks like a bell. To keep the same amount of sleep time, you can press and drag the orange band.

5. Tap the Options button in the upper-left corner to reconfigure the settings for Bedtime (see Figure 16-21). You can adjust the days the Bedtime feature is used, the reminder time, the Wake Up Sound, and the volume for the Wake Up Sound. Tap Done when finished (or Cancel if you didn't make any changes).

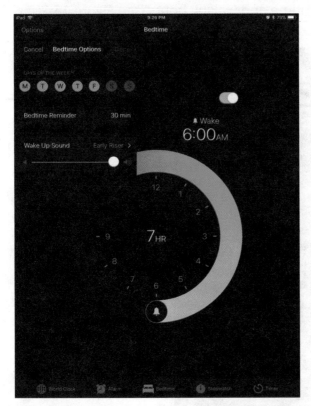

FIGURE 16-21

6. Tap the Bedtime toggle switch to Off to disable or On (green) to enable.

Use Stopwatch and Timer

Sometimes life seems like a countdown or a ticking clock counting the minutes you've spent on a certain activity. You can use the Timer and Stopwatch tabs of the Clock app to do a countdown to a specific time, such as the moment when your chocolate chip cookies are done cooking or to time an activity, such as reading.

These two work very similarly: Tap the Stopwatch or Timer tab from Clock's screen and then tap the Start button (see Figure 16-22). When you set the Timer, iPad uses a sound to notify you when time's up. When you start the Stopwatch, you have to tap the Stop button when the activity is done.

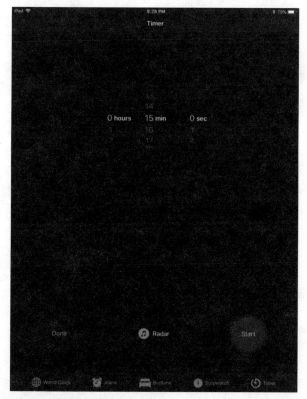

FIGURE 16-22

TIP

Stopwatch allows you to log intermediate timings, such as a lap in the pool or the periods of a timed game. With Stopwatch running, just tap the Lap button, and the first interval of time is recorded. Tap Lap again to record a second interval, and so on.

» Scheduling a reminder

» Syncing reminders and lists

» Completing or deleting
reminders

» Setting notification types

» Viewing notifications

» Opening apps from Cover Sheet

» Setting up Do Not Disturb

Chapter **17**

Working with Reminders and Notifications

T he Reminders app and Cover Sheet (formerly known as Notification Center) features warm the hearts of those who need help remembering all the details of their lives.

Reminders is a kind of to-do list that lets you create tasks and set reminders so that you don't forget important commitments.

You can even be reminded to do things when you arrive at or leave a location. For example, you can set a reminder so that when your iPad detects that you've left the location of your golf game, an alert reminds you to pick up your grandchildren, or when you arrive at your cabin, your iPad reminds you to turn on the water . . . you get the idea.

CHAPTER 17 **Working with Reminders and Notifications** 359

Cover Sheet allows you to review all the things you should be aware of in one place, such as mail messages, text messages, calendar appointments, and alerts.

If you occasionally need to escape all your obligations, try the Do Not Disturb feature. Turn this feature on, and you won't be bothered with alerts until you're ready to be.

In this chapter, you discover how to set up and view tasks in Reminders and how Cover Sheet can centralize all your alerts in one easy-to-find place.

Create a Reminder

Creating an event in Reminders is pretty darn simple:

1. Tap Reminders on the Home screen.

2. On the screen that appears, tap Reminders from the list on the left and then tap a blank slot with a plus sign to the left of it in the displayed list to add a task (see Figure 17-1). The onscreen keyboard appears.

3. Enter a task name or description using the onscreen keyboard and then tap Done in the upper-right corner of the Details dialog.

The following task shows how to add more specifics about an event for which you've created a reminder.

Note that when you first use Reminders, you have only the Reminders list to add tasks to. However, you can create your own list categories. See the task "Create a List," later in this chapter, to find out how to do this.

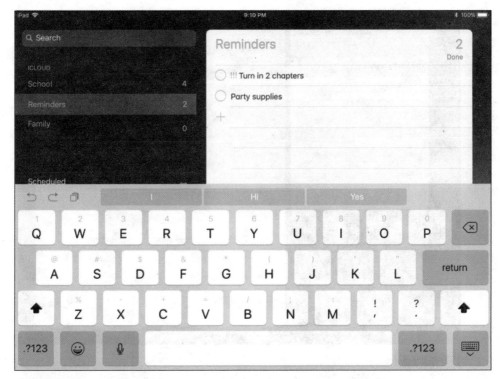

FIGURE 17-1

Edit Reminder Details

To edit the details of a reminder:

TIP

1. Tap a reminder and then tap the Details button (an *i* in a circle) to open the Details dialog, shown in Figure 17-2.

I deal with reminder settings in the following task.

2. Tap a Priority — None, Low (!), Medium (!!), or High (!!!) — from the choices that appear.

3. Tap Notes and enter any notes about the event using the onscreen keyboard (see Figure 17-3).

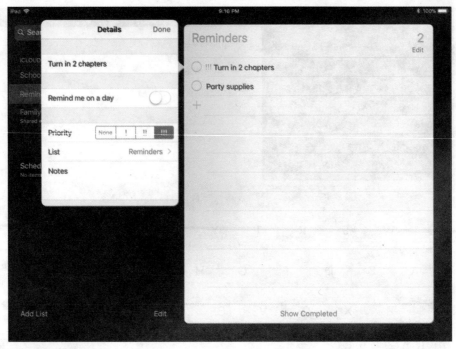

FIGURE 17-2

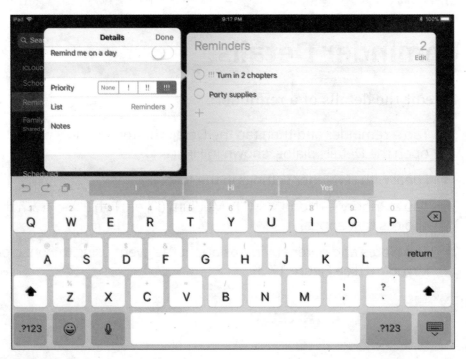

FIGURE 17-3

4. Tap List and then tap which list you want the reminder saved to, such as your calendar, iCloud, Exchange, or a category of reminders that you've created. Tap Details to return to the Details screen.

5. Tap Done to save the task.

Priority settings display the associated number of exclamation points on a task in a list to remind you of its importance.

Schedule a Reminder
by Time or Location

One of the major purposes of Reminders is to remind you of upcoming tasks. To set a reminder, follow these steps:

1. Tap a task and then tap the Details button that appears to the right of the task.

2. In the dialog that appears (refer to Figure 17-2), toggle the Remind Me on a Day switch to turn the feature to On (green).

3. Tap the Alarm field that appears below this setting (see Figure 17-4) to display date settings.

4. Tap and flick the day, hour, and minutes fields to scroll to the date and time for the reminder.

5. Tap Done to save the settings for the reminder.

If you want a task to repeat with associated reminders, tap the Repeat field in the Details dialog and from the dialog that appears, tap Every Day, Every Week, Every 2 Weeks, Every Month, Every Year (for those annual meetings or great holiday get-togethers with the gang), or create a Custom interval. Tap Details and then tap Done to save details for the task.

To stop the task from repeating on a specific date, tap the End Repeat field, tap End Repeat Date, and select a date from the scrolling calendar.

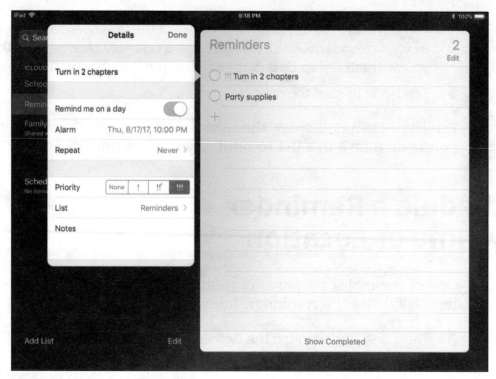

FIGURE 17-4

Create a List

You can create your own lists of tasks to help you keep different parts of your life organized and even edit the tasks on the list in List view.

1. Tap Reminders on the Home screen to open it.

2. Tap Add List in the lower-left corner to display the New List form, shown in Figure 17-5.

3. Tap New List and then enter a name for the list.

4. Tap a color; the list name will appear in that color in List view.

5. Tap Done to save the list.

6. Tap a blank line to enter a task.

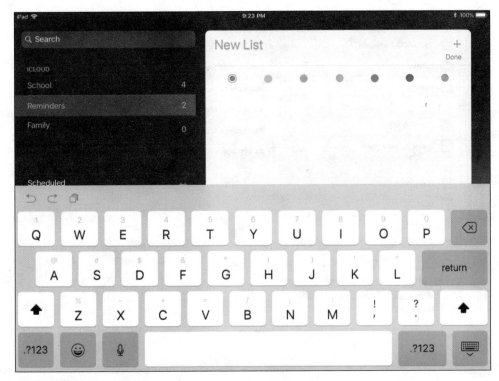

FIGURE 17-5

Sync with Other Devices and Calendars

To make all these settings work, you should set up your default Calendar in the Settings ⇨ Calendar settings and set up your iCloud account to enable Reminders (Settings ⇨ Apple ID [top of the screen] ⇨ iCloud).

TIP

Your default Calendar account is also your default Reminders account.

1. To determine which tasks are brought over from other calendars (such as Outlook), tap the Settings button on the Home screen.

2. Tap your Apple ID and then tap iCloud. In the dialog that appears, be sure that Reminders is set to On (green).

3. Scroll down the Settings list on the left and then tap Reminders.

4. Tap the Sync button and then choose how far back to sync Reminders (see Figure 17-6).

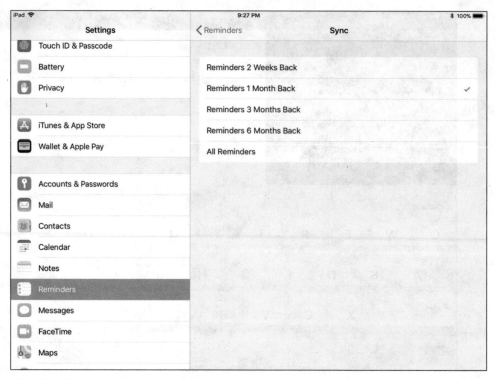

FIGURE 17-6

Mark as Complete or Delete a Reminder

You may want to mark a task as completed or just delete it entirely.

1. With Reminders open and a list of tasks displayed, tap the circle to the left of a task to mark it as complete. When you tap Show Completed at the bottom of the list, the task now appears as completed; when you next open Reminders, it will have been removed from the Reminders category.

2. To delete more than one reminder, with the list of tasks displayed, tap Edit. In the screen shown in Figure 17-7, tap the red minus icon to the left of any task and tap Delete. Alternatively, tap Delete List at the bottom of the screen and tap Delete in the confirming dialog to delete all the events on the list.

3. Tap Done when finished.

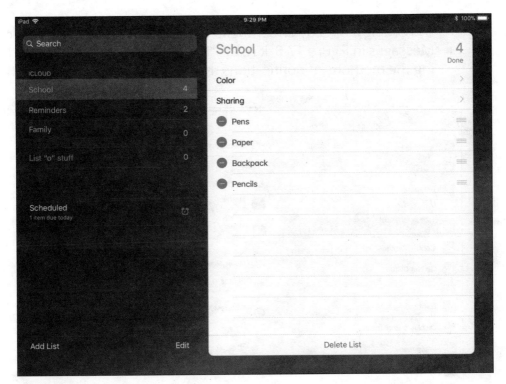

FIGURE 17-7

Set Notification Types

Cover Sheet is a list of various alerts and scheduled events; it even provides information (such as stock quotes) that you can display by swiping down from the top of your iPad screen. Cover Sheet is on by default, but you don't have to include every type of notification there if you don't want to; for example, you may never want to be notified of incoming messages but always want to have reminders listed here — it's up to you.

Some Cover Sheet settings let you control what types of notifications are included. To set notification types:

1. Tap Settings and then tap Notifications.

2. In the settings that appear (see Figure 17-8), you see a list of items to be included in Cover Sheet. You can view the state of an item

by reading it directly under the item's name. For example, under Messages in Figure 17-8, it reads "Badges, Sounds, Banners," indicating the methods of notifications that are enabled for that app.

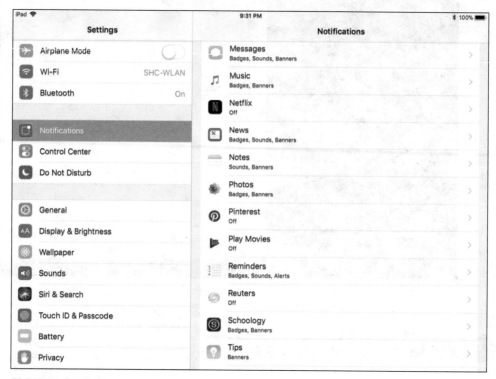

FIGURE 17-8

3. Tap any item. In the settings that appear, set an item's Allow Notifications switch (see Figure 17-9) to On or Off in order to include or exclude it from Cover Sheet.

4. Tap Options in the Alerts section to choose to have no alert, view a banner across the top of the screen, or have a boxed alert appear.

TIP

If you enable Banners, it will appear and then disappear automatically if you tap the Temporary style. If you choose Persistent, you have to take an action to dismiss the alert when it appears (such as swiping it up to dismiss it or tapping to view it).

5. If you want to be able to view alerts when the lock screen is displayed, turn on the Show on Lock Screen setting.

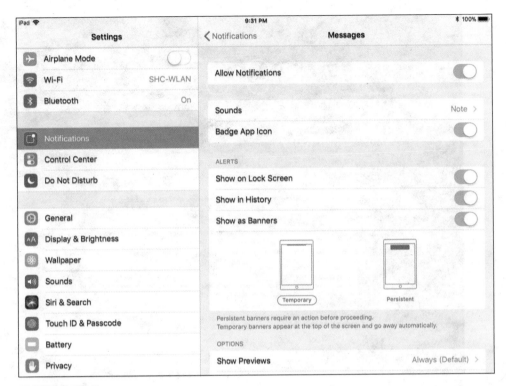

FIGURE 17-9

6. Tap Notifications in the upper-left corner to return to the main Notifications settings screen. When you've finished making settings, press the Home button.

TIP

You can drag across or tap an alert displayed in Cover Sheet to go to its source, such as the Reminders app, to see more details about it.

View Cover Sheet

After you've made settings for what should appear in Cover Sheet, you'll regularly want to take a look at those alerts and reminders.

1. From any screen, tap and hold your finger at the top of the screen and drag down to display Cover Sheet (see Figure 17-10).

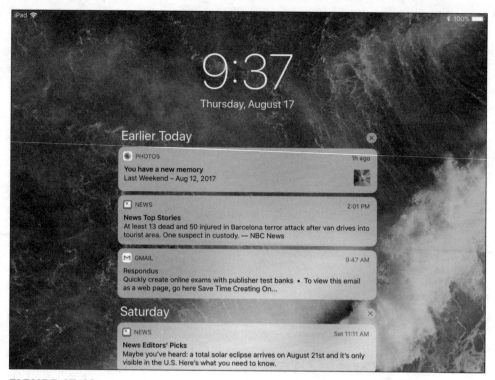

FIGURE 17-10

TIP

Swipe from left to right on the date at the top of the Cover Sheet to view other notifications, such as weather, reminders, Siri app suggestions, and more. Swipe from right to left on the date at the top to return to app notifications.

2. To close Cover Sheet, swipe upward from the bottom of the screen.

TIP

To determine what is displayed in Cover Sheet, see the previous task.

There are two sections in Cover Sheet for you to play with: Notifications and Today.

1. Swipe down from the top of the screen to open the Cover Sheet. The Notifications section is displayed by default.

2. Swipe from left to right on the date/time at the top of the Cover Sheet to access the Today tab to view information in widgets that pertain to today, such as Reminders, weather, stock prices, Calendar items, and other items you've selected to display in Cover Sheet (see the preceding task).

You select which widgets appear in the Today tab by tapping the Edit button at the bottom of the Today screen and then selecting the items you want to see. Tap Done to return to the Today screen.

3. Swipe from right to left on the date/time at the top of the Cover Sheet to visit the Notifications section to see all notifications that you set up in the Settings app. You'll see only notifications that you haven't responded to or deleted in the Notifications section or that you haven't viewed in their originating app.

Work with Notifications in the Cover Sheet

You will receive notifications on your Cover Sheet when a message has been received or you've missed a FaceTime call, for example. You can respond to notifications in several ways. You'll need to begin by swiping down from the top of your screen to open Cover Sheet.

You don't have to unlock your iPad if you're viewing your lock screen; just tap and drag down from the Status bar to view Cover Sheet.

>> Tap an item, and you're taken to the originating app, where you can take the appropriate action: create and send a return message, initiate a FaceTime call, or whatever. Swiping from left to right on a notification and tapping the Open button produces the same affect.

If you're on the lock screen, you'll have to use Touch ID or enter your passcode to view the notification in its app.

» Swiping from right to left on a notification will yield two options: Clear and View.

- Tap Clear to remove the notification from the Cover Sheet. No worries, though: The item is still available for viewing in its originating app.

- Tap View to open a window in Cover Sheet offering an expanded view of the notification, as shown in Figure 17-11. Tap the X to clear the notification, tap the notification window to open the notification in its app, or tap outside the notification window to return to the Cover Sheet.

FIGURE 17-11

Get Some Rest with Do Not Disturb

Do Not Disturb is a simple but useful setting you can use to stop any alerts, text messages, and FaceTime calls from appearing or making a sound. You can make settings to allow calls from certain people or several repeat calls from the same person in a short time period to come through. (The assumption here is that such repeat calls may signal an emergency situation or urgent need to get through to you.)

1. Tap Settings and then tap Do Not Disturb.

2. Set the Do Not Disturb switch to On (green) to enable the feature.

3. In the other settings shown in Figure 17-12, do any of the following:

    - Toggle the Scheduled switch to On (green) to allow alerts during a specified time period to appear.

    - Tap Allow Calls From and then, from the next screen, select Everyone, No One, Favorites, or Groups, such as All Contacts.

    - Toggle the Repeated Calls switch to On to allow a second call from the same person in a three-minute time period to come through.

    - Choose to silence incoming calls and notifications Always or Only while iPad is locked.

4. Press the Home button to return to the Home screen.

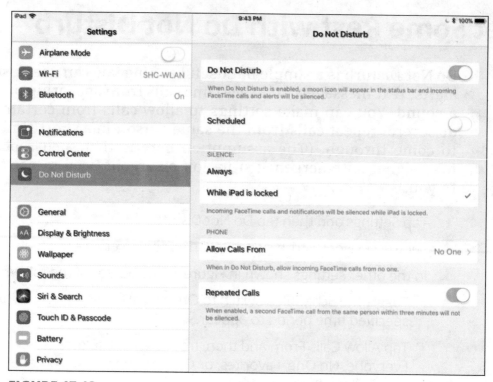

FIGURE 17-12

Chapter **18**

Making Notes

Notes is the app that you can use to do everything from jotting down notes at meetings to keeping to-do lists. It isn't (yet) a robust word processor (such as Apple Pages or Microsoft Word), but for taking notes on the fly, jotting down shopping lists, or writing a few pages of your novel-in-progress while you sit and sip a cup of coffee on your deck, it's a useful option.

In this chapter, you see how to enter and edit text in Notes and how to manage those notes by navigating among them, searching for content, or sharing or deleting them. I also help you explore the short-cut menu that allows you to create bulleted checklists, add pictures and drawings to notes, and apply styles to text in a note. iOS 11 also incorporates into Notes the ability to scan and mark up documents directly, as opposed to needing third-party options for such tasks.

Open a Blank Note

To open a blank note:

1. To get started with Notes, tap the Notes app icon on the Home screen. If you've never used Notes, it opens with a blank Notes list displayed. (If you have used Notes, it opens to the last note you were working on. If that's the case, you may want to jump to the next task to display a new, blank note.) You see the view shown in Figure 18-1.

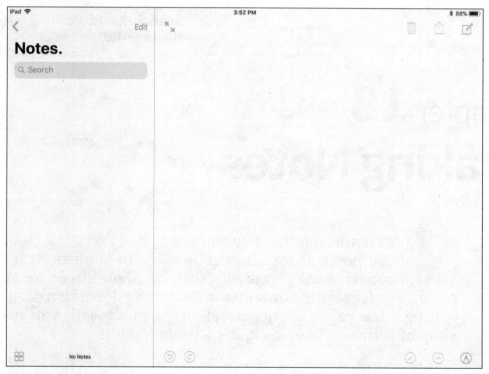

FIGURE 18-1

2. Tap the New button in the upper-right corner of the open note (looks like a piece of paper with a pencil writing on it). A blank note opens and displays the onscreen keyboard, shown in Figure 18-2.

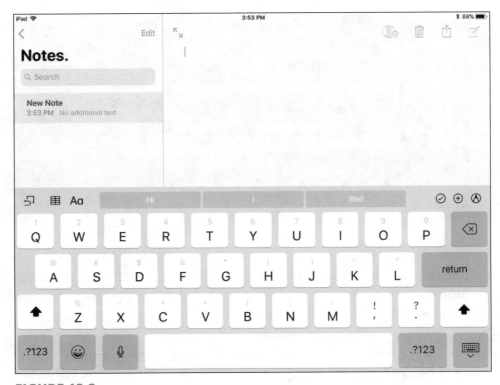

FIGURE 18-2

TIP

Notes can be shared among Apple devices via iCloud. In Settings, both devices must have Notes turned on under iCloud. New notes are shared instantaneously if both devices are connected to the Internet; this makes it easy to begin a note on one device and move to another device, picking up right where you left off.

3. Tap keys on the keyboard to enter text or, with Siri enabled, tap the Dictation key (the one with the microphone on it) to speak your text. If you want to enter numbers or symbols, tap the key labeled .?123 on the keyboard (refer to Figure 18-2). The numeric keyboard, shown in Figure 18-3, appears. Whenever you want to return to the alphabetic keyboard, tap the key labeled ABC.

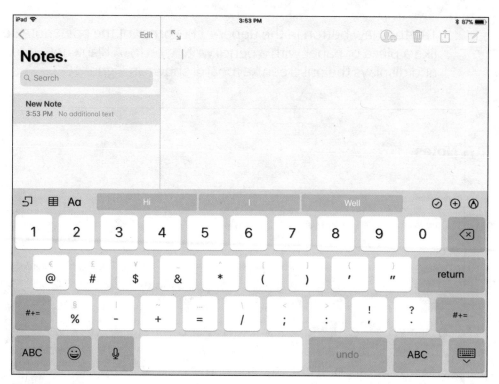

FIGURE 18-3

TIP

When you have the numerical keyboard displayed (refer to Figure 18-3), you can tap the key labeled #+= to access more symbols, such as the percentage sign or the euro symbol, or additional bracket styles.

TIP

iOS 11 introduces a cool new trick to the keyboard: the ability to access alternate characters on a key with a pull-down. For example, if you need to type the number 4, simply touch and pull down on the R key, as opposed to engaging the numerical keyboard.

4. To capitalize a letter, tap the Shift key that looks like a bold, upward-facing arrow (refer to Figure 18-2) and then tap the letter. Tap the Shift key once again to turn the feature off.

TIP

You can activate the Enable Caps Lock feature in Settings ⇨ General ⇨ Keyboard so that you can then turn Caps Lock on by double-tapping the Shift key. (This upward-pointing arrow is available only in the alphabetic keyboard.)

5. When you want to start a new paragraph or a new item in a list, tap the Return key (refer to Figure 18-2).

6. To edit text, tap to the right of the text you want to edit and either use the Delete key (refer to Figure 18-2) to delete text to the left of the cursor or enter new text. No need to save a note — it's kept automatically until you delete it.

You can press a spot on your note and, from the menu that appears, choose Select or Select All. Then you can tap the button labeled BIU to apply bold, italic, or underline formatting.

Use Copy and Paste

The Notes app includes two essential editing tools that you're probably familiar with from using word processors: Copy and Paste.

1. With a note displayed, press and hold your finger on a word.

To extend a selection to adjacent words, press one of the little handles that extend from an edge of the selection and drag to the left, right, up, or down.

2. Tap Select or Select All in the options that appear.

3. On the next toolbar that appears (see Figure 18-4), tap the Copy button.

4. Tap in the document where you want the copied text to go and then press and hold your finger on the screen.

5. On the toolbar that appears (see Figure 18-5), tap the Paste button. The copied text appears (see Figure 18-6).

If you want to select all text in a note to either delete or copy it, tap the Select All button on the toolbar shown in Figure 18-5. All text is selected, and then you use the Cut or Copy command on the toolbar, shown in Figure 18-4, to delete or copy the selected text. You can also tap the Delete key on the keyboard to delete selected text.

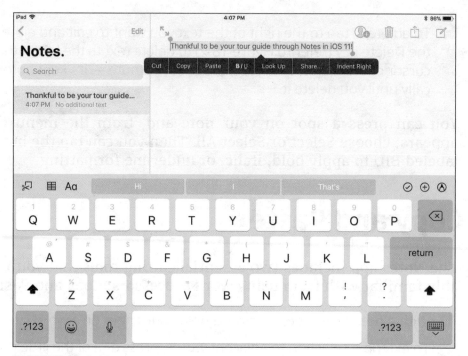

FIGURE 18-4

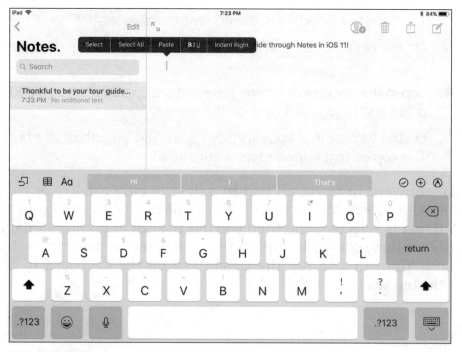

FIGURE 18-5

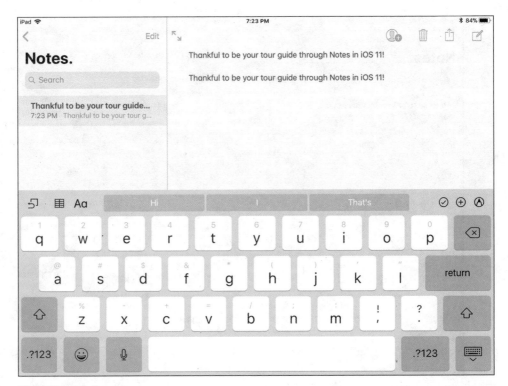

FIGURE 18-6

Insert a Picture

To insert a photo into a note:

1. Tap the + button above the keyboard. In the menu that appears, tap Photo Library.

2. Tap Photo Library (see Figure 18-7) to insert a picture you've already taken and choose the photo you want to insert.

3. Tap Choose, and the photo is inserted into your note.

TIP

If you want to take a photo or video, tap Take Photo or Video in Step 2 and take a new photo or video. Tap Use Photo to insert it in your note.

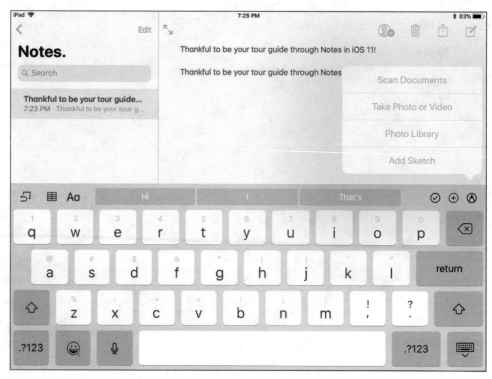

FIGURE 18-7

Add a Drawing

Notes has advanced to the point where you can now create a drawing to add to your note.

1. With a note open, tap the + button above the keyboard to display the shortcut toolbar.

2. Tap Add Sketch in the options and the drawing tools, shown in Figure 18-8, appear.

3. Tap a drawing tool (Pen, Marker, or Pencil). The selected tool will be the tallest among the group.

4. Tap a Color button in the color palette.

5. Tap a color and then draw on the screen using your finger, as shown in Figure 18-9.

FIGURE 18-8

FIGURE 18-9

6. When you've finished drawing, tap Done in the upper-left corner.

7. You can delete a drawing from a note by pressing the drawing until the toolbar appears. Tap the Delete button, shown in Figure 18-10, to remove the drawing.

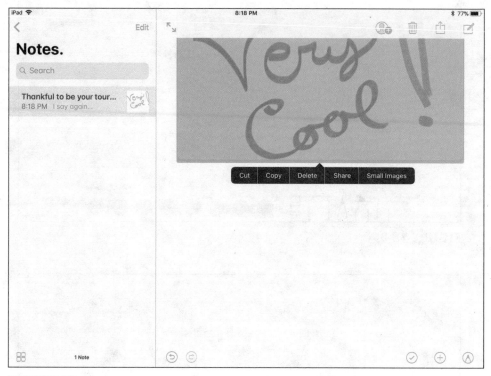

FIGURE 18-10

TIP

Tapping the Ruler tool places a ruler–shaped item on screen that you can use to help you to draw straight lines.

Apply a Text Style

Text styles, including Title, Heading, Body, Bulleted List, Dashed List, and Numbered List, are available on the shortcut toolbar (which is just sitting on top of the onscreen keyboard). With a note open and the shortcut toolbar displayed, press on the text and choose Select or Select All.

Tap the Text Style tool on the shortcut bar (labeled with Aa) and then tap to choose a style from the options, shown in Figure 18-11.

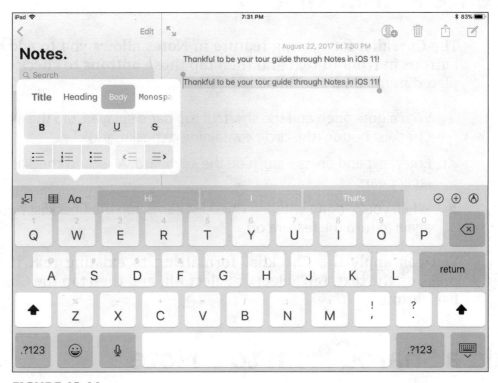

Notes is a very nice application and is getting better with every iOS iteration, but it's limited when compared to full-blown word processing apps. So if you've made some notes and want to graduate to building a more robust document in a word processor, you have a couple of options. One way is to download the Pages word-processor app for iPad and copy your note (using the copy-and-paste feature discussed earlier in this chapter). Alternatively, you can send the note to yourself in an email message, sync it to your computer, or use the Share button to send it your computer via AirDrop. Open the note and copy and paste its text into a full-fledged word processor, and you're good to go.

Create a Checklist

The Checklist formatting feature in Notes allows you to add circular buttons in front of text and then tap those buttons to check off completed items on a checklist.

1. With a note open and the shortcut toolbar displayed, tap the Checklist button (the circle containing a checkmark).

2. Enter text and press Return on the keyboard. A second checklist bullet appears.

3. When you're done entering Checklist items, tap the Checklist button again to turn the feature off.

TIP

You can apply the Checklist formatting to existing text if you press on the text, tap Select or Select All, and then tap the Checklist button.

Add a Shared Item to a Note

In iOS 11, you can share items to a note. For example, if you're displaying a map in Maps or a photo in Photos, you can tap the Share button and then choose Add to Notes (seen in Figure 18-12).

When you do, in the dialog that appears (see Figure 18-13), you can either add text to the note and save it or select an existing note to add the item to.

FIGURE 18-12

FIGURE 18-13

Scan Pages into Notes

You can also scan pages into Notes:

1. With a note open, tap the + button above the keyboard to display the shortcut toolbar.

2. Tap Scan Documents in the options, and the scanner window shown in Figure 18-14 appears.

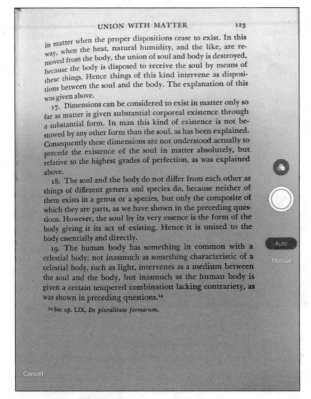

FIGURE 18-14

3. Position the document you want to scan in the scanner window.

4. Tap the white Scan button to scan the document.

5. Drag the handles in the corner of the scan selection (the lightly shaded area) to select the portion of the document you want to capture, as shown in Figure 18-15.

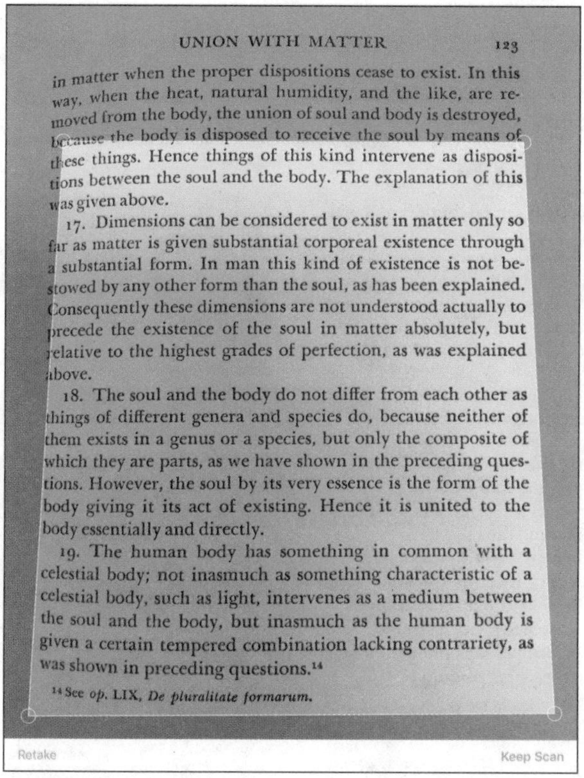

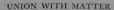

UNION WITH MATTER   123

in matter when the proper dispositions cease to exist. In this way, when the heat, natural humidity, and the like, are removed from the body, the union of soul and body is destroyed, because the body is disposed to receive the soul by means of these things. Hence things of this kind intervene as dispositions between the soul and the body. The explanation of this was given above.

17. Dimensions can be considered to exist in matter only so far as matter is given substantial corporeal existence through a substantial form. In man this kind of existence is not bestowed by any other form than the soul, as has been explained. Consequently these dimensions are not understood actually to precede the existence of the soul in matter absolutely, but relative to the highest grades of perfection, as was explained above.

18. The soul and the body do not differ from each other as things of different genera and species do, because neither of them exists in a genus or a species, but only the composite of which they are parts, as we have shown in the preceding questions. However, the soul by its very essence is the form of the body giving it its act of existing. Hence it is united to the body essentially and directly.

19. The human body has something in common with a celestial body; not inasmuch as something characteristic of a celestial body, such as light, intervenes as a medium between the soul and the body, but inasmuch as the human body is given a certain tempered combination lacking contrariety, as was shown in preceding questions.[14]

14 See op. LIX, De pluralitate formarum.

Retake   Keep Scan

FIGURE 18-15

TIP

Try to make the scan selection as square as possible to maintain the correct aspect ratio, which makes for a cleaner scan.

6. Tap the Keep Scan button in the lower right of the screen (refer to Figure 18-15).

7. When the scanner window opens again, you can repeat Steps 3 to 6 to scan more pages or tap the Save button in the lower-right corner to save the scan.

8. To share your scan or save it as a PDF, tap the scan in Notes, tap the Share button in the upper-right corner, and select a method of sharing or tap Create PDF, all shown in Figure 18-16.

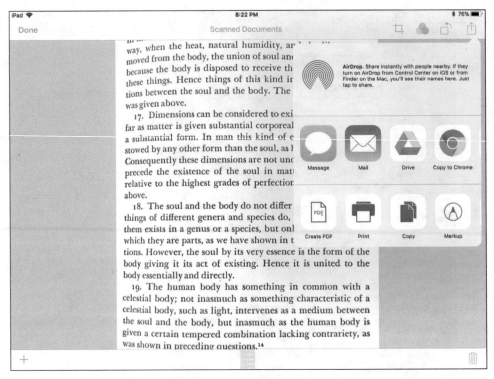

FIGURE 18-16

Move Among Notes

To move among notes, follow these steps:

1. Tap the Notes app icon on the Home screen to open Notes.

2. With the Notes list displayed (see the previous task), tap a note to open it.

3. To move among notes, tap the Notes button in the top-left corner and then tap another note in the list to open it. Of course, if you have a lot of notes, simply swipe up and down your screen to browse the list.

Notes names your note, using the first line of text. If you want to rename a note, first display the note, tap at the start of the first line of text, enter a new title, and press Return on the keyboard; the new first line is now reflected as the name of your note in the Notes list.

TIP

Because Notes lets you enter multiple notes with the same title — which can cause confusion — name your notes uniquely!

Search for a Note

You can search to locate a note that contains certain text. The Search feature lists only the notes that contain your search criteria, and it highlights only the first instance of the word or words you enter when you open a note.

1. Tap the Notes app icon on the Home screen to open Notes.

2. Tap the Search field in the Notes list on the left, and the onscreen keyboard appears. If you don't see the Search field, just swipe down on the Notes list to reveal it.

3. Begin to enter the search term. All notes that contain matching words appear on the list, as shown in Figure 18-17.

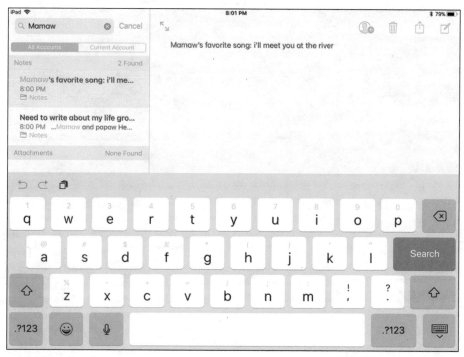

FIGURE 18-17

4. Tap a note to display it with the first instance of the search term highlighted; locate other instances of the matching word the old-fashioned way — by skimming to find it.

Share a Note

If you want to share what you wrote with a friend or colleague, you can easily use AirDrop (iPad 5 or later), Mail, or Message to send the contents of a note.

1. With a note displayed, tap the Share button at the top right of the screen and a popover appears, as shown in Figure 18-18.

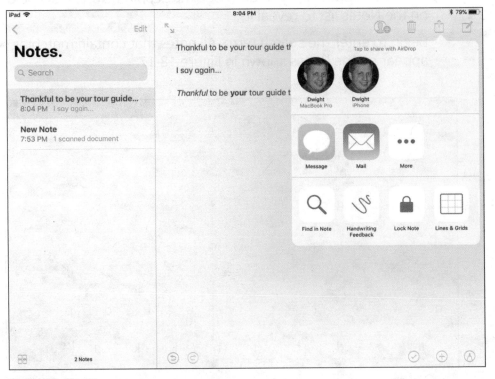

FIGURE 18-18

2. Tap Mail or Message. In the email or message form that appears, type one or more addresses in the appropriate fields. At least one address must appear in the To field.

3. If you need to make changes to the subject or message, tap in either area and make the changes.

4. Tap the Send button, and your email or message is sent.

To leave an email before sending it and save a draft so that you can finish and send it later, tap Cancel, and then tap Save Draft. The next time you tap the Mail button with the same note displayed in Notes, your draft appears.

5. To send via AirDrop to an AirDrop-enabled device (including Macs running OS X Yosemite or later with an AirDrop Finder window open) nearby, tap AirDrop in Step 2 and then tap the detected device to which you want to send the note.

If you want to print a note, in Step 2, choose Print rather than Mail (you may have to swipe over a bit to find it in the options). Complete the Printer Options dialog by designating an AirPrint-enabled wireless printer (or shared printer on a network that you can access using AirPrint) and how many copies to print; then tap Print.

Delete a Note

There's no sense in letting your Notes list get cluttered, making it harder to find the ones you need. When you're done with a note, it's time to delete it.

1. Tap Notes on the Home screen to open Notes.

2. Tap a note in the Notes list to open it.

3. Tap the Trash button, as shown in the upper-right corner of Figure 18-19. The note is deleted.

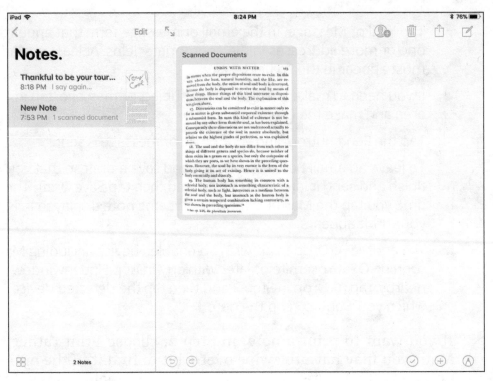

FIGURE 18-19

An alternative method to delete a note is to swipe to the left on a note in the Notes list and then tap the Delete button that appears (it looks like a trash can). You could also move the note to another folder or lock the note to prevent it from being viewed. If you lock the note, you'll want to provide a password, and perhaps even use Touch ID, to secure it from prying eyes (see Figure 18-20).

Should you like to retrieve a note you've deleted, tap the Back button in the upper-left corner of the screen until you get to the Folders list and then tap Recently Deleted. Tap the Edit button in the upper-right of the Recently Deleted list, tap the note or notes you'd like to recover, tap Move To in the lower-left corner, and then select a Notes list to relocate the selected items. Notes not removed from Recently Deleted will be permanently deleted in 30 days.

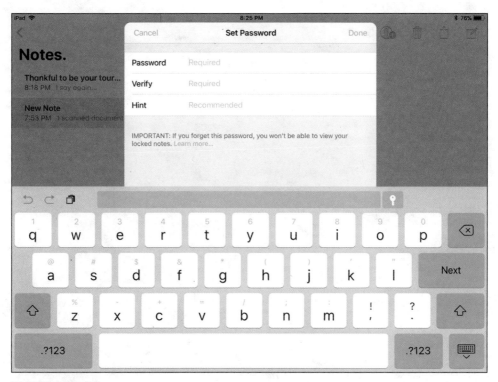

FIGURE 18-20

IN THIS CHAPTER

» **Reading the news**

» **Selecting Favorites**

» **Exploring channels and topics**

» **Finding news**

» **Saving news stories**

Chapter **19**

Getting the News You Need

The News app is a news aggregator, meaning that it gathers news stories that either match your news reading habits or match the channels and topics you've selected. You can choose which news sites are your favorites, search for news on a particular topic, and save news stories to read later. In this chapter, you get an overview of all these features.

Read Your News

Whether kicking off your day or calling it a night, reading the news is a great way to catch up on world and local events. Here's how to get the latest scoop on your iPad:

1. Tap the News app icon to get started. The first time you open it, you'll be asked a few questions to set up the app — customization of notifications and whether to deliver news to your Inbox, for example. Continue through the initial screens until you get to the news stories.

When you first open News, it will ask your permission to access your location. The purpose of knowing your location is to provide more accurate searches and local weather information. If you prefer more accurate info and weather, tap Allow when prompted; if not, tap Don't Allow.

2. The For You tab of news stories appears by default, though whichever tab you last chose will appear the next time you open the app.

3. Swipe up or down on the screen to browse the stories of the day in categories like Trending Stories (seen in Figure 19-1).

FIGURE 19-1

4. Tap a story to open it.

5. If you like a story, tap the Like button (looks like a heart) to help News understand which kinds of stories you enjoy (see Figure 19-2). If you despise the story, tap the Dislike button (looks like a heart with a slash) to discourage News from showing stories like it (also in Figure 19-2).

Back button

Dislike button

Like button

Text Size button

FIGURE 19-2

6. Tap the Text Size button in the upper-right corner to adjust text size for easier reading (refer to Figure 19-2).

7. Tap the Back button (left-pointing arrow) in the upper-left corner to go back to the For You list (refer to Figure 19-2).

When you're reading a story you like, you can tap the Share button at the bottom of the screen to share via Mail, Message, Twitter, Facebook, and a multitude of other options.

TIP

See Who or What Is in the Spotlight

The Spotlight tab, seen in Figure 19-3, features a topic or story of the day that Apple's News editors handpick for further exploration. The topic can be anything from as light as Emmy or Academy Award nominations to sports (the Super Bowl, for example) to heavier political fare.

FIGURE 19-3

Follow Favorite Channels and Topics

The Following tab allows you to select the topics and channels you prefer to include in Your News, as well as manage notifications from news sources.

1. With the News app open, tap the Following button at the bottom of the screen. The screen shown in Figure 19-4 appears.

FIGURE 19-4

2. Scroll down the screen to find suggestions from Siri based on your searches, favorite channels, and topics that appeal to you. You can also search for topics and channels using the search field at the top of the screen.

3. Items with small bell icons (like those in Figure 19-5) allow you to set a notification when stories become available; tap the bell to enable (blue) or disable (gray) notifications.

4. Tap an item to view it.

5. Tap Edit in the upper-right corner of the screen to edit the Following list.

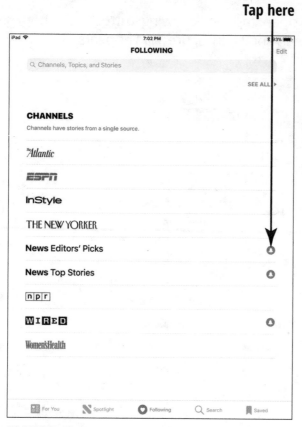

Tap here

FIGURE 19-5

6. To delete an item, tap the red circle containing the – and then tap the Delete button that appears to the right (see Figure 19-6). Tap Done in the upper-right corner when you finish editing the list.

7. Scroll to the top of the screen and tap the blue +Browse button to see a list of channels you designate as favorites, as shown in Figure 19-7.

8. Scroll up and down the page to find items that interest you and tap them to make them favorites. (The heart on the icon will turn red for favorites; tap again to remove a favorite.)

9. Tap Done at the bottom of the screen to exit the Favorites list.

10. Scroll to the bottom of the Following screen to see Manage Notifications. Tap Manage Notifications to scroll through a list of channels and toggle the bell icon to enable (blue) or disable (gray) notifications for a news outlet.

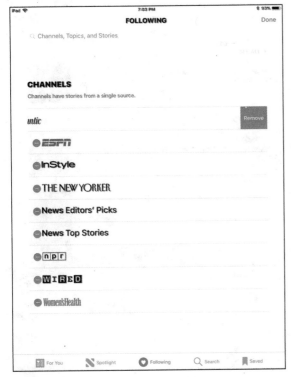

FIGURE 19-6

FIGURE 19-7

TIP

You can preview stories before opening them, which saves some download time. In Settings, tap News and then be sure the Show Story Previews switch is set to On (which it is by default).

Search for News

If you have a particular news story you'd like to follow, you can search for it from within News.

1. With the app open, tap the Search button at the bottom of the screen. You're presented with a Search field as well as some Suggestions (see Figure 19-8).

2. Enter a search term or phrase and press Enter or tap an item in the search results (see Figure 19-9).

FIGURE 19-8

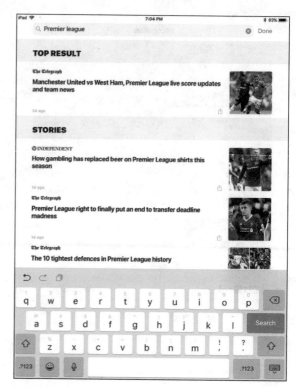

FIGURE 19-9

TIP If you don't find what you want in the results, tap the Show More Topics or Show More Channels links in the results list.

Save or Share News Stories

It's handy to be able to save news stories to read offline at any time and to share items that interest you with others who might also like them.

1. In the News app, open a news story using any of the methods described in this chapter.

2. Tap the Share button in the top-left corner.

3. In the Share dialog (see Figure 19-10), share your story via any of the methods listed — for example, Message or Mail.

4. To save your story for reading offline later, tap the Save button (see Figure 19-10). To remove a saved story from your Saved list, tap the Don't Save button (appears only if the story has previously been saved).

5. To view saved stories, return to the News app by tapping the Back button and then tap the Saved button. Your saved stories are displayed (see Figure 19-11).

Save button

FIGURE 19-10

FIGURE 19-11

Chapter **20**

Troubleshooting and Maintaining Your iPad

iPads don't grow on trees — they cost a pretty penny. That's why you should learn how to take care of your iPad and troubleshoot any problems it might have so that you get the most out of it.

In this chapter, I provide some advice about the care and maintenance of your iPad, as well as tips about how to solve common problems, update iPad system software, and even reset the iPad if something goes seriously wrong. In case you lose your iPad, I even tell you about a feature that helps you find it, activate it remotely, or even disable it if it has fallen into the wrong hands. Finally, you get information about backing up your iPad settings and content using iCloud and the fingerprint reader feature, Touch ID.

Keep the iPad Screen Clean

If you've been playing with your iPad, you know (despite Apple's claim that the iPad has a fingerprint-resistant screen) that it's a fingerprint magnet. Here are some tips for cleaning your iPad screen:

» **Use a dry, soft cloth.** You can get most fingerprints off with a dry, soft cloth, such as the one you use to clean your eyeglasses or a cleaning tissue that's lint-and chemical-free. Or try products used to clean lenses in labs, such as Kimwipes (which you can get from several major retailers, such as Amazon).

» **Use a slightly dampened soft cloth.** This may sound counter-intuitive to the previous tip, but to get the surface even cleaner, very (and I stress, very) slightly dampen the soft cloth. Again, make sure that whatever cloth material you use is free of lint.

» **Remove the cables.** Turn off your iPad and unplug any cables from it before cleaning the screen with a moistened cloth, even a very slightly moistened one.

» **Avoid too much moisture.** Avoid getting too much moisture around the edges of the screen, where it can seep into the unit. It isn't so much the glass surface you should worry about, as it is the Home button and the speaker holes on the top and bottom of the iPad.

» **Don't use your fingers!** That's right, by using a stylus (or an Apple Pencil if you have an iPad Pro) rather than your finger, you entirely avoid smearing oil from your skin or cheese from your pizza on the screen. Besides the Apple Pencil, a number of top-notch styluses are out there; just search Amazon for "iPad stylus," and you'll be greeted with a multitude of them, most of which are at a very reasonable price.

» **Never use household cleaners.** They can degrade the coating that keeps the iPad screen from absorbing oil from your fingers. Plus, you simply don't need to go that far since the screen cleans quite easily with little or no moisture at all.

TIP

Don't use premoistened lens-cleaning tissues to clean your iPad screen! Most brands of wipes contain alcohol, which can damage the screen's coating. Be sure whatever cleaner you do use states that it's compatible with your model iPad, as there are differences in screen technology between models.

Protect Your Gadget with a Case

Your screen isn't the only element on the iPad that can be damaged, so consider getting a case for it so that you can carry it around the house or around town safely. Besides providing a bit of padding if you drop the device, a case makes the iPad less slippery in your hands, offering a better grip when working with it.

Several types of covers and cases are available, but be sure to get one that will fit your model of iPad because their dimensions and button (and camera) placements may differ, and some models have slightly different thicknesses. There are differences between covers and cases:

» **Covers tend to be more for decoration than overall protection.** While they do provide some protection, they're generally thin and not well-padded.

» **Cases are more solid and protect most, if not all, of your iPad.** They're usually a bit bulky and provide more padding than covers.

You can choose covers from such manufacturers as Griffin (www.griffintechnology.com), or you can also check out Apple's range of silicone and leather covers (www.apple.com/shop/ipad/ipad-accessories/cases-protection).

Cases range from a few dollars to $70 or more for leather (with some outrageously expensive designer cases costing upward of $500). Some provide protection for the screen, back, and sides, while others protect only the back and sides. If you carry your iPad around much, consider a case with a screen cover to provide better protection for the screen or use a screen overlay, such as InvisibleShield from Zagg (www.zagg.com/us/en_us/invisibleshield). If you're the literary type, try the BookBook case that looks like a well-worn leather book (www.twelvesouth.com/product/family/bookbook).

Extend Your iPad's Battery Life

The much-touted battery life of the iPad is a wonderful feature, but you can do some things to extend it even further. Here are a few tips to consider:

TIP

» **Keep tabs on remaining battery life.** You can estimate the amount of remaining battery life by looking at the Battery icon on the far-right end of the Status bar, at the top of your screen.

» **Use standard accessories to charge your iPad most effectively.** When connected to a recent-model Mac or Windows computer for charging, the iPad can slowly charge. However, the most effective way to charge your iPad is to plug it into a wall outlet using the Lightning-to-USB cable and the USB power adapter that came with your iPad.

Third-party charging cables usually work just fine, but some are less reliable than others. If you use a third-party cable and notice that your iPad is taking longer than usual to charge, it's a good idea to try another cable.

» **Use a case with an external battery pack.** These cases are very handy when you're traveling or unable to reach an electrical outlet easily. However, they're also a bit bulky and can be cumbersome.

» **The fastest way to charge iPad is to turn it off while charging it.** If turning your iPad completely off doesn't sound like the best idea for you, you can disable Wi-Fi or Bluetooth to facilitate a faster recharge. Better yet, simply activate Airplane Mode and turn both Wi-Fi and Bluetooth off at the same time.

» **The Battery icon on the Status bar indicates when the charging is complete.** The icon will be totally filled in when the battery is fully charged.

TIP

Your iPad battery is sealed in the unit, so you can't replace it yourself the way you can with many laptops or other cellphones. If the battery is out of warranty, you have to fork over about $99 to have Apple install a new one with AppleCare coverage. See the "Get Support" task, later in this chapter, to find out where to get a replacement battery.

TIP

Apple offers AppleCare+. For $99, you get two years of coverage, which even covers you if you drop or spill liquids on your iPad (Apple covers up to two incidents of accidental damage). If your iPad has to be replaced, it will cost you only $49, rather than the $250 it used to cost with garden-variety AppleCare. You can purchase AppleCare+ when you buy your iPad or within 60 days of the date of purchase. See `http://www.apple.com/support/products/ipad.html` for more details.

Find Out What to Do with a Nonresponsive iPad

If your iPad goes dead on you, it's most likely a power issue, so the first thing to do is to plug the Lightning-to-USB cable into the USB power adapter, plug the USB power adapter into a wall outlet, plug the other end of the cable into your iPad, and charge the battery.

Another thing to try — if you believe that an app is hanging up the iPad — is to press the Sleep/Wake button for a couple of seconds and then press and hold the Home button. The app you were using should close.

You can always try the tried-and-true reboot procedure: On the iPad, you press the Sleep/Wake button until the red slider appears. Drag the slider to the right to turn off your iPad. After a few moments, press the Sleep/Wake button to boot up the little guy again.

If the situation seems drastic and none of these ideas works, try to force restart your iPad. To do this, press and hold the Sleep/Wake button and the Home button at the same time until the Apple logo appears onscreen. This may take ten seconds or more, so be patient.

TIP If your iPad has this problem often, try closing out some active apps that may be running in the background and using up too much memory. To do this, press the Home button twice, then from the screen showing active apps, tap and drag an app upward. Also check to see that you haven't loaded up your iPad with too much content, such as videos, which could be slowing down its performance.

Update the iOS Software

Apple occasionally updates the iPad system software, known as iOS, to fix problems or offer enhanced features. You should occasionally check for an updated version (say, every month). You can check by connecting your iPad to a recognized computer (that is, a computer that you've used to sign into your Apple account before) with iTunes installed, but it's even easier to just update from your iPad Settings, though it can be just a tad slower:

1. Tap Settings from the Home screen.

2. Tap General and then tap Software Update (see Figure 20-1).

3. A message tells you whether your software is up-to-date. If it's not, tap Download and Install and follow the prompts to update to the latest iOS version.

TIP If you're having problems with your iPad, you can use the Reset feature to try to restore the natural balance. Follow the preceding set of steps and then tap the Reset button instead of the Software Update button in Step 2.

Tap here

FIGURE 20-1

Restore the Sound

My wife frequently has trouble with the sound on her iPad, and sub–
sequently we've learned quite a bit about troubleshooting sound
issues, enabling us to pass our knowledge on to you. Make sure that

>> **You haven't touched the volume control buttons on the side
of your iPad.** They're on the left side of the iPad.

WARNING

Be sure not to touch the volume decrease button and inad-
vertently lower the sound to a point where you can't hear it.
Pushing the volume buttons will have no effect if the iPad is
sleeping, so don't worry about this happening while the iPad is
just sitting in a purse or backpack.

- » **The speakers aren't covered up.** No, really — they may be covered in a way that muffles the sound.

- » **A headset isn't plugged in.** Sound doesn't play over the speakers and the headset at the same time.

- » **The volume limit is set to On.** You can set up the volume limit for the Music app to control how loudly your music can play (which is useful if you have teenagers around). Tap Settings on the Home screen and then, on the screen that displays, tap Music and then tap Volume Limit under the Playback section if it is set to On. Use the slider that appears (see Figure 20-2) to set the volume limit. If the slider button is all the way to the left, you've set your volume limit too low (all the way down, as a matter of fact).

Slider button

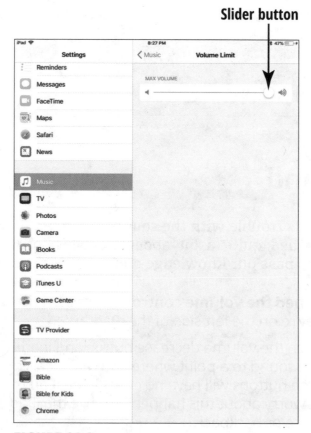

FIGURE 20-2

TIP

When all else fails, reboot. This strategy worked for us — just press the Sleep/Wake button until the red slider appears and then drag the slider to the right. After the iPad turns off, press the Sleep/Wake button again until the Apple logo appears, and you may find yourself back in business, sound-wise.

Get Support

Every single new iPad comes with a year's coverage for repair of the hardware and 90 days of free technical support. Apple is known for its high level of customer support, so if you're stuck, I definitely recommend that you try it. Here are a few options that you can explore for getting help:

- » **The Apple Store:** Go to your local Apple Store (if one is handy) to see what the folks there might know about your problem. Call first and make an appointment at the Genius Bar to be sure to get prompt service.

- » **The Apple support website:** It's at http://support.apple.com/ipad. You can find online manuals, discussion forums, and downloads, and you can use the Apple Expert feature to contact a live support person by phone.

- » **The iPad User Guide:** You can download the free manual that is available through iBooks from the iBooks Store. See Chapter 12 for more about iBooks.

- » **The Apple battery replacement service:** If you need repair or service for your battery, visit www.apple.com/batteries/service-and-recycling and scroll down to the iPad Owners section. Note that your warranty provides free battery replacement if the battery level dips below 50 percent and won't go any higher during the first year you own it. If you purchase the AppleCare+ service agreement, this is extended to two years.

WARNING

Apple recommends that you have your iPad battery replaced only by an Apple Authorized Service Provider.

Find a Missing iPad

You can take advantage of the Find My iPhone (even though you have an iPad, the app is still called Find My iPhone) feature to pinpoint the location of your iPad. This feature is extremely handy if you forget where you left your iPad or someone steals it. Find My iPhone not only lets you track down the critter but also lets you wipe out the data contained in it if you have no way to get the iPad back.

You must have an iCloud account to use the Find My iPhone feature. If you don't have an iCloud account, see Chapter 3 to find out how to set one up.

If you're using Family Sharing, someone in your family can find your device and play a sound. This works even if the volume on the iPad is turned down. See Chapter 11 for more about Family Sharing. Also, see Apple's support article on "Family Sharing and location" at `https://support.apple.com/en-us/HT201087` (as of this writing) for help with this service.

Follow these steps to set up the Find My iPhone feature:

1. Tap Settings on the Home screen.

2. In Settings, tap your Apple ID at the top of the screen and then tap iCloud.

3. In the iCloud settings, tap Find My iPad and then tap the On/Off switch for Find My iPad to turn the feature on (see Figure 20-3).

4. From now on, if your iPad is lost or stolen, you can go to `www.icloud.com` from your computer, iPad, or another iPad and enter your Apple ID and password.

5. In your computer's browser, the iCloud Launchpad screen appears. Click the Find iPhone button to display a map of your device's location and some helpful tools (see Figure 20-4).

Tap here

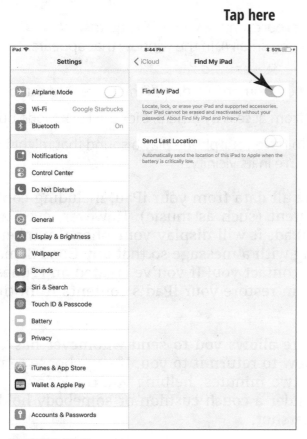

FIGURE 20-3

FIGURE 20-4

6. Click the green circle representing your iPad and then click the Information button (the small *i*). In the window that appears, choose one of three options:

- To wipe information from the iPad, click the Erase iPad button.
- To lock the iPad from access by others, click the Lock Mode button.
- Tap Play Sound to have your phone play a sound that might help you locate it if you're in its vicinity.

TIP Erase iPad will delete all data from your iPad, including contact information and content (such as music). However, even after you've erased your iPad, it will display your phone number on the Lock screen along with a message so that any Good Samaritan who finds it can contact you. If you've created an iTunes or iCloud backup, you can restore your iPad's contents from those sources.

TIP The Lost Mode feature allows you to send whomever has your iPad a note saying how to return it to you. If you choose to play a sound, it plays for two minutes, helping you track down your iPad in case it fell under a couch cushion or somebody holding your iPad is within earshot.

Back Up to iCloud

You used to be able to back up your iPad content using only iTunes, but since Apple's introduction of iCloud with iOS 5, you can back up via a Wi-Fi network to your iCloud storage. You get 5GB of storage for free or you can pay for increased storage (a total of 50GB for $.99 per month, 200GB for $2.99 per month, or 2TB for $9.99 per month).

TIP You must have an iCloud account to back up to iCloud. If you don't have an iCloud account, see Chapter 3 to find out more.

To perform a backup to iCloud:

1. Tap Settings from the Home screen and then tap your Apple ID at the top of the screen.

2. Tap iCloud and then tap iCloud Backup (see Figure 20-5).

3. In the pane that appears (see Figure 20-6), tap the iCloud Backup switch to enable automatic backups. To perform a manual backup, tap Back Up Now. A progress bar shows how your backup is moving along.

FIGURE 20-5

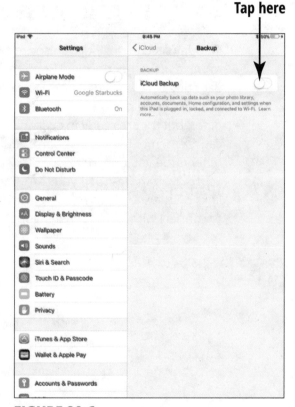

Tap here

FIGURE 20-6

TIP

If you get your iPad back after it wanders and you've erased it, just enter your Apple ID and password, and you can reactivate it.

TIP

You can also back up your iPad using iTunes. This method actually saves more types of content than an iCloud backup, and if you have encryption turned on in iTunes, it can save your passwords as well. However, this method does require that you connect to a computer to perform the backup. Unfortunately, you can't back up to both iTunes and iCloud. However, if you do back up and get a new iPad down the line, you can restore all your data to the new phone easily.

APPLE ID AND PASSWORD SUPPORT

In today's technology-driven society, it seems you need a username and password to wake up in the morning! Remembering usernames and passwords can be a daunting task, and your Apple ID and password are no exceptions. Thankfully, Apple is at the ready with your solution, but it's not one-size-fits-all; situations differ, but they're ready in every case. Whether you've forgotten your Apple ID, can't remember your password, your Apple ID account is locked, or just about any other issue you can come up with, Apple's got your answer at https://support.apple.com/apple-id. If you can't find what you're looking for by using any of the links on the site, scroll down to the bottom and click the blue Get Support button to connect with Apple's stellar support team.

Index

About the Author

Dwight Spivey has been a technical author and editor for a decade, but has been a bona fide technophile for more than three of them. He's the author of *iPhone for Seniors For Dummies*, 6th Edition (Wiley), *Idiot's Guide to Apple Watch* (Alpha), *Home Automation For Dummies* (Wiley), *How to Do Everything Pages, Keynote & Numbers* (McGraw-Hill), and many more books covering the tech gamut.

Dwight is also the Educational Technology Specialist at Spring Hill College. His technology experience is extensive, consisting of macOS, iOS, Android, Linux, and Windows operating systems in general, educational technology, desktop publishing software, laser printers and drivers, color and color management, and networking.

Dwight lives on the Gulf Coast of Alabama with his wife, Cindy, their four children, Victoria, Devyn, Emi, and Reid, and their pets, Rocky and Samwise.

Dedication

To my Mamaw, Faye Alexander.

I love and miss you, sweet lady.

Author's Acknowledgments

Heartfelt thanks to my agent, Carole Jelen of Waterside Productions, for keeping me working on such great projects!

Great editing and beautiful graphic design are two elements that set *For Dummies* books apart, and the crew behind this book was truly critical to its completion. I want each individual involved at every level to know how grateful I am for their professionalism, dedication, hard work, and their patience in putting together this book. Special gratitude and thanks to the following amazing people, from the bottom of my heart: Amy Fandrei, Kelly Ewing, and Aaron Crabtree.

Publisher's Acknowledgments

Senior Acquisitions Editor: Amy Fandrei

Project Editor: Kelly Ewing

Copy Editor: Kelly Ewing

Sr. Editorial Assistant: Cherie Case

Reviewer: Aaron Crabtree

Production Editor: G. Vasanth Koilraj

Cover Image: © LDProd / iStockphoto